DATE DUE

AG 4 97			
OC 27 '97			
DE 17 '01			
DE 19 08			

DEMCO 38-296

Todd Gitlin

The Twilight of Common Dreams

☾

Why America Is Wracked by Culture Wars

METROPOLITAN BOOKS

Henry Holt and Company • New York

Metropolitan Books
Henry Holt and Company, Inc.
Publishers since 1866
115 West 18th Street
New York, New York 10011

Metropolitan Books℠ is a division of Rowohlt
and an imprint of Henry Holt and Company, Inc.

Library of Congress Cataloging-in-Publication Data
Gitlin, Todd.
The twilight of common dreams: why America is wracked
by culture wars / Todd Gitlin.—1st American ed.
        p.   cm.
Includes bibliographical references (p.   ) and index.
   1. Pluralism (Social sciences)—United States.
2. Multiculturalism—United States.   3. United States—
        Social conditions—1980–   I. Title.
E184.A1G48   1995   95-22321
305—dc20   CIP

ISBN 0-8050-4090-0

Henry Holt books are available for special promotions and
premiums. For details contact: Director, Special Markets.

First Edition—1995

Designed by Paula R. Szafranski

Printed in the United States of America
All first editions are printed on acid-free paper. ∞

3   5   7   9   10   8   6   4   2

To Laurel

Contents

III. The Aggrandizement of Difference

IV. The Poignancy of Multiculturalism

The slaveholder, were he kind or cruel, was a slaveholder still, the every-hour violator of the just and inalienable rights of man, and he was therefore every hour silently but surely whetting the knife of vengeance for his own throat. He never lisped a syllable in commendation of the fathers of the republic without inviting the sword, and asserting the right of rebellion for his own slaves.

—FREDERICK DOUGLASS

Preface

The culture wars have produced shelves of war stories. There is something of a standard script and, indeed, a standard narrator: the conservative writer who deplores "the closing of the American mind," "political correctness," "illiberal education," "thought police," the "dictatorship of virtue." Pundits and politicians denounce the depredations of affirmative action and multicultural history. Newsmagazine cover stories cry panic against Afrocentric know-nothings and restrictive "hate speech" codes. The presumption is that, in the not too distant past, an incontestable consensus reigned, and deserved to reign, about the virtue of Western civilization, the nature of merit and authority, the rules of reason, the proper constitution of canon and curriculum, the integrity of American history, the civility of men. Now, however, the grand old consensus is under assault from the battering rams of irrationalists, totalitarians, reverse racists, anti-Americans, and their ilk. Millions of people thus labeled plead innocent, hunker down, reverse the terms, claim the mantle of victimhood, resist self-questioning, and cry out against racism and sexism, against white males, against fraudulent claimants to objectivity.

Who or what is at the root of these distempers? In the standard script, the facts speak for themselves, and the decisive facts are that the subversives of the Left are back, aliens in our nest, Sixties radicals all, refugees from the rigors of civilization, having burrowed into the Modern Language Association, the National Endowments for the Arts and the Humanities, the English department at Duke, the black studies department at the City College of New York, the Whitney Museum, the Smithsonian Institution . . . and so on. With Communism dead everywhere in Europe and hanging on in China only by dint of a boom in private investment, writers on the Right have found a surrogate enemy to brandish. Mao is dead, now Mapplethorpe is the devil king.

Citizens of the United States have been given to purification crusades from the moment there was a United States to purify—indeed, earlier. In the Alien and Sedition Acts of 1798, the nativist upsurges of the 1840s, and many subsequent classification movements, those who have imagined themselves to be *real* Americans, *normal* Americans, have declared that various groups of abnormal or hyphenated Americans threaten the integrity of the nation. The tired, the poor, the huddled masses yearning to breathe free have had to strain to prove that they could be trusted to breathe in the approved rhythms. Nor are Americans uniquely stringent—far from it: every nation's nationalism is the search for a principle that distinguishes insiders from outsiders and elevates the former over the latter.

But Americans are not only, perhaps not even primarily, exclusive. They have frequently been at odds over exclusiveness. For a long time, an important part of being an American has been to take sides in culture wars over what it means to be an American. Americans have stared endlessly in the mirror, inspected and classified themselves, marveled at or decried what they saw there, argued about whether the mirror was accurate and whether they needed a new one. Almost always they have felt uncertain just what it is to be a member of the American nation. Indeed, lacking a founding nationality in which the political structure is rooted, Americans came up with a term to signal that they were a nation after all, or were steadily trying to form one—this very term *American* that vexes Latin Americans and Canadians, who feel equally entitled to it. Thus, unlike the Mexicans or Australians, the French or the Chinese, we have one term for our political entity, the *United States,* and a linguistically quite independent one for the people who inhabit it.

The premise of this book is that the culture wars do not settle disputes or explain themselves. As honest partisans of all stripes declared in the Sixties, "The issue is not the issue." Most of the offenses and defenses have strong points—and gaping holes—but none is self-evident, none can be taken at face value. Pressures for "political correctness" and attacks on "political correctness"; revisions of American history and attacks on those revisions; disputes within the academic hothouse and the fact that these are the disputes of the day—*all* the obsessions need scrutiny. For the culture wars have more sources than their partisans own up to. Some are relatively recent: the end of the Cold War, demographic changes, political choices of Left and Right. Some go deeper: economic dislocations, long-running identity muddles, and philosophical currents. Taking positions is fine, exposing petty orthodoxies virtuous, pointing out historical error necessary. I am not averse to rooting for good guys. But my chief aim is to understand where our symbolic melodramas come from, and what these distortions and distempers reveal and conceal about perennial dilemmas of American identity and the contemporary incapacity of American politics.

Most of all, this book is about the fates of two ideas: that of America as a force for individual freedom, and that of the Left as a force for equality. It may seem odd that I should want to discuss them together. The collapse of Soviet Communism and the end of the Cold War have been claimed by the trumpeters as a victory of "the market" and so the end of the Left's long and treacherous road. America has triumphed and therefore the Left has declined—so sounds the chorus, in a clangor as shrill as the sense of national malaise is pervasive. The irony is that, partly because the enemy broke down, whatever consensus existed about the direction and meaning of American history has also loosened, and the pressures against a single, coherent American identity, always strong, have intensified.

Strange to tell, the idea of the Left and the idea of America share a history—I am tempted to say also a destiny. They are the two great, heavily burdened ideas of the Enlightenment. They have at times competed, at times overlapped. They arose from the same stock, these beliefs in progress and redemption: rival claimants to the heritage of freedom, equality, and the rest of the promises of the modern world. During their battered—and battering—histories, they have provided pictures of the whole, offered meanings for sacrifice, laid out compass points for a turning world, promised that human beings could take hold of their destinies and, together, transcend blood and accident and economic station and become more than themselves, more, even, than their local communities, members of something encompassing and enduring. If today the two classical stories have both worn thin—if they often seem virtually incomprehensible, especially to the young, if they are embattled, or greeted with grimaces and shrugs, if reverence for their heroes looks like nostalgia or stupidity, or both—we should try to understand how this happened.

I.

The Problem

It is bad to arrive too quickly at the one or
the many.

—PLATO, *Philebus*

1

A Dubious Battle
in Oakland

Columbus Day of 1992 should have been the perfect occasion for teaching schoolchildren about American Indians or, as the city of Oakland, California, officially calls them, Native Americans. Oakland, with an African-American plurality and a white minority in its population and on its city council, was no partisan of the conquering ex-hero from Imperial Spain, who was now frequently held an author of genocide. Indeed, the Oakland Board of Education had resolved that schools should "focus the October 12th curriculum of every year on Native American culture, contributions and history."

Moreover, after much travail, the State of California had just adopted a new kindergarten-through-eighth-grade history–social science textbook series published by Houghton Mifflin, offering little comfort to traditionalist partisans of Columbus or, indeed, to anyone inclined to see American history as the unbroken progress of benign Europeans across a savage and underutilized continent. Of the pages devoted to historical narrative in Houghton Mifflin's fourth-grade book, *Oh California!*, 15 percent went to sympathetic accounts of several California Indian nations. In the eighth-grade text, *A More Perfect Union,* an insert in chapter 3 entitled "Understanding Eurocentrism" cautioned against regarding American history simply as the saga of triumphant European "discovery." ("As you read more about the colonial period, try to imagine how American history might have been different if European settlers had been more open to the ways of other cultures.") The text declared: "Although their names and discoveries live on in romantic stories, most of the conquistadors acted ruthlessly in their search for riches and power. They treated the native inhabitants of America cruelly, enslaving them and often killing them. The conquistadors left a trail of slaughter as they searched for lost cities of gold."

The politics of textbook adoption in California, as in a number of other states, are intricate. The process could be called messy and political, or it could be called democratic. To be adopted by California schools, textbooks have to pass through several filters. Roughly every seven years, the state chooses a list of acceptable textbooks. The texts must be written in accordance with a "framework" approved by the state board of education. After public hearings, they must be cleared by the board's curriculum commission, then certified by the board itself. Once certified as eligible for adoption, they are referred to local school boards for further open hearings. All these hurdles have to be passed before textbooks are voted on by local school boards.

In the summer of 1990, when the Houghton Mifflin series came up for certification by the state's curriculum commission in Sacramento, one might have expected Christian fundamentalists, long dismayed by what they saw as a dangerous undermining of American verities, to rise in righteous indignation against so "politically correct" a dismantling of the "we came, we saw, we conquered" version of American history. After all, attacks from the cultural Right have long been a staple of textbook adoption proceedings. But on this occasion, although one Christian fundamentalist, wielding the psychological jargon that has become routine on these occasions, did maintain that the new textbooks "could be very damaging to the self-esteem of a fundamentalist Christian child" because they implied that fundamentalists are "emotional and hysterical," the complaint was easily addressed, was not followed up, and had no great effect.

Rather, the focus in Sacramento, and in the media, was on the groups of the cultural Left. To great media fanfare, a number of group representatives testified passionately that the books were "racist," religiously discriminatory, and otherwise demeaning. Muslims, Jews, Chinese Americans, gays, and, most vigorously, African Americans objected. A group calling itself Communities United against Racism in Education (CURE) offered eighty-five single-spaced pages of objections to the kindergarten through fifth-grade books alone, charging that they contain "stereotypes, omissions, distortions, exaggerations, and outright lies about peoples of color"; that they are "unidimensional" and "Eurocentric," taking "the side of colonialism and exploitation," "uncritically extol[ling] the white supremacist concept of Manifest Destiny" and "anthropologiz[ing] indigenous peoples"; that they "justify and trivialize . . . some of the most vicious social practices in our history," and "marginalize the lives and struggles of women, working and poor people, people with disabilities, and gay and lesbian people." In CURE's view, Houghton Mifflin "places the white establishment at the center of the universe and all the rest of us as their 'burden.' The insidious message is: in order for some children to be proud of their histories, other children must be made ashamed of theirs."

CURE pointed to some genuine instances of establishment bias, and to a number of places where the books were uncritical in a Dick-and-Janeish way, even arguably jingoistic in a traditional civics-book manner. They did find occasional passages in the books that could reasonably be read as subtle or not-so-subtle disparagements of foreign and minority cultures—for example, a European's jocular account of lengthy Chinese names. They rightly objected to a traditional account of Thanksgiving for failing to mention that Puritans and other colonists killed Indians. They chastised the third-grade book for calling John Wesley Powell "one of the first people to explore the Grand Canyon" when, of course, he was one of the first *white* people to do so. They pointed to a literature excerpt that contained the line: "She had blue eyes and white skin, like an angel." They argued that telling the children to make simulated Kwakiutl masks trivialized the spiritual qualities of Kwakiutl ceremonies—though they neglected to note that textbooks customarily trivialize the spiritual quali-

ties of *everybody's* ceremonies. Where a teacher's edition referred to help-
ful police, CURE wrote: "In many communities, specifically communities
of color, police officers are regarded not as helpers, but as people to fear."

But CURE and other critics did themselves no favors by interspersing
valid criticisms among scores of indiscriminate ones. The majority of
CURE's charges were trivial and hypersensitive. They were so eager to
find ethnocentrism in these texts that they seemed to quarrel with the
notion that there was or is a dominant American culture. They objected to
the profusion of American flags in the texts' pages. They objected that in
the kindergarten book's illustrations people of color looked "just like
whites, except for being tinted or colored in," and that when photographs
of children of color appeared, "there was no discussion of their respective
ethnic identities and specific contributions." When the books singled out
minorities' customs, CURE saw disapproval; when the books didn't single
them out, they saw neglect. They saw cultural bias against Cambodia
when the second-grade book mentioned that a Cambodian child living in
Boston plays in the snow when he couldn't have done so in Cambodia,
since it "never snows there." They again cried bias when the second-
grade book traced an African-American family back one generation less
than a family of German descent, and chastised the book, written for
seven-year-olds, when it failed to discuss the details of sharecropping.
They denounced a passage on the baseball player Roberto Clemente for
not mentioning that Jackie Robinson opened the way for him, and objected to a list of inventions because all were invented by white men.
They criticized an exercise inviting students to write a personal story from
a slave's point of view, on the ground that it is impossible "to imagine
being enslaved."

In Sacramento, however, CURE's and related objections grabbed the
mighty attention of the media. So did flamboyant statements like that of
an African-American woman calling the books "Eurocentric pap—
slanted, racist, and wrong" and maintaining that they contributed to a
"mental holocaust" of "self-esteem problems" for black children. Such
claims were supported by the Black Caucus of the state assembly. So
were Chinese Americans' complaints that the books trivialized the exploitation of the Chinese laborers imported to build the transcontinental rail-
roads. There were Muslim objections to a description of Mohammed—

strictly forbidden in Islam—as well as to a suggestion in a teacher's edition that a student play the part of Mohammed in a skit. Another strong objection was that in the world history volume, a diagram of a camel and its trappings was used to illustrate the "Moment in Time" capsule contained in the chapter on "The Roots of Islam"—the only animal used for such a purpose.

Nowadays, people of color have no monopoly on hypersensitivity. The California Jewish Community Relations Council brought its own list of offenses against the sixth-grade book, *A Message of Ancient Days*. They argued that the text presented Judaism as a passing prologue to Christianity. They objected to capitalizing the Christian "God" while the Jewish "god" was lower-case. They objected to treating the Jews as a people of laws and rituals, invidiously compared to Christians with their belief in kindness and love. They objected to the phrase "Old Testament," wishing it changed to "Hebrew Bible"; they deplored one lesson title, "An Age of Transition," and a reference to "His [Jesus'] Resurrection." They objected to the book's version of the story of the Good Samaritan, on the grounds that the bad neighbors were identified as Jews. Unremarked, however, on the same page, the source of this parable was referred to as "a popular Jewish teacher named Jesus."

The protesters were unimpressed by the fact that the seventh-grade world history volume included fifty-three pages on sub-Saharan Africa (10.6 percent of the entire narrative), fifty-six pages on Islam (11.2 percent), thirty pages on China (6.0 percent), and thirty-four pages on Japan (6.8 percent). As a memo from California's Superintendent of Public Instruction Bill Honig later pointed out, where a previously adopted world history text had devoted only one of its forty chapters to African history and ancient American Indian cultures combined, one-eighth of the new seventh-grade book was devoted to the Indians, or Native Americans, alone—an increase by a factor of ten. Nor did the critics seem to care that the textbooks frequently represented a radical departure from the history taught in earlier decades. The same seventh-grade book that offended some Muslims with the camel picture also noted that "Christian and Muslim sources portrayed the crusaders differently," and declared: "Traditionally, we learn history from the point of view of the winners." (Of course, the crusaders were losers in the short run, but Europe's storytellers have traditionally awarded them the righteous victory and not dwelt on the embarrassing dénouement.)

For their part, the authors plausibly defended the accuracy of their text on the great majority of points but agreed to a list of corrections on others—John Wesley Powell as the first *white* man to travel down the Grand Canyon, the Central Pacific railroad hiring "thousands," not "hundreds" of Chinese, and so on. The pictures of Mohammed were deleted, and the suggestion that a student play the role of the prophet replaced by the suggestion that a student interview a Muslim scholar. Gary B. Nash, the UCLA historian who was one of the authors of the series, later acknowledged to me that the offending camel was "a mistake. We thought it would be neat to show how an animal could be a means of diffusion of culture. Our mistake was that it's the only capsule which shows an animal. From the orthodox Moslem point of view, it plays on the stereotype of the Arab as a 'camel jockey.' The camel will go as soon as we revise the seventh-grade book." One sentence disliked by the Christian Right was revised. As for the Jewish objections, "Old Testament" became "Hebrew Bible," "An Age of Transition" became "Religious Developments," and an insert was added on developments in Judaism after Christ. The story of the Good Samaritan was modified to note that the man beaten by robbers was also a Jew. But some corrections were inconsistent. Many of the references to the Israelites' "god" were shifted to the upper case, but many—at times on the same page—were not. (Christianity's God was now consigned to the lower case only once.)

With the disputatious hearings completed, the state curriculum commission recommended adoption of the Houghton Mifflin books, subject to corrections. In October 1990, the state board of education approved the revised Houghton Mifflin books at every grade level, along with an eighth-grade text published by Holt, Rinehart & Winston. Local school boards were free to choose whichever they preferred for the eighth grade. At other grade levels, local boards would have to accept the Houghton Mifflin books or seek a state waiver to use funds that would otherwise be spent on textbooks to acquire their own materials, pending state approval.

Opponents now turned to the local adoption proceedings. Over the next few months, Los Angeles and San Francisco school boards, among many others, held their own contentious hearings, and ended up approving the Houghton Mifflin series. The opponents' only victory in a big city came in Oakland, the sixth-largest school district in the state. One consequence was that when Columbus Day rolled around in 1992, Oakland's fourth-, fifth-, and seventh-grade teachers had no textbooks at all to help them teach about California's Indians or, indeed, about anyone else.

The textbook battles took place in circumstances that were primed for rancor and inauspicious for education. Years of fiscal crisis had taken their toll on resources available for public services in California. A tax revolt kindled with the passing of the 1978 citizens' initiative called Proposition 13 had accelerated with the passing of several sequels. The result had been the slashing of the revenues available to local governments, and state funds had failed to make up the shortfalls. In addition, a downturn in California's economy not only worsened the social conditions that demoralize children but cut state school funds, gutted art, music, and other academic programs, closed libraries, and crowded the classrooms. In Oakland, for example, teachers were routinely responsible for more than thirty students at a time. Between 1969 and 1994, California slid in per-pupil school allocations from among the top ten states to forty-first. Still, the state had allocated money for new textbooks. Moreover, Bill Honig, the energetic reformer who was the state's top school official, was committed to a curriculum that would take account of the multiple cultures of America. Long before the time came to purchase new textbooks, Honig had established a commission to draw up a new "framework"—a slate of specifications that publishers would have to meet by 1990 to qualify for statewide approval.

That framework, approved in 1987, was a brave attempt to square the pedagogical circle. It required that grade school history be taught with an emphasis on the multiplicity of historical experiences while stressing the "centrality of Western civilization." At the same time, it insisted that history be integrated with social studies and literature, and told as a coherent story. It required that the K–8 curriculum include three full years of world history—one of which was to cover the ancient world—along with three years of American history and one of California history. It insisted that the study of religion be integrated into the historical curriculum. (Perhaps it was this provision that placated the right wing.) The framework's coauthors were Charlotte Crabtree, a professor of education at UCLA, and Diane Ravitch, a professor of history at Teachers College of Columbia University, a leader of the fight against "Afrocentrism" in New York State's curriculum, subsequently assistant secretary of education in the Bush administration, and a political lightning rod. "Diane Ravitch was chosen to do a sneaky end-run," Toni Cook, then vice president (and later president) of the Oakland Board of Education, told me later. "She wanted to put things in the books which were very kindred to what the conservative forces were trying to do in New York. For example, this idea that all Americans are immigrants."

Though California accounts for 11 percent of America's textbook sales and offers a market of more than $50 million, the $20 million cost of a new series was such that the only publisher willing to meet the deadline with an entire line of new books was Houghton Mifflin, which lacked a history series of its own. Houghton Mifflin linked up with a group of textbook entrepreneurs called Ligature Inc. Ligature's education experts wanted to break with one of the hoariest of textbook traditions, namely, stodginess. Their designers, trained at the Rhode Island School of Design, specialized in dazzling wake-up devices—overlapping illustrations, questions stuffed into the margins, colored inserts alternating with black-and-white segments, visuals dripping down and across the pages, full-page drawings encapsulating "Moments in Time." When they showed a prototype segment to focus groups of California teachers, the teachers approved.

For two years, Gary Nash told me, "we just went hell-for-leather." Given the elaborate back-and-forth process of outlines and drafts, comments from experts and teachers, and redrafts, Nash agreed that two years was just not enough time to compile ten books (kindergarten through eighth grade, in addition to an alternative fourth-grade book for possible use outside California). "Each of the four authors was supposed to read everything," Nash said, "though it was impossible." Nash himself was teaching a full load at UCLA and trying to finish two other books. His coauthors, Beverly J. Armento, director of the Center for Business and Economic Education at Georgia State University, Christopher L. Salter, chairman of the geography department of the University of Missouri, and

Karen K. Wixson, a professor of education at the University of Michigan, were not historians. Nash played his main role in the earlier stages—setting up extensive outlines and trying to insure that the books would, in fact, be multicultural. Much of the carelessness of the texts, he said, the lines attacked for racism and bad faith, came from the rush job.

In any event, with the books accepted at the state level, Gary Nash thought the worst was over. He had not anticipated much flak in the first place. He was, after all, well known as a multiculturalist, as well as one of the most prolific American social historians of a cohort trained in the 1960s and devoted to reconstructing American history, in the words of an early revisionist slogan, "from the bottom up." Nash's books included *Red, White, and Black: The Peoples of Early America,* which, in the words of his introduction, "proceed[ed] from the belief that to cure the historical amnesia that has blotted out so much of our past we must reexamine American history as the interaction of many peoples from a wide range of cultural backgrounds over a period of many centuries." In 1970, when (under Governor Ronald Reagan) the regents of the University of California fired the activist Angela Davis from her philosophy post at UCLA, Nash headed her defense committee, which raised enough money to pay her salary. That same year, he helped redesign the introductory course in American history at UCLA, turning it into the history of an interaction of peoples. He had already written a popular textbook for eleventh-grade American history that many districts, including Oakland's, had adopted unopposed.

At fifty-nine, the sandy-haired, neatly bearded Nash was wearing a work shirt and stonewashed jeans when I spoke to him at his comfortable Pacific Palisades home. The art on the wall was Mexican, the lunch was burritos. Nash was now president-elect of the Organization of American Historians—with the support of colleagues of all colors—and was being considered for the position of head of the National Endowment for the Humanities. During a four-hour period, his phone rang five times for conversations about other textbooks he was working on.

Nash has the easy, welcoming manner California has made famous, although he grew up in Philadelphia. During the interview, he spoke deliberately, in an unruffled tone, until one of two subjects came up. The first: the downgrading of ordinary people in the old-fashioned version of history. Then he accelerated. "What does it tell our kids, to say that only great men make history?" He swept passionately into an example of a person he wanted to write about when the Houghton Mifflin books were first being outlined: Fred Korematsu, an ex-welder and high school graduate who had tried to enlist in the U.S. Army during World War II and who, when the authorities came to intern him along with his Japanese-American compatriots, refused to comply, was arrested, tried, convicted, and appealed his internment all the way up to the Supreme Court. "Or take the sixth-grade book, *A Message of Ancient Days,* on world religions," Nash went on. "In the course of the school year, you don't even get to Europe until February. Just by doing it this way, we broke the mold."

The second subject that aroused Nash's ire was the attack on his textbooks as "racist." Like many another—especially many another white—who identifies with the universalist tradition of the Left, he was stunned. He did not fully grasp how his ecumenical position could have come under such intense, downright unheeding fire. In his incomprehension, Nash was, and is, in good company. In the heat of the battle, it is hard to grasp why people who care about justice strike so venomously against those who, whatever their differences, stand closest to them. During recent years, many men and women of goodwill have had trouble understanding why they, of all people, have been singled out as enemies. They are rationalists. Confronted with unbalanced, ungenerous, sometimes downright bizarre accusations, they go on trying to meet them with straightforward arguments: Jews did *not* dominate the slave trade; melanin in skin pigment does *not* increase intelligence. But this was not the project white leftists were supposed to have signed up for! They were supposed to be teaching about conquest and slavery, struggles for freedom, and how history goes on from there. Nash, like many another man and woman of the Left, didn't know what hit him.

Nowhere was the outcome more shocking than in Oakland. With an elected school board composed of four African Americans, two Chinese Americans, and one white leftist; a school superintendent of African-American and Latino descent; and a teaching staff almost half nonwhite (and largely left-of-center in disposition) responsible for teaching a student body that in 1990 was 46.9 percent black, 24 percent white, 18.8

percent Asian and Pacific Islander, and 15.2 percent Hispanic, Oakland might have been the very model for what is called, these days, multicultural education. Moreover, school administrators had decided that, for the first time, teachers at the various grade levels would make their own text recommendations, and for the most part, the teachers liked the new books. So Nash was not prepared for the eruption that greeted him when, on March 18, 1991, he flew to Oakland to address an open meeting sponsored by the Berkeley and Oakland school boards at Claremont Middle School in a middle-class, largely white section of Oakland near the Berkeley city line. (The Oakland and Berkeley school boards were debating the books simultaneously.) All the seats were taken long before the meeting began and the room was overflowing with more than a hundred people. Some were parents, but at least as many, by various accounts, were ethnic studies students, mainly black, from San Francisco State University across the bay. The hall was festooned with placards bearing slogans like STOP POISONING YOUNG MINDS! Mary Hoover, a professor of ethnic studies at San Francisco State (now a dean at Howard University), was Nash's principal antagonist, accusing the books of "sheer Eurocentric arrogance." Hoover focused on a passage in *A Message of Ancient Days* in which an early "naked dark-skinned" human on the east African plains carries a "bloody bone" that "oozes . . . red marrow." Hoover maintained that there was an implication that these early Africans were cannibals.

"She misrepresented the books," says Steven Weinberg, an eighth-grade history teacher who, when I spoke to him, had spent twenty-four years at Claremont Middle School and supported the adoption of the Houghton Mifflin books. "I said, they're not talking about cannibalism. They're *carnivorous.*" (By the time the books were published, the "bloody marrow bone" had become, simply, "a bone" containing, incidentally, marrow, and the naked persons were no longer specified as "dark-skinned.") "The way she distorted these books," Weinberg says, "they were like something out of the eugenics movement. It was as if they were worse than Goebbels. There was cheering and yelling. It was really ugly. The attacks on Gary Nash were ridiculous and *ad hominem.* He was trying to establish his credentials, and he said he had been on the Angela Davis defense committee. Someone got up and said, 'We have to remember that there were plenty of people on that who did not have Angela Davis's best interests at heart.' "

"It was an auto-da-fé, a one-sided battle," maintained Harry Chotiner, a former UC Santa Cruz professor of American history and member of the editorial board of *Socialist Review* who now teaches at the private College Preparatory School in Oakland. Chotiner had accompanied a friend, an Oakland curriculum official, to the meeting because, he told me, "Gary Nash had been a hero of mine. When I was a graduate student in history, I had a lot of respect for what he'd written about Native Americans and blacks, the new social history. It was a pilgrimage for me." Chotiner was shocked, therefore, to find that "not one speaker was willing to give him or the editors the benefit of the doubt. No one said, 'I like this about the book, but on the other hand I don't like that.' Instead, the objections ranged from the thoughtful to the silly to the scurrilous." The point about the camel Chotiner agreed was thoughtful. An example of the silly was the objection that a section on black history in one volume didn't focus on Jackie Robinson, Martin Luther King, Jr., or Malcolm X. (This particular volume stopped at the year 1900, Nash responded.) An example of the scurrilous was the contemptuous charge from an African-American student that the use of the term *Afro*-American at one point in the series was "clear evidence of deep-seated racism, and so he as a white man and a racist had no business trying to teach her."

Chotiner estimated that there were twenty or thirty of the silly and scurrilous attacks. "In most cases, bad motives were assumed, and Gary and the editors were the enemy. People would have spoken in the same tone if the authors had been George Wallace, Ross Barnett, and Bull Connor. There were no attempts to bridge gaps, to find common ground. I was really stunned by the anger. It wasn't even an anger of betrayal— 'How dare you do this when we share something in common?' The anger was, 'This is just what we expected.' I was completely intimidated by their anger. I thought, this is outrageous, but I couldn't get up and talk. My legs would not support me, my arm would not go up into the air. If you asked me, Why not? Were they going to beat me up? No. Were they going to slash my tires? No. Throw a rock through my window? No. I think I would have been heckled, and I don't think my comments would have made a difference."

"I wasn't expecting a dispute in which the critics declaim but they don't point to evidence," Nash said later. There was, for example, the charge that the books "trivialized" slavery. The seventh-grade book includes, among other descriptions of the horrors of slavery and the endurance of slaves, a graphic two-page passage from Frederick Douglass's autobiography. "Just fifteen years ago," Nash says, "the textbooks were full of happy slaves grateful to have been lifted up out of barbarian Africa. Getting an accurate account of slavery into the textbooks is the whole point of my career." He was, moreover, incredulous when a Japanese-American woman stood up to charge that the books trivialized the suffering of her people during World War II internment, saying: "We want our history written by our people." In truth, the seventh-grade book does sweep through its discussion of the relocation camps in a few lines. But these lines call the camps "prison-like" and point out that the internees were forcibly dispossessed (in a section entitled "The Ongoing Struggle for Justice"). In the fourth-grade book on California history, lesson 1 of the chapter "California in Wartime" begins with two pages on the internments—almost half the entire lesson.

Nash acknowledges that some criticisms were legitimate, in particular the accusation by some Chinese-American parents that not many pages were devoted to their ancestors in the California history volume. Still, he defended his choices. "My response was, you can't produce a book which is all-inclusive. You can't emphasize the Chinese in San Francisco *and* the Armenians in Fresno *and* the Portuguese in San Pablo *and* the Italians in North Beach *and* the Koreans in L.A. You can't write the history of every ethnic group in California. You certainly can't do it for the entire country." Arguably, the experience of the Chinese in America was more significant than the others. In any event, Nash's point is not likely to be persuasive to some minority parents convinced that their children, systematically humiliated by their exclusion from public imagery, need to find exemplars who look like them in history books.

Despite the criticism that they are not inclusive enough, the books as they stand already strain at the seams to enfold two contradictory stories. The master contours of American history are the traditional ones. "In fact," Nash affirms, "the way the story is told does follow the Europeans, [for] that is the story of how power worked." Here, shifting the ground of his argument, Nash subscribes to a conventional historical sequencing and choice of topics. History should be neither a feel-good exercise nor a census of the experiences of preferred peoples. It should not be simply an inventory of "contributions," as if the historian's mission were to distribute party favors. Its purpose is not to make anyone "proud" of any group's historical record. Whether one likes the status quo or not, history should be, in important part, the record of what power has done. A student who does not know how the powerful acted—indeed, often over the objections of the weak and oppressed—cannot begin to understand why the world has become what it is. Like it or not, the decisions that shaped America's political, legal, and economic institutions were largely made by Europeans and their descendants.

Nash's texts, on the other hand, do try to make their peace with history from below. They frequently interrupt their master narrative for snippets of social history. They indicate what women were doing. They pause to tell stories about the people who were not movers and shakers, people rolled over by "progress," people who had to fight for their places in the American sun. History from above rolls forward with seeming relentlessness. History from below is always stopping, retracing its steps, moving sideways, shifting back and forth, pausing to say "meanwhile" and "despite."

The disjointedness of the books, their occasional self-contradiction, their jumpiness as they juxtapose one historical account with another— all this is a direct consequence of working in both keys at once for fear of being dismissive. Disjointedness is built into their nature as the product of two rival traditions. In this, they are typical of the textbooks that followed the 1960s. Starting in the 1970s, as Frances FitzGerald observed in *America Revised,* textbook writers frequently slapped revisionist views of the European conquest, of slavery and capitalism, onto the old triumphalist upward-and-westward story. The Houghton Mifflin books illustrate her point that the result is riddled with inconsistencies. Thus, in Houghton Mifflin's eighth-grade book, lesson one speaks of the "discovery of the new world," says that "America was different promises to different people," and declares that the conquistadors "subdued whole civilizations of native peoples." In lesson two, the reader is invited to identify with a Spaniard on his ship; in lesson three, with an Indian. ("Europeans were not the first to discover the 'new' world.") Downright inconsistencies passed through the revision net. When I mentioned to Nash that, despite the argument against the discovery myth, a reference to "the discovery of New World" appeared on page four, he was surprised to see it. The books total, after all, more than three thousand pages, and they were hurried into shape to meet a bureaucratic deadline. Any scrupulous or—depending on your point of view—nit-picking reader could find grist for his or her sense of injury. Activists took offense—they *chose* to take offense—at what seemed to them a casual quality to some of the books' reminders that American history has long been marked by contempt and discrimination directed at people of color.

The books' thematic disjointedness is embodied in, and intensified by, their format, which gives them the look of scrapbooks. Even Sheila Jordan, an Oakland teacher formerly on the city school board (and later elected to the Oakland City Council) who voted for adoption and used the Houghton Mifflin books in the lower grades, acknowledged to me that "they're fragmented. There are too many color patches, too many little synopses and boxes. They don't flow easily. The layout gets in the way in an attempt to be hip, multimedia, and all that. The books don't put the fragments together."

Indeed, to anyone raised on linear texts, these books bear a disconcerting resemblance to MTV. The master text is frequently broken up by tinted paragraphs of quotations. Even teachers who thought the series an advance on what had come before didn't like everything about them. The "narrative" that starts each lesson runs no longer than two paragraphs— for example: "Thunderclouds rise like mountains off to the east. The once calm ocean has suddenly grown restless, loudly thumping the ship's prow. You're crossing the Atlantic Ocean in the mid-1500s . . ."—before the generalizations kick in. Although many teachers and students found the books useful, others demurred. One bright eleven-year-old of my acquaintance found the sixth-grade book lacking "enough of a story." Nash accepted some of this criticism. "There were so many 'features,' they interfered with the story. I objected, but I almost always lost."

However, incoherence was not the charge leveled against the Houghton Mifflin textbooks when the dispute surfaced in Oakland. The charge was, in fact, coherence—coherent racism by inclusion, exclusion, and, at times, intention. Frequently, this was joined to a charge that most teachers deferred to the texts, that they used them as crutches, even that they were downright lazy; they should have been out writing or rustling up their own materials—as, in fact, some of the most conscientious teachers did. I spoke with one of these, Carol Chinn, a fourth-grade teacher at Malcolm X School in neighboring Berkeley, who supplemented textbook lessons by assigning literature on Indians and other groups and leading field trips to missions and museums as a way of satisfying the framework's demands. To present a unified history, Chinn would focus on a single period and come at it from various angles at once so that, for example, while teaching the Gold Rush, she was also asking what was happening to women, to Chinese miners, to Indians, rather than having ethnic groups pop up here and there and then vanish for long stretches. "I've been doing this for a long time," she told me. "I feel strongly that these children have to live in the year 2010, when a majority of California will be nonwhite. I wasn't willing to accept bias at all."

Oakland's teachers, who had never before been so involved in selecting school textbooks, were not uncritical of the Houghton Mifflin series. Even a supporter like curriculum official Shelley Weintraub noted that the fourth-grade California history book lost interest in the California Indians after the Gold Rush, and gave scant attention to Americans of Asian origin. Many teachers found the eighth-grade book too difficult, as well as confusing at times. On such grounds, and in the belief that there were better alternatives at hand, Oakland teachers opposed adoption of the Houghton Mifflin books for kindergarten through third grades and for the eighth grade. They endorsed the others—the seventh-grade teachers by more than 90 percent, the fourth-, fifth-, and sixth-grade teachers narrowly. The Oakland school superintendent, Richard ("Pete") Mesa, supported the teachers.

When opponents proposed to devise their own substitute materials—a decision the school board eventually endorsed—the teachers' reaction was, according to Steven Weinberg, "Who are they kidding?" There was no time, they thought, to do a serious job of assembling comprehensive equivalents. But many teachers held a more relaxed view of what textbooks were for in the first place. They knew that textbooks were intrinsically limited. Still, they wanted to get them into the students' hands—at least as the source of homework assignments. As Weinberg said, "A textbook is not a course. Just because a textbook leaves something out doesn't mean that the course has to leave it out." The Oakland school board could have adopted the books as flawed but useful tools—so that, at the very least, teachers had them in place for background—and at the same time promoted the use of supplements. In the end, this is what the Los Angeles school board did. In the course of the debate there, Nash agreed to edit a set of primary source materials by Americans of indigenous, African, Hispanic, and Asian origin, 172 pages' worth, which Houghton Mifflin included with the textbooks at no extra charge. By law, this very same supplement had to be available to every school district in the state. When I interviewed her a year after the fight, Toni Cook, of the Oakland school board, called this "a responsible compromise."

But when push came to shove in Oakland, the opponents were not in the market for "a responsible compromise." They wanted all or nothing. The debate was not about actual textbooks to be used as practical instruments of schooling but about symbols, overloaded with emotional meaning, totems of moral conviction. For many people—administrators, teachers, and parents—textbooks are symbols to start with: signs that some larger community exists. The community exists, so the assumption goes, insofar as it shares collective knowledge. The textbook is therefore a carrier of the publicness of the public schools. It suggests the possibility—indeed, the actuality—of a shared collective identity. This is why textbooks are revised, why they are defended and fought over.

When the Oakland teachers endorsed most of the Houghton Mifflin books, some of the early critics changed their positions. Thus school board member Sheila Jordan, who had shared in a unanimous board decision calling on the state to reject the books when they had first come under attack by CURE, had become a vociferous defender and, for her pains, was falsely accused of taking Houghton Mifflin money for her successful city council election campaign. Jan Malvin, a Jewish psychologist and parent who had brought the issue of the depiction of Judaism to the Oakland board's attention in the first place, was swayed by the teachers' vote. Since the teachers had endorsed the books as amended, she was willing to defer to their judgment.

But despite such accommodations, when the Oakland school board met to make a decision in June 1991 the atmosphere was acrimonious—not much different from the atmosphere at the Claremont Middle School meeting three months earlier. One school board member was heard to say beforehand, "We're going to mau-mau Gary Nash." An *Oakland Tribune* op-ed article by two leading opponents of the texts, San Francisco State University's Mary Hoover and Kitty Kelly Epstein, an associate professor of education at Oakland's Holy Names College, sounded off, though they offered only two specific criticisms of the books. The fifth-grade book, Hoover and Epstein wrote, referred to the frontier as "unexplored"—a case, they charged, of ethnocentric wording. The other example, however, was something else. "The essence of the books' portrayal of American history," Hoover and Epstein wrote, "is captured in the title of the fifth-grade text, 'The U.S., A Nation of Immigrants,' . . . [which] does not capture the experience of a huge part of the American population. Native Americans, Mexican Americans and African Americans were not lucky immigrants but victims of some of the worst murder and pillage in human history." When junior high school history teacher Steven Weinberg rose at the school board meeting to say that the claim was false, that the fifth-grade book was not, in fact, entitled *The U.S., A Nation of Immigrants,* that it was, in fact, entitled *America Will Be,* from a Langston Hughes poem, the crowd booed him down, Weinberg recalls, "with shouts of 'Put on a swastika' and 'You're quoting out of context.' How can you quote a title out of context?" A white teacher defending the books was told, "Shut up, white bitch." "What do you mean, 'white bitch'?" she said. "Well, you are *white,*" was the reply.

Everything about Steven Weinberg is trim—his beard, his V-neck sweater, his gold-rimmed glasses, his manner of speaking—but for his frayed white collar. "The Muslims are usually faceless hordes," Weinberg says. "Not in this book. This book, in fact, teaches that the Muslims were more tolerant than the Christians. This was the first time you had any reference to important people in Muslim history. The Muslim kids in school can see references to the people they're named after. In the eighth-grade book, Mexican soldiers are called 'brave,' while the Americans are given no adjective. I was surprised, in fact, that there was no right-wing attack on these books. I said to myself, Be happy for small favors." Weinberg describes himself as a moderate Democrat and "a pluralist in almost all dimensions." A year before the debate, he had used his own money to buy his students copies of *Dragonwings*, a novel by Lawrence Yep about a Chinese-American aviator. "I really believe in having many voices in the curriculum. I don't feel myself naturally allied with people who say that we should teach traditional American history. I don't like being lumped with them."

When I interviewed Weinberg, the walls of his classroom at Claremont Middle School were festooned with questions scrawled in childish lettering on signed white sheets of paper: "What group of Indians were the first ones to live in America?" "Why are blacks treated so poorly?" "Why are people so obsessed with money and power?" "Why don't the U.S. have women as President?" "Why did the U.S. take over Mexico's land?" "Who makes rules for America?" The children, Weinberg explained, chose the questions they wanted to see answered by the end of the school year.

I asked Weinberg how he taught Columbus. He showed me one of his assignments: Write a paragraph saying whether we ought to celebrate Indigenous People's Day or Columbus Day. The next week, he gave his students two statements to refute. The first said: "The American Indians were uncivilized barbarians. They had no religion. They had no art. They were disorganized, with no laws or governments. They were half-naked and lived in flimsy huts. They created nothing of value." The second: "All Native Americans lived in harmony with nature and in peace with each other before the European invasion began in 1492."

"It's very hard to do this right," Weinberg added. "What makes sense to a student from Cambodia? I have a boy from Ethiopia in my class. We have people from South America. It constantly forces me to rethink, because I don't want simply to teach what I was taught. I spent a lot of time trying to teach the Alamo accurately. The traditional view minimizes slavery in Texas. I found something that speaks to interracial harmony: the Anglo and Hispanic Texans who were long-term Texans were the ones trying to avoid the war in the first place."

◆ ◆ ◆

On June 5, 1991, the Oakland school board voted against adopting the Houghton Mifflin books that the teachers had wanted for grades four through seven. For kindergarten through third grade and for the eighth grade, they selected other books. At the sixth-grade level, the board voted in favor of an older book published by Scholastic, a book that they did not consider in detail, that they chose largely because it was not from Houghton Mifflin, and that one white teacher involved in curriculum matters considers "far more racist than Houghton Mifflin." "I haven't heard of any teacher who likes" the sixth-grade Scholastic book, Renee Swayne, a third-grade teacher in Oakland who supported the Houghton Mifflin books, told me. "The board needed to be clear what they were voting on," she said. "If they were opposed to a racist text, some of the previously adopted materials that they were instructing us to continue to use were even more racist." Swayne, an African American and a twenty-year veteran of the Oakland schools, resented the opponents' attitude. "They presuppose that there is only one black ideology, and if you spoke against it you were hissed, harassed, and humiliated. I don't like that kind of intimidation. I don't like that overzealous quality. I consider myself to be liberal but I don't toe the line. It put me in a funny position to be aligned with the quote unquote 'establishment.' But I tried to come up with a decision that was in the best interests of the children. There's no safe, single, easy solution."

I asked Swayne how she approached Columbus. "I taught the Columbus myth so I could debunk it," she said. "I read them the story and then we began to question it. I asked the students: How can you discover a place where people already live? What if you invite someone home and they take over the room? Can they say they discovered it? We talked about the concept of value, how gold meant something to the Europeans but not to the Indians. The Indians were not stupid, they just had other values." I asked if she thought her students had ended up confused. "I told them it wasn't a matter of right and wrong. They talked about whether Columbus was a hero or a villain. There was a point at which they were beginning to model themselves after my opinions. It was more important to get them to reason than to come to a specific conclusion. If one kid becomes a questioner, you've achieved something. But now, without the books, I think there are classrooms where no social studies is being taught."

Just beneath the surface of such disputes lies the wound in all American dreams, the question of race. To the most vigorous opponents, the deep issue was simple: the schools ill-serve African-American youth. One leading anti–Houghton Mifflin activist, Fred Ellis, a husky, affable African American who has been teaching hard-to-teach children for thirty years, says: "Textbooks are one reason why kids have dropped out of school. If you don't believe me, listen to rap artists. Some of what they say is vulgar, but they're sometimes relevant. Public Enemy came out and said young people should be the teachers. I've worked with kids who are dropouts. You can't use material that is irrelevant. These kids sleep on the street, they're abandoned, they have experiences I haven't had."

Another activist, Kitty Kelly Epstein, was the particular bane of many textbook supporters. A slender, intense woman in her forties, Kitty Epstein was a veteran of the Marxist Left and had worked with Sheila Jordan to democratize the American Federation of Teachers and in a campaign against school vouchers. But in recent years, she has been fired by the conviction that "progressivism doesn't mean anything." Attacks on the Oakland school board—there had been corruption charges—were, in her eyes, covers for racism. The fact that a majority of Oakland's teachers wanted the Houghton Mifflin textbooks did not cut much ice with Kitty Epstein: she dismissed textbooks as "crutches," adding that many teachers don't even use them anymore. Epstein said scornfully: "There are teachers who say, 'Oh, my God, what shall we do for these poor kids?' We don't think about them that way. We don't pity them. They're smart. We're excited about these kids. We don't think these are poor little kids the way a lot of the teachers do. I've talked to these kids. These are the most intellectually exciting conversations I've had in my life."

Still, I asked, wouldn't it have been better to have the Houghton Mifflin books available for classroom use as references, sources of homework assignments, baselines for class discussion? But the books, Epstein and Ellis insisted, lacked "positive materials." They assumed that the self-esteem of children is at risk unless they can be taught history peopled by exemplary figures who look like themselves. Renee Swayne, on the other hand, thought the books did well enough at that, and applauded the books for being true to a terrible history: "I don't think slavery is anything to be unproud about. Some people don't want to teach slavery. But we are survivors! We should be appalled by slavery, but it's nothing to be embarrassed about." I asked Steven Weinberg to respond to the argument that "irrelevant" textbooks are one reason why black students drop out of school. "I think that may be true of some kids at the high school grade levels," he said. "Very few at eighth grade. I think this image is extrapolated from high school and college, when they've seen enough of the world to feel alienated."

Accused of offering no alternatives to the Houghton Mifflin textbooks, the opponents took the position that they could develop their own homegrown substitute curriculum in a hurry. For this purpose, they would use the state money that the school board would save by not adopting state-sanctioned textbooks—$18 to $30 per child, depending on the grade level. "It's very easy to develop a new curriculum," Epstein told me. The Oakland school board thought so too, and agreed to let Ellis and Epstein recruit teachers and others to write new materials to compensate for the missing textbooks. During the summer of 1991 Ellis, Epstein, and their allies did work up parts of a surrogate curriculum. But many were less history than contemporary polemics. Even the NAACP, which had supported the original protest, objected to a caricature of Clarence Thomas that appeared in one curriculum segment.

In the tenth and eleventh straight years of Republican rule in Washington and the ninth of Republican rule in the governor's mansion in Sacramento, why did committed people devote so much energy to mobilizing against the most pluralist textbooks ever brought before the State of California? Why were they able to command so much of the public debate on educational subjects overall? How could one gay activist have accused the books of "extermination" for failing to take note of Americans who had loved people of the same sex? Why so vehement? Even allowing the books' flaws, why the urge to demonize them?

The bitterness of the attack on the textbooks in Oakland was, by any stretch of the imagination, out of all proportion to the real stakes. In this, it was typical of many (not all) of the recent multicultural donnybrooks. In the background, whether noted directly or not, were intractable facts: a stupefying degree of inequality in American society and, in particular, of poverty among African Americans. Wealth in the United States has sometimes trickled, sometimes cascaded upward for a quarter of a century so that, to put the matter in raw statistical terms, in 1989, the wealthiest 1 percent of American households owned 39 percent of total household wealth, and 48 percent of the sum of all bank accounts, stocks, and bonds. The median nonwhite household, which in 1983 owned 9 percent of what the median white household owned, owned only 5 percent in 1989. In 1989, 35 percent of nonwhite and Hispanic families had zero or negative net worth, compared with 12 percent of whites. In 1993, 46 percent of black children were living below the poverty line. Between 1984 and 1989, the life expectancy gap between white and black males widened from 6.3 years to 8.2 years; according to the most recent data available, males in Bangladesh have a better chance of living past age forty than males in Harlem.

While most Americans deplore these facts, and at least outside (admittedly, growing) white supremacist and Social Darwinist circles it is generally bad form to insist that they are in the natural order of things, there is no political consensus about what to do and no vigorous political movements welling up from those populations most affected. Those who suffer most are often most quiescent. As Clara Sue Kidwell, a professor of Native American studies at the University of California, Berkeley, told me at the time of the 1992 protests against Columbus, "We have tremendous issues to deal with: jobs on the reservation, health issues, the dropout crisis. No political agenda comes out of the attack on Columbus. Instead, there's the assumption that all our problems follow from Columbus." Instead of moving to organize against rock-bottom class inequalities and racial discrimination, many activists choose to fight real and imagined symbols of insult. They do not know what else to do, and they are not trying to find out. Their critics do not offer a convincing means to heal America's wounds, either.

Dedicated people like Fred Ellis and Kitty Epstein resort to a deeply censorious assumption: in the beginning and in the end is the Word. They assume that school is omnipotent, that pride develops from talk of pride, that guilt is the engine of political change. The assumption of the textbook opponents is that more "relevant" textbooks make alienated youth less alienated, keep them in school, thus help them succeed. They agree with textbook advocates, in fact, that better textbooks—whatever they mean by "better"—will make a significant difference in keeping up the morale of Oakland's students and thereby equip them to fare better in a future economy that will have less need of the less skilled. But genuflections are made toward these arguments in the absence of strong evidence.

Or against the evidence. John U. Ogbu, a professor of anthropology at the University of California, Berkeley, and his colleagues concluded after much research that neither the ideal of a common curriculum defended by conservatives nor the ideal of multiculturalism defended by liberals "is likely to enhance appreciably the academic achievement of those minority groups who have not traditionally done well in school." The disturbing possibility raised by this research is that poor students are put off less by the tilt of the textbooks than by the fear that their peers will define any academic success as "acting white."

There is also the disconcerting question of how much academic success the American economy could actually abide. If all African-American youth in Oakland graduated from high school with a B average or better, would there be jobs for them anywhere but McDonald's? For that matter, would there be places for them to continue their education? One thing was certain: with community college fees rising by 290 percent between 1990–91 and 1994–95, student fees in the nineteen-campus California State University system rising by 103 percent and in the nine-campus University of California system by 134 percent, with experienced professors being seduced into early retirement and courses being eliminated accordingly to cut costs, there wouldn't be room for most of these high school graduates in the moldering halls of California's college system.

During years of tax revolt, declining revenues, state budget crisis, and educational cutbacks, much of the popular energy and commitment it would have taken to fight for the preservation—let alone the improvement—of public education was channeled into acrimony among potential allies. Oakland's school fight was a shadow play at the edge of the precipice.

"It was a symbolic fight," said Sheila Jordan, who was the only educator on the school board. "They won a symbolic victory but they lost a piece of the struggle. If we had gotten these textbooks, they could have used any supplementary materials they wanted. I'm not against a certain Afrocentricity, I'm not against distributing political material—let the kids have anything that could help. There had never been such a wide representation of teachers in the selection process. Previously, a much smaller group of teachers had made recommendations, and they were being lobbied by the publishers. I think most parents wanted the books. But the issue became so politicized. If you were for the Houghton Mifflin books, you were called 'racist.' "

Shelley Weintraub put it this way: "I thought the textbook debate was totally misplaced. You pick false symbols, you call each other names, you stifle real debate. There's virtually no connection between the rage that the opponents are feeling and the object of their attack. They can't affect the federal government, they can't affect the state government, so they're going to trash the local school board."

Weintraub is herself a Berkeley veteran of the antiwar and women's movements. "I regard myself as a multiculturalist," she said, "and I think this is the prevailing view among teachers. To give an accurate understanding of American history, you have to give an accurate picture of the Chinese working on the railroad, and a lot of other groups doing a lot of other things. But I'm not a big one for basing the curriculum on self-esteem. It's hippie-dippy. My sense of my students is that they gain self-esteem when they develop skills and feel their power, and not because they had someone to look up to. I'm not against role models and heroes, but I think it's ahistorical to base a curriculum on that. My kid came home from kindergarten with a badge that said, I FEEL SPECIAL. I think there are other ways."

I asked Steven Weinberg what he thought was driving the protest. "The important thing is that most of the testimony wasn't about the textbooks, actually. People were recounting experiences of racism: their children were beaten up, called names. The testimony was real heartfelt. A lot of people took a leap of faith that there was some connection between this and the textbooks." This is the leap of faith that makes for the wrong fight on the wrong grounds. Weinberg continued: "Something else happened. I said, If we don't have textbooks, it's going to be harder to keep our best teachers. This year, we have all new faces teaching the seventh grade. Anyone who could went to the eighth grade, where we had a textbook, or went to another subject. Or retired early. This is hard work. You don't have time to develop a curriculum. You need all the help you can get." He pointed to an inch-thick stack of papers he had to grade over the weekend.

"Two things anger me," Weinberg added. "There are all the untruths that were told about the books. And all of that made the job harder for some awfully good teachers, and in that way the protest hurt the education of the kids."

Two years after the Columbus quincentenary, Oakland's fourth-, fifth-, and seventh-grade classes still had no history textbooks.

All family fights are different, but Oakland's textbook fight has a familiar ring. Who by now isn't used to atrocity tales in the culture wars? But why is there so much bitterness on all sides? Why such hypersensitivity? Why have so many people who have suffered grievously from the West's many abrogations of Enlightenment reason lost faith in the Enlightenment? What has become of the ideal of a Left—or, for that matter, of a nation—that federates people of different races, genders, sexualities, or for that matter, religions and classes? Why has this ideal been neglected or abandoned by so many of the poor and minorities who should share the Left's ideal of equality? Why are so many people attached to their marginality and why is so much of their intellectual labor spent developing theories to justify it? Why insist on difference with such rigidity, rancor, and blindness, to the exclusion of the possibility of common knowledge and common dreams?

Today it is the conservatives who claim common culture and color blindness as their special causes and who denounce the obsession with difference—as it is frequently right and necessary to do. It suits them to identify the Left as a whole with the illiberality that they often properly despise. Yet they miss the fact that much of the energy of the party of difference is, in fact, directed not against conservatives but against the left wing of the party of commonality. One of the striking features of the Oakland dispute is that it was, in so many respects, internecine. Many of those who confronted each other so harshly were veterans of the 1960s Left. They had shared a radical ambiance and fought together for civil rights, peace in Vietnam, the strengthening of public support for schools, welfare, and job creation. Once again, in the not-so-grand tradition of the Left, some leftists targeted other leftists (who now called themselves "progressives") and dominated the discussion by dint of their fury. Sheila Jordan had been a Trotskyist. Toni Cook had been an activist in the Black Student Union and a supporter of the black nationalist Ron Karenga as a student at UCLA in the late 1960s—at the same time Gary Nash was a prominent member of UCLA's faculty Left.

The leaders of both camps were not Republicans. None sided with the party of tradition, the nationalists who, in this country, we call conservatives, whose cultural passion is to shore up conventional forms of authority. No, Oakland's days as a Republican stronghold are long gone—mainly because of a steady influx of African Americans and, even more, a linked exodus of whites (who declined from 50.5 percent of the population in 1970 to 28.3 percent in 1990). The textbook dispute does, however, display the incapacity of the so-called Left. There is no *it* there. What we have instead is an ill-fitting sum of groups overly concerned with protecting and purifying what they imagine to be their identities. Yet the conscience they still tug on is the conscience of the Left. The energies they drain are the energies of the Left. What we are witnessing in the culture wars is not the triumph of the Left but its decline.

The cautionary tale with which I have begun is a severe case of a larger wrongheadedness, a misplacement of energies. True, part of the reason why textbook politics took the course it did in Oakland was local. The

San Francisco Bay Area has nourished many a mass social movement, from labor in the 1930s to the student and antiwar insurgencies of the 1960s, each asserting the right of citizens to organize and clamor and intervene in the workings of institutions. Mobilization against tradition is itself a tradition there. Precisely because the population—if hardly the economy or the media—is dominated by racial minorities, political culture in the Bay Area tilts toward a recognition that America is inhabited by a multiplicity of cultures, each with its own legitimate social, political, and cultural claims.

But there is a crucial imbalance. Whatever the protestations about the glories of "multiculturalism," there is only a weak sense of collectivity that claims the loyalty of citizens across racial and ethnic grounds. There are, rather, on many issues, "communities"—African-, Chinese-, and Japanese-American, the many Spanish-speakers lumped together as Latino, gays, lesbians, and radical feminists . . . each with its activists, its lineage, its injuries, its martyrs, and its claim to justice. Each, to some degree, encompasses particular habits and assumptions, yet at the same time partakes of an unacknowledged and shared American way of life. One thing that some group members can claim in common is enemies real or imputed. Where better to find them than among the ranks of the different who are often more prosperous, yet closest to their hopes? In the current climate, there are no impediments to the demonization of white left-liberals, males in particular. Rather, there is breathing space for the kind of sectarianism that claims attention and resources, and often enough succeeds by mobilizing small, visible, passionate groups against the very idea that commonality might be as important as, even more important than, difference.

Episodes of intellectual and cultural secession, of flagrant disregard for the truth and flagrant contempt for the common enterprise, are not necessarily slated to succeed. If anything, as the historian Sean Wilentz has pointed out, many if not most campaigns of what might be called extravagant multiculturalists are beaten back. The Houghton Mifflin books were adopted almost everywhere in California. In Los Angeles, notorious for its ethnic antagonisms, all parties to the textbook controversy were willing to compromise on adding to the curriculum primary-source supplements by writers from racial minorities. Eventually the tempest in the teapot blew itself out. But win or lose, these dubious battles show no sign of subsiding, and win or lose, they derail what slender chances might exist for a left-wing version of commonality. They demoralize the proponents of commonality, choke off the forbearance, the reciprocity, and, yes, the deal-making that are the prerequisites of a successful democratic politics in a complicated society. They help undermine the only basis for a politics of equality that might succeed on a national scale—a majoritarian spirit. Often enough, they target as enemies those they need as allies, if not friends.

In the meantime, the conservative nationalists who defend their own version of a politics of commonality have also staked out their exclusivity. Virtually every party to such disputes feels like an embattled guardian on the ramparts of American culture. The result is a universality of defensiveness, a generalized resentment, and a feeling that, if one is definitively limited by minority status, there is nothing better to do than secede—or to draw fast the wagons and get yours. The white heterosexual male, feeling besieged or abandoned by blacks, or feminists, or gays, abandons *them*—unless they agree with him. Blacks feeling disrespected by whites, gays feeling embattled by straights (and AIDS), the handicapped feeling unfairly treated by the able-bodied—all feel they have been silent too long while their people suffer. The result is a cacophony without much listening or the sympathy needed to keep up a common conversation. There are those who secede in the name of self-defense, hoping to protect their people from more oppression, and those who secede in the name of universal rights—using their belief that they stand for the common good to justify turning their backs on their own defaults, and on the oppressed.

The result is petty—and sometimes more than petty—aggression and deafness, an obsession with purifications. The squandering of energy on identity politics, the hardening of the boundaries between groups, the insistence that individuals are no more than their labels, is an American tragedy. But no tragedy is simple, and this one, too, has a philosophy and a history. Even if the alarm about "political correctness" is too shrill— and even if the exaggerations themselves require explanation—the tragedy slowly playing out in the obsession with separate identities is consuming the energy and imagination we are going to need if there is to be any way at all out of a deep trap that has been a long time in the making. Identity politics is a very bad turn, a detour into quicksand, but it did not come out of the blue. Rather, it is a set of false solutions proclaimed for real problems—false solutions that began with a certain plausibility. The oddity is that the Left, which once stood for universal values, seems to speak today for select identities, while the Right, long associated with privileged interests, claims to defend the common good. How the terms have been reversed is what I hope to explain.

II.

The Exhaustion of Commonality

What meaning . . . can continue to attach to
such a term as the "American" character?—
what type, as the result of such a prodigious
amalgam, such a hotch-potch of racial
ingredients, is to be conceived as
shaping itself?

—HENRY JAMES, *The American Scene*

There is a religious war going on in this
country, a cultural war as critical to the kind of
nation we shall be as the Cold War itself, for
this is a war for the soul of America.

—at the 1992 Republican
National Convention

2

"A Prodigious Amalgam"

1. The Dream, the Pot,
and the Popular Front

The attack on the Houghton Mifflin textbooks could only have been so fierce if the old saga of a common America had already, in good measure, unraveled. What resulted was a dispute between two new versions of the American story. Gary Nash and his allies strained to enfold racial and other social differences within a recognizable common history. They were, in effect, the left wing of the party of commonality. Differences, insists the party of commonality, exist within a whole history that *doesn't* differ. The same history may, and should, be told from different vantage points, and should attend to diverse, indeed divergent experiences; but these diverse histories take place in history—a history that speaks to, and for, everyone, and in the name of which Americans contend. The experience of slavery does not belong to African Americans alone; nor the conquest and the reservation system to native peoples alone; nor economic growth to the wealthy alone. Whatever milieu you come from, you do not know American history unless you know the victims as well as the victors.

The textbook supporters tried—not impeccably—to be sensitive to the complexity of perspectives and interests represented among their readers. Their work was, of course, like the work of all textbook writers, political, though not in any direct polemical way. They sought to cultivate the common ground beneath all understanding. They believed that there is not only shareable knowledge about America, but a story held in common—a story of progress. Some version of this story is shared by people of many different persuasions, from the enlightened left-liberalism of Gary Nash to the elitist conservatism of Allan Bloom ("Our story is the majestic and triumphant march of two principles: freedom and equality"). In Nash's progressive version, American history rests on a shared constitutional faith. In the name of that faith, the weaker go up against the stronger and fight, neither easily nor irresistibly, to extend democratic rights against concentrations of power. In this view, the multiple claims of rival groups in a democracy can be decently adjudicated if (and only if) care is taken to preserve the sense of a common interest on which the interests of the various parts must rest. The textbooks' mission, then, is to cultivate this common interest by telling a single tale—that of the American struggle to extend constitutional rights to the oppressed and unrecognized and to achieve greater equality. In this view, common culture is not ancestor worship, but it is common knowledge in the cause of justice.

Yet the disjointed and self-contradictory quality, the very cumbersomeness of these textbooks, indicates something about their vulnerability to attack. They look basted together. They *are* basted together, like the nation they chronicle. They are gaudy, but they lack confidence. They do not sound the brass for the unquestioned pieties of yore, for what Tom Engelhardt has called "victory culture." They are not jubilant celebrations of the melting pot or of a westward-flowing empire. The America of these books is haunted. American culture is no longer celebrated for its splendid uniqueness, but turns out to be, rather, just one culture (and a loosely bound one, at that) among many. The flow of the narrative is so disrupted as to stutter. The lingering sense of a saga of unending progress that culminates in the United States of America is forced. "America," the books maintain, *"will* be." The lingering insistence that America the coherent, the good, and the just, lies in the future—that is to say, that it does not exist—only halfheartedly conceals the revelation that the old firm America was not really there in the past where it was supposed to be and where once, in the textbooks, it was unquestionably assumed to be.

This lack of confidence, anxiety, even incoherence about what the national identity is and ought to be, or even whether there ought to be one at all, today crops up everywhere in American culture. In the spring of 1994 it was widely reported that a school board in Florida was insisting that teachers instill in their students the belief that America's basic values are "superior to other foreign or historic cultures." But the truly remarkable thing—all the more remarkable for being unremarked upon—was that this was a newsworthy story in the first place. Not so many decades ago, it would have been taken for granted that America was the pinnacle of civilizations. Now, this insistence on the superiority of America was controversial, treated by the national media, at least, as a newsworthy oddity, a man biting a dog. Soon thereafter, moderate Republicans who pledged to repeal the Florida school board decision were elected to replace the conservative Christian majority who had supported it. Thus does the new anxiety, sometimes called "multiculturalism," circulate throughout American society, especially through the mass media, which, even in a time of centrifugal motion, still capture such common images as exist.

One tip-off on the rise of such anxieties came on the cover of the issue of *Time* magazine that was on newsstands on July 4, 1991—an issue published at the end of the season when those wicked little letters *PC* had gained media currency and howls were being heard from many quarters about the suppression of thought by know-nothing vigilantes on the nation's campuses. Instead of celebrating the national holiday in full bombast, with yet another unity rally against the barbarians, *Time* chose for its cover a most untraditional Revolutionary icon: a fife-and-drum corps whose white male drummer is flanked by a headbanded Native American and a black woman playing an African drum. Bringing up the rear are a dark-skinned person of indeterminate sex or ethnicity and an Asian woman. The entire tableau is emblazoned with these less-than-stirring words: "Who Are We?" The subhead reads: "American kids are getting a new—and divisive—view of Thomas Jefferson, Thanksgiving and the Fourth of July."

Compare, for example, *Time*'s July 4 cover of 1987, with a gallery of various American types emblazoned "We The People"; or 1986's Ronald Reagan portrait against a backdrop of fireworks bursting in air; or bicentennial 1976's "THE PROMISED LAND: AMERICA'S NEW IMMIGRANTS," in old-timey lettering; or 1955's portrait of Dwight David Eisenhower, identified solely as "THE PRESIDENT OF THE U.S.," against a backdrop of the Liberty Bell. That the national ideology's onetime flagship of received opinion, whose founder famously declared the coming of "The American Century" in 1941, should admit to such uncertainty—admit to it and also, perhaps, express a certain pride in 'fessing up—suggests the agitation so evident in the corridors of established opinion. Who are we indeed? What do we belong to, and what belongs to us? Obsessive questions that come up again and again these days, along with the rustle of two linked questions just behind: Who qualifies as insulted and injured? And what are they owed by those who are not injured, at least not as badly?

Who are we? The acrimony is as intense as the quarrels are predictable. Follow the script of each battle in the culture wars and before long you arrive at the same tangle of questions: What is America anyway, and who wants to know? Who gets to say, and with what consequences? Are we finding ourselves through or despite our differences, or are we falling apart despite what we hold in common? Do we become more equal as we become more antagonistic? Is separateness the necessary prologue to a commonality that can only be attained once the most oppressed secede to cultivate truths that the majority long suppressed? Are there bridges worth building?

These disputes have enough roots for an entire ideological forest, but there is a surprising connection among all the contending parties, an unacknowledged commonality. They share more than they want to acknowledge. It is normal to be perplexed and dismayed by questions of belonging and respect. How American, this passion for respect, this fear of exclusion, this need to belong, this anxiety about worthiness! To express and cope with these questions has been a perennial democratic problem, for one thing Americans have long respected is a certain *dis*respect. The United States is that paradoxical nation where people are taught that they deserve respect; in which many feel deprived of respect; in which many of these, in turn, find it legitimate to complain that they are so deprived; and in which many also find the demand for respect, at least in its blustery form when it comes from somebody else's lips, funny. We cultivate egalitarian irreverence.* Our culture, to be sure, has its strongly conformist side, but one thing it conforms to is the presumption that no one is so high as to be above scrutiny, no one so low as to be beneath dignity. America: land of slavery, abolitionism, slave revolts, Emancipation, segregation, a civil rights movement, and drastic racial inequalities with respect to wealth, longevity, and virtually every other measure of life condition.

There have been both reformist and pluralist versions of the principle of equal respect. The reformist version fuels democratic movements. For all the many inequalities and oppressions in American history, the egalitarian streak in American ideology has buttressed the antislavery, women's suffrage, civil rights, feminist, gay rights, and other reform movements. That most contentious program, affirmative action, has a root in the Declaration of Independence's commitment to equality from birth, minorities and women having generalized the principle of *one person, one vote* to *one group member, one job.* The pluralist streak, meanwhile, undergirds our famous multiplicity of civic organizations. It was, according to Alexis de Tocqueville, our special genius to cultivate the organization of interested groups. Of the enduring nations of the last two centuries, it is America, uniquely depicted as a "democracy of nationalities," that is the most inviting to the pressures of group affirmation and also, perhaps, the most accommodating to them. In retrospect, it is difficult to believe that a nation of immigrants, slaves, and conquered natives, a nation run by Europeans but claiming a universal mission, a nation ostensibly liberal in its belief that people make their own destinies yet subjecting

---

* I understood vividly how distinctive this concept is as I was about to give a lecture containing the phrase in Taiwan in December 1993. (The subject was the spread of American popular culture.) To iron out translation difficulties, I was meeting beforehand with the interpreters, at their request. What did I mean, *egalitarian irreverence*? one of them asked. Or was this a typographical error and did I perhaps mean *reverence*? No, I explained, what is singular about America is the widespread respect for the *disrespect* of authority.

whole categories of people to special oppressions and humiliations, could have postponed forever a protracted convulsion over the question, "Who Are We?"

Time's urgent question fairly quivers with anxiety. Are we no more than a muddle? Is there a "we" at all? And if not, or if "we" are uncertain, then what? Such a question, asked so insistently, answers itself: we are a people who don't know who we are. "We" bother to ask such a question only because we suspect, to say the least, that this "we" is problematic. According to *Time*, "we" might be able to construe ourselves as a unity if we work at it, but we are going to have to work at it, because we begin as a plurality. No sooner have we asked about commonality than we have to acknowledge difference. And so the question of collective identity, however simple it appears, is actually compound. It leads to other questions: Who are my kind of people, who are the other kinds, and what do we or should we have to do with each other? What shall I, from within my segment, render unto the whole?

There is a lineage to this anxiety, for Americans have frequently worried about where our essence lies—and lashed out at people who seemed to challenge it, whatever it was. American history is, in no small part, the bloody ground of these fights. From the seventeenth century onward, future Americans spoke a multiplicity of languages and held to a multiplicity of religions. Gaining access to an abundance of land, they encouraged not only broad property-holding but continuing immigration from the nations of Europe. All these factors combined with geographical remoteness from Europe to weaken the hold of any religious or secular bonds imposed from abroad.

Quickly, however, pressures toward uniformity emerged. Although an American nation is never once mentioned in the Declaration of Independence, the peculiar term "un-American" is in use, at least by a visiting Englishman, as early as 1818—the same year that Congress rejected a petition from the Irish societies of New York and Philadelphia for a western land grant. Periodically, under popular pressure, the nation's governing classes have erected boundaries dividing the ins from the outs. Americans have often been fearful that, as a whole, the nation does not really exist, or that it will not last. Conservatives arise frequently to complain about centrifugal motion: thus, the eighteenth-century Tory Jonathan Boucher's comment that "every observant man who has resided in America must have seen that men are less attached to each other, and the bond of social or political union is looser there than in almost every other country." On July 4, 1845, long before "Native Americans" became the label of choice for many former "Indians," the Native American Party met in Philadelphia "for the purpose of devising a plan of concerted political action in defence of American institutions against the encroachments of foreign influence," decrying the presence of "a foreign body of citizens," a "swarm" of strangers committed "to perpetuate foreign clannishness among adopted citizens of the United States, in contravention of that spirit of union and nationality, without which no people can legitimately claim a place among the nations of the earth." The Native American Party faded fast, but its preoccupations have never been long absent from American life. The fear lest national integrity be weakened by interlopers has remained a fixture of national culture.

If the common identity of a people derives in important part from their sense of a common past, tied to their sense of a common present condition, Americans have good reason for perplexity, and a long history of it. America, Walt Whitman's "Nation of many nations," *is* unusual, if not unique, in this respect. The country was settled by refugees, adventurers, conquered peoples, and slaves—in sum, by peoples, not by a singular people claiming a common root. With less than 2 percent of its population deriving from pre-Colombian tribes or Mexicans conquered in the Mexican war, and some 12 percent of its population descended from African slaves, the United States today owes the great majority of its ethnic diversity to neither federation (like Switzerland) nor conquest (like the former USSR) but to never-ending mass migrations. Well into the twentieth century, a relatively weak national government was in no position to enforce any uniform identity. In fact if not in ideology, America was multinational, multicultural, multilinguistic, multiracial. In ideology if not in fact, it was seen by its thinkers—and by at least some of its citizens—as a nation unlike all others. We exhibited a "composite nationality"; we were "not a nation, so much as a world"; we were, or harbored, or had, oddly, a "way of life" and a "dream."

At the beginning of the republic, we were not quite Horace Kallen's "democracy of nationalities"—certainly not equally so: the European nationalities monopolized the privilege. But there was in principle, at least, the possibility that we would become a unity, one rising from many, and this was so partly *because* the common nation's roots in the past were relatively shallow. Founded without the unifying assurances that other nations have derived, at least at times, from blood ties of long duration, thoughtful and influential Americans frequently claimed that our commonality derived from imagined and yet unrealized potentials. Like Marx's hypothetical revolutionaries, Americans would take their poetry from the future, not from the past. American history is thick with proclamations to the effect that Americans are coming into existence *but have not yet arrived*. Here is John Quincy Adams writing in 1819 of German immigrants: "They must look forward to their posterity rather than backward to their ancestors." In 1845, Emerson declares in his diary that "in this continent—asylum of all nations, the energy of Irish, Germans, Swedes, Poles, & Cossacks, & all the European tribes—of the Africans, & of the Polynesians, will construct a new race, a new religion, a new state, a new literature, which will be as vigorous as the new Europe which came out of the smelting-pot of the Dark Ages, or that which earlier emerged from the Pelasgic & Etruscan barbarism." In 1908, Israel Zangwill has the hero of his influential play *The Melting-Pot* ask: "What is the glory of Rome and Jerusalem where all nations and races come to worship and look back, compared with the glory of America, where all races and nations come to labour and look forward! . . . The real American has not arrived. He is only in the Crucible, I tell you—he will be the fusion of all races, the coming superman." In 1936, Langston Hughes, acutely conscious of the harshness of the American past and present, affirms: "America will be!" In 1960, Walter Lippmann writes: "The bond of American union has not been piety and reverence for the past but a conviction of purpose and of the destiny it would bring for posterity. America has always been not only a country but a dream." In 1980, that keen student of the American audience, Ronald Reagan, says: "Americans live in the future."

If we are to be bound and known by what has not yet taken place, no wonder we set out, we Americans, with a built-in uncertainty about what exactly it is to be American. When the entity that one belongs to has not yet arrived but perpetually shimmers in a state of becoming, in a future that may, for all we know, recede forever, then the very concept of identity fails to take on a very clear shape. The journey ("purpose") is everything, the destination ("destiny") murky. Metamorphosis is all. Opportunity is at least as important as achievement; potential, at least as important as actuality.

Pause for a moment on this central cliché of American rhetoric, "the American dream." Has any other nation, even an empire, ever identified itself so closely with a dream? Is there a Spanish or Pakistani dream? Was there a Roman dream? a T'ang dream? a Hapsburg or Napoleonic dream? It is one thing to have a "vision," to invoke glory or reason, or for that matter Aryan supremacy, as a national purpose; it is quite another to identify the nation with something so insubstantial as a dream. A dream may be evocative, illuminating, fascinating, or frightful, but one thing it is not is a fait accompli. It is incapable of verification. It invites revision. Intrinsically ambiguous, it begs for interpretation and reinterpretation. A dream, after all, is the most private and invisible of experiences. So, to paraphrase Lippmann: America is not yet. It is a collective anticipation. But how does one identify with a potential?

What a collective dream gains in vividness, it loses in fixity. In America, the very idea of the nation is free of the nationality that weighs down the definition of every other nation—enough so that freedom from definition is central to the definition of Americanness. At least, Americans believe that it is their dream that sets them apart—not their blood, like the Germans, or their language, like the French, or even their political institutions, which are in bad odor. True enough, the official civic ideal is a compound of relatively stable attachments: to the social equality of individuals; to the preeminent value of personal freedom; to official symbols of union like the flag; to some rough idea of a national community. But intrinsic to American freedom is the absence of a requirement that Americans do things the way they or their forebears did in their old countries. "The way we do things here" is an opening to diversity. Each attempt to arrest the flux of Americanness, to pin down once and for all the nature of national membership, has failed.

Perhaps it is foolish even to contemplate compressing the sense of what it is to be an American into a single procrustean idea. One reason is that, in a country lacking ethnic coherence, the idea of the United States of America has been ideological, and far from seamless. We, if there is a "we," are a people of ideas. We were formed by documents, above all the Declaration of Independence and the Constitution. The United States, in theory, was to be the homeland of an idea: a democracy of free individuals. This *new* nation was to be more than *another* nation, it was to be the homeland of liberty, showing the rest of the world that what it wanted to be was, in fact, America. In its most liberal, least nativist version, America was the truth of the world unveiled, a decisive moment in the revelation of humanity to itself.*

But American ideology was also intrinsically strained. Its main ideas clashed. Dissolving the bands that tied them to the British Empire, the American founders felt impelled to justify themselves to the entire world not only by itemizing their grievances against George III but by stating first their conviction that "all men are created equal" and that they are "endowed by their Creator with certain inalienable rights." Not "all colonists," not "all whites" not even "all North Americans," but "all men"— the idea of equal rights setting a standard against which to measure all injustice, all brutality, all concentrations of illegitimate power, although it was to take decades of suffering and political clamor to pry open the definition of "men" to include enslaved African Americans and women. From the beginning, Americans fought over who precisely was entitled to life, liberty, and the pursuit of happiness; which *men,* precisely, were created equal; which authorities, precisely, were illegitimate; and therefore whose rebellion was justified. The phrase "life, liberty, and the pursuit of happiness" is at war with itself; as the abolitionists insisted, the liberty of the slave owner steals the happiness of the slave.

To some, we were the people who disliked authority; to others, the people who embraced the republican idea and civic virtue. Later, to some we would be the people of economic liberty above all; to yet others, the people bound together by white supremacy or Christianity. This slackness

---

* As if to prove the point, thirteen years later, with the help of the Marquis de Lafayette and his American-inspired rhetoric, French revolutionaries produced a "Declaration of the Rights of Man and Citizen"—not a "Declaration of the Rights of Frenchmen"—declaring men equal "in respect of their rights," though again distinctly failing to take women into account.

of definition was in turn rooted in a huge material fact. The conquest of an entire continent and the forcible removal of its indigenous peoples meant that cheap land was widely available to settlers, which made for a large number of property owners—large in contrast to other societies of the time—which, in turn, made possible a relatively high order of political democracy and an openness to political and ideological experimentation. Millenarian religious awakenings also weakened secular authority and hence fixed identity. A fierce utopian streak in the nineteenth century— from Robert Owen and Brook Farm to Mormonism and Edward Bellamy —was yet another sign of the provisional and unfinished quality of much of America's political culture.

But from the start, foreign menaces helped greatly to consolidate the idea of the nation. The nation understood itself to have been conceived under siege from the Indians in the first place. One grievance recorded in the Declaration of Independence was that the king inflamed "the merciless Indian Savages, whose known rule of warfare, is an undistinguished destruction of all ages, sexes and conditions." Then, from the birth of the republic onward, if intermittently, actual and potential European adversaries bound the United States into a community that felt entitled to demand a certain uniformity of its citizens. Nations born in revolution feel pressures from real and fancied enemies, and the United States was no exception. Jefferson, the great promulgator of liberty, embraced the Alien and Sedition Acts in 1798. By the War of 1812, alarms had been sounded over French revolutionaries and Spaniards as well as over the Indians and the British. The march westward heightened the sense of nationhood. The Civil War—or rather, in Lincoln's formulation, the war to preserve the Union—led to a further burst of nationalist sentiment.

Consider, for example, Edward Everett Hale's famous "The Man Without a Country," published in *The Atlantic* in 1863, with half a million copies reprinted within a year. The story was set in 1807, when a cocky naval officer named Philip Nolan is supposed to have been convicted for supporting the treasonous Aaron Burr. Nolan cries out "in a fit of frenzy,—'Damn the United States! I wish I may never hear of the United States again!' " To explain Nolan, Hale tells us that he "had grown up in the West of those days, in the midst of 'Spanish plot,' 'Orleans plot,' and all the rest." He had been brought up among foreigners (a Spanish officer, a French merchant, an English tutor). He had dwelt on the margins of national life: "He had spent half his youth with an older brother, hunting horses in Texas; and, in a word, to him 'United States' was scarcely a reality." He had not, in short, been acculturated into national attachments. But most of all, Nolan's offense is civic, not cultural: he violated his duty. Hale tells us: "He had sworn on his oath as a Christian to be true to 'United States.' It was 'United States' which gave him the uniform he wore, and the sword by his side." Nolan is condemned to spend the rest of his life on a prison ship, never again to see the name of the United States, or to hear its name. The story's very conceit suggests that attachment to the American nation was something to be achieved and not (yet) taken for granted.

Yet what common condition could be ascribed to the whole of this multiple, contentious people? Unifiers frequently attempted to compress differences into a single national character: Americans were sturdy, brave, God-fearing, freedom-loving, devoted to work, committed to the civil covenant. This core could enfold components as distinct as the rectitude of the banker, the revivalism of the evangelist, and the republicanism of the radical artisan. Moreover, throughout the nineteenth century and intermittently since, school textbooks assumed that a combination of European "racial stock" and pioneer character made for superiority. The nation composed of such persons was destined to increase the freedom of its citizens in the process of becoming more unified. The slaves were reduced, in effect, to un-Americans on American soil. In this light, more than two centuries of African slavery were an inconvenient exception to the general freedom.

To further complicate the quest for unity, the American experience was relatively open to encounters and collisions with newcomers—as long as they were white. America's binges of nativist and antiradical intolerance were, throughout the nineteenth century, relatively shallow and short-lived. The Alien Act was allowed to expire in 1800 without the deportation of any flesh-and-blood aliens, and it wasn't until the 1880s, in the midst of labor organizing and anti-anarchist panics, that immigration was first restricted on racial and ideological grounds. Successive generations who might have thought that they had settled the question of who they had become, that they had arrived at some final resting place of

Americanness, have had to contend not only with contradictions in their own thought but with the unsettling presence of those *other* Americans, the newcomers and claimants, the enslaved and the radicals, the millenarians and schismatics, those who were unwilling, or had not been permitted, to transform themselves into *normal* Americans, and tried to transform or at least bend the ideal.

While national identity has never been altogether immobile for long, there have been periods of greater or lesser firmness. The Union victory in the Civil War became the linchpin of an American victory saga. It was after the Civil War, and especially toward the end of the nineteenth century, that one heard a growing clamor to the effect that the United States had become a nation. The transcontinental push on the iron rails, the defeat of the Indians, the opening of the territories westward to the Pacific, together generated a new identity—to be American was to feel implicated in the idea of the frontier; it was to hold a share in the continental territory, to partake of the struggle by which civilization slowly but steadily liberated a continent from the forces of backwardness and barbarism. Outside the suppressed cultures of "Indians," blacks, and some others, American identity was stable enough that pressures for consolidation and uniformity needed not be so intense. Groups were free to remain unassimilated by standing apart from the whole. Neither the national state nor the national economy was strong enough to overcome centrifugal tendencies, not least the massive immigration from Europe, which scattered hybrid and hyphenate American identities around the country, where immigrants could, if they wished, cultivate a certain separateness. "Prior to 1917," the historian Gary Gerstle writes, "an ethnic group could choose, if its members desired, to remain separate from the American cultural mainstream and to cultivate its Old World traditions; the American landscape was dotted with insular ethnic communities, whose cultural life remained remarkably autonomous of the Protestant, republican, and commercial culture around them." Immigrants clustered in towns and neighborhoods and organized fraternal and burial societies, festivals, newspapers, schools, and theaters alongside work and commercial associations that were themselves frequently kin-based. In nineteenth-century Cincinnati, schools taught German half the day. Between 1860 and 1890, the German piano manufacturer William Steinway established a distinct German-American town at College Point, Long Island, in part to avoid unions. Within and aside from ethnic communities, myriad radical groups and religious movements flourished.

It was around the turn of the century that advancing uniformity transformed the terms of American identity. As the historian John Higham has written about the 1890s: "Under the inroads of industrial bureaucracy and specialized knowledge, the self-sufficiency of the 'island communities' was irretrievably passing. As national organizations crisscrossed an increasingly crowded terrain, more and more of the American people became integrated into economic networks and status hierarchies that drastically reduced the significance of the local arena." There is no need to dwell here on the relative significance of the various interwoven factors at work—industrial growth, labor shortages, mass production, war, technical improvements in transportation and communication, the rise of bureaucracy, the growth of national associations. The result can be summarized: as an economy and a culture, America was nationalized. Racial segregation forced on blacks and Chinese, in particular, no other choice but to live in distinct subcultures; but white enclaves were dissolving into a mainstream. An awareness of differences fueled an intense desire to police deviants. America's cultural authorities grew harsher, more puritanical. Thus the heightened attacks on immigrants and the vigorous purification crusades directed against prostitution, alcohol, drugs, the movies, and other sinful pursuits. The crusades were not automatically successful—New York City harbored a thriving gay world overlapping with a larger Bohemia from the 1890s through the 1920s—but the pressure for a conformity of manners and mores was generally fierce. This cultural pressure was intensified by new patriotic rituals of "Americanization": it was in 1892, for example, to celebrate the Columbus quadricentennial that President Benjamin Harrison declared October 12 a national holiday and instituted the Pledge of Allegiance.

But the American catechism was to be imparted through more than schools and political rituals. To become an American was coming to mean to embrace the promise of better living through the acquisition of consumer goods. The consolidation of corporations, the rise of both "scientific management" and the marketing apparatus, abetted by national communications—movies, radio, news wires, magazines—offered a vast, efficient market to meet the growing desire for an improved way of life. Genuflections were made to the virtues of free speech and tolerance, but to a great degree, freedom came to be understood as access to consumer choice: the right to acquire purchasing power and to dispose of it as one liked. In the course of the twentieth century, a new formula for becoming a real American came to prevail: work hard, consume well, marry properly, and stay out of trouble. Once freedom, that most explosive element in American identity, had been safely redefined as the ability to acquire things, a uniform American identity could be baptized in a sanctioned history of heroes: the Puritan pilgrims, the Founding Fathers, Lincoln, and selected gunslingers of the Old West. The new identity was not force-fed to unwilling victims; it was, by and large, welcomed—if not with enthusiasm, at least with a sense of inevitability.

Add to these standardizing pressures the fact that differences actually were diminishing. The Civil War eradicated one significant regional distinction, though the defeat of Reconstruction and its replacement by white rule throughout the South preserved an essential difference from the North. The Indian wars and the white (and, let it not be forgotten, black) settlement of the West, along with the mystique of the West enshrined in the popular culture of the latter decades of the nineteenth century, bulked up the sense of what was distinctive about America, Frederick Jackson Turner famously declaring in 1893 that "in the crucible of the frontier, the immigrants were Americanized, liberated and fused into a mixed race." From now on, differences would be seen as dangerous, especially when they resulted from the infiltrations of foreign enemies. The subversive became an American—that is, "un-American"—type, that which no law-abiding, self-respecting American should permit him- or herself to be.

War is the health of uniformity. It was the coming of World War I that moved the United States to a crest of fierce nationalism indistinguishable from xenophobia. Now we were at risk from aliens. It was during the war that "The Star-Spangled Banner" was adopted by the U.S. Army as a national anthem, although the words had been written to declare America "the land of the free and the home of the brave" a century earlier. Soon the meanings of both freedom and bravery were to be brutally clarified, as was the price of failing to be an authentically color-coded—true-blue, red-blooded—American. Spasms of anti-German patriotism alerted Americans that the test of Americanness was opposition to the Hun. In the interest of self-defense and the extension of democracy, Americans were now to be molded into liberators, Kaiser-haters, English-speakers. In 1916, Wilson had made a point of repudiating the "hyphenate vote." In the spirit of uncomplicated loyalty, Theodore Roosevelt frequently denounced "hyphenated Americans," demanding in 1917 that his countrymen—even recent "British-American" immigrants—acknowledge that "we Americans are the children of the crucible."

Not surprisingly, it was an opponent of the war, Randolph Bourne, who made one of the early arguments for what today would be called multiculturalism, maintaining that the true American destiny was to be "trans-national." His principle was impeccable but his timing inauspicious. Free speech and antiwar advocates were brutalized, tarred and feathered, lynched, driven out of towns, arrested, jailed, prosecuted, deported, their periodicals banned from the mails and shut down, their elected representatives expelled from legislatures. From the wartime repression of pacifists, socialists, and anarchists, it was only a short step to a postwar red scare, race riots against the growing numbers of northern urban blacks, and still tighter limits on immigration. The spirit of the antiradical crackdowns enshrined paranoia as a feature of Americanization—to be a proper American now required that one be vigilant against Communists, immigrants from the wrong countries, the unassimilated, and other "foreign" influences.

With World War I, then, all the elements were in place for an American identity combining affirmation and negation, plenitude and panic, built on an American way of electricity and mobility, promising the opportunity for personal success, and dignified with words like *freedom, equality,* and *opportunity*—and not only the words, but also a substantial, if scarcely universal, experience of these words in action. Whites were invited to sit at the grand table and partake of the luscious fruits, and at the same time stand ready lest *they,* out there, take them away. The good life among good things was the American ideal that would fill the movies, the magazines, and the other symbolic treasuries of culture during most of this century.

This image of a singular "American way of life" came into circulation

coupled with the image of Americans "re-formed" in the melting pot—
"born again," to borrow a later usage. Total immersion, consecration,
baptism, alchemy—the melting down of inferior coinages "to begin the
world over again" (Thomas Paine)—this was the American promise, and
it was usable for manifold purposes. As president, Theodore Roosevelt
had wholeheartedly embraced this symbol of bully nationalism, crying out
from his box at the 1908 American premiere of Zangwill's play, "That's a
great play, Mr. Zangwill, that's a great play." (Roosevelt promptly agreed
to let Zangwill dedicate the published version to him, writing him: "I do
not know when I have seen a play that stirred me as much." Roosevelt did
not seem to mind that this exponent of the American ideal was an English
Jew.) In 1916, the same year Wilson was rejecting the hyphenate vote,
the virulently anti-Semitic Henry Ford was running his immigrant employees through "Ford English School Melting Pot" rites in Detroit, symbolic baptisms in which, under a sign reading E PLURIBUS UNUM, the
newcomers relinquished their Old World belongings, stepped into a des-
ignated "melting pot" and emerged dressed in American clothes and
waving American flags. (What the proto-Nazi Ford made of the fact that
the phrase was popularized by a universalist-feminist Jew who believed
passionately in miscegenation is unfortunately not revealed by the
records.)

But boiling as it was, the pot was not thought to be capable of melting
just anyone. The descendants of African slaves were a caste to be kept
out. State laws forbade race mixing. Moreover, the crude nationalism of
World War I, larded with the rigmarole of "scientific" race theory, fueled
a racist version of the antiforeigner panic. In 1921 and 1924, Congress
imposed national quotas on immigrants. Asian immigration, already heavily constrained, was essentially ended altogether, and northern, paler,
Protestant Europeans were privileged over the Catholic and Jewish, the
Mediterranean and eastern. The national origin principle for preserving
the ethnic dimensions of the American population would last almost forty
years. The pot melted its ore selectively, and for that reason alone served
as a useful metaphor for national identity. It promoted amnesia and saved
embarrassment. This kept the color-caste system compatible with hymns
to American liberty.

Yet, in the same year that Henry Ford was melting the ethnics down,

John Dewey, America's principal philosopher of democracy, was opposing narrow racist and nativist varieties of nationalism, defending instead a democratic version of Americanism. In this popular view, the war was admirable because it was designed to "make the world safe for democracy." Dewey's wager was that, in the wake of the war, a newly powerful national government would be vulnerable to appeals for the extension of political rights; that one result of the wartime mobilization would be an invigorated ideal of Americanism. Old World customs would be discarded, not simply for the customs of Americanization, but for more expansive political values.

Enter that influential offshoot, *democratic* Americanism, which required the extension of political rights to all citizens. Women's suffrage followed, although during the Republican years that ensued, the dominant idea was that no further rights were necessary. It took the Depression to shatter the belief that the free flow of capital was itself the guarantor of economic well-being. When Franklin D. Roosevelt came into office in 1933, democratic Americanism flowered into the New Deal, whose premise was that government initiative was needed to benefit the common man (and woman). The welfare state, inaugurated first for soldiers and mothers, was generalized.

The cultural side of democratic Americanism was an amalgam of populism, Progressivism, militant industrial unionism, and sentimental leftism that united the New Deal and the Communist Party into the Popular Front. The photography of Dorothea Lange and Walker Evans, among others, celebrated the unfamous. Song and story celebrated the virtues of little guys who found themselves up against hardhearted bankers and corrupt politicians. Frank Capra honored John Doe and Mr. Smith; Carl Sandburg sang the praises of *The People, Yes;* Communist Party leader Earl Browder smoothly retailed the slogan, "Communism is twentieth century Americanism"; Frank Sinatra and Paul Robeson inhabited a "House I Live In" devised by two Communists, celebrating "the little bridge at Concord where freedom's fight began." On this view, true patriotism was a love of equality. The Working Class melted into The People. "If you like America . . . if you like its Rocky Mountains, its Storm King highway, its low-priced automobiles, the hot and cold running water in your well-tiled bathroom," declared an ad in the Communist *New Masses,* then American Communism was for you.

Here was a nationalism that invited entry into an open Americanness on the ground that, as Woody Guthrie put it, "this land is your land, this land is my land . . . this land was made for you and me." In the left-wing version of Americanism, being Polish, Finnish, Jewish, or German was a route into the democratic political amalgam. How to be black and American was the most tortuous problem, of course, since the boundary was racial and not simply ethnic, and there was a most virulent racism to combat. No more than anyone else did the Left know just how to square the circle, allowing space for autonomous black life while encouraging a shared culture. The key, in any event, was tolerance in the interest of composing a popular commons—a "people's America" against "the interests." One of the most original of American Marxists, Leon Samson, went so far as to argue, in 1933, that Americanism was a sort of moral equivalent of socialism, "a substitute for socialism . . . and that is why the socialist argument falls so fruitlessly on the American ear."

Democratic Americanism, a sort of ethnocentrism from below, was an ideology splendidly tailored for the Great Depression. This period of desolation made visible the cliché so resonant it seems always to have been with us: *the American dream.* In print, at any rate, this indelible phrase appears the product of the scion of an impeccably white, Anglo-Saxon, Protestant family, one of whose forebears was an indentured servant in Virginia who rose to landowning status. James Truslow Adams had no ties to the Left—he was far and away too much the aristocrat for that —but he was close to the Progressive tradition and was as deeply suspicious of business as he was enamored of immigrants. In his best-selling popular history *The Epic of America,* published in 1931, Adams rhapsodized about "that American dream of a better, richer, and happier life for all our citizens of every rank which is the greatest contribution we have as yet made to the thought and welfare of the world. That dream or hope has been present from the start. Ever since we became an independent nation, each generation has seen an uprising of the ordinary Americans to save that dream from the forces which appeared to be overwhelming and dispelling it." This embattled dream, Adams wrote, was of "a land in which life should be better and richer and fuller for every man, with opportunity for each according to his ability or achievement." He meant not only opportunity but also social equality, for he followed this line with an anecdote about a French visitor who, on being asked what struck him most about America, answered: "The way that everyone of every sort looks you right in the eye, without a thought of inequality." Still, Adams was no fool. He knew the dream had been disfigured by "ugly scars," by "three centuries of exploitation and conquest." The dream that had drawn tens of millions of immigrants, a dream of being "unrepressed by social orders which had developed [elsewhere] for the benefit of classes rather than for the simple human being of any and every class . . . has been realized more fully in actual life here than anywhere else, *though very imperfectly even among ourselves.*" He denounced the greed of big businessmen and proposed a more equitable distribution of wealth. Such reforms were necessary to bring the dream to fruition.

Adams concluded his book with a long quotation from Mary Antin, the immigrant Russian Jew who published a best-selling book called *The Promised Land* in 1912, animated by fulsome images of the future: "The endless ages have indeed throbbed through my blood, but a new rhythm dances in my veins. . . . The past was only my cradle, and now it cannot hold me, because I am grown too big. . . . America is the youngest of the nations, and inherits all that went before in history. . . . Mine is the whole majestic past, and mine is the shining future." Placed below Mary Antin's rapturous words, on Adams's last page, was a woodcut. A godlike muscular male, an Adamic figure, waded through the ocean, lifting an airplane on its flight. Mary Antin, meet Charles Lindbergh. The Jewish author of *The Promised Land* shared the page with Charles Lindbergh, the lone master of the machine (and future isolationist and pro-Nazi): two versions of Americanism, each embodying "the dream."

Adams's version prefigured many another variation on the theme of the Popular Front. The mission of America was to serve as a refuge for minorities, who may have looked or sounded different but were all the same under the skin, willing and even eager to assimilate, to make themselves at home in an America that would earn their assimilation and not humiliate them. America would honor outsiders by absorbing them into the mainstream. As Mary Antin wrote in her next book, subtitled *A Com-*

plete Gospel of Immigration (1914), in this way Americans could play out their world mission of "hasten[ing] the climax of the drama of unification" in which all peoples "merg[e] their interests, their cultures, their bloods."

But, of course, not all Americans were the descendants of voluntary immigrants. The awkward truth about the celebrants of this American merging was that it was premised, almost exclusively, on the whiteness of all the merging parties. Rhapsodic invocations of de-hyphenated Americans usually left the descendants of Africans out of consideration. African Americans did not have the luxury of merger fantasies. Rather, their fate was twoness, that famous compound identity named by W. E. B. Du Bois: "this sense of always looking at one's self through the eyes of others, of measuring one's soul by the tape of a world that looks on in amused contempt and pity," the knowledge that one is "an American, a Negro; two souls, two thoughts, two unreconciled strivings; two warring ideals in one dark body, whose dogged strength alone keeps it from being torn asunder." The despised outsiders had to make homes in the margins of the world from which they were excluded. One of the classic themes of their literature has been the ordeal of outsiders who try to honor the whole of their multiplicity: to cling to their origins even as they find themselves churning around and alongside and against the so-called mainstream. Outsiders produced yet another American tradition: the tales of the unmelted, the torn, the compound identity.

2. Red Blood, Green Lawns, and the Grand Creed

War revived unifying Americanism just when it might have slackened. Sometimes World War II invoked xenophobia and uniformity, sometimes the democratic values of the Popular Front. For the most part, government propaganda discouraged the expression of difference. The voices of uniformity said: Whatever your separateness, transcend your tribe; or rather, fold it into the whole. In the commanding words of one government poster, "DON'T SPEAK THE ENEMY'S LANGUAGE! SPEAK AMERICAN!"

Popular culture enlisted in the war effort. In books and pamphlets, movies and radio, popular artists and social scientists produced an image of a unified, finally fused America. America embraced an identity that gained coherence from the fact that it was under assault. A good many of the propagandists were liberals and leftists. This was, after all, a war against fascism and racial subjugation (even if the Japanese were racially demonized in the process). Ethnicity was inducted into the team. Popular Front consciousness became virtually obligatory in the multiethnic platoons of World War II movies ("O'Hara! Antonelli! Goldberg! Martinez! Washington!"), where mutual reliance is the bond that distinguishes the good guys from the Nazis. As film historian Jeanine Basinger writes, the clear moral of this kind of movie was: "We are a mongrel nation—ragtail, unprepared, disorganized, quarrelsome among ourselves, and with separate special interests, raised, as we are, to believe in the individual, not the group. At the same time, we bring different skills and abilities together for the common good, and from these separate needs and backgrounds we bring a feisty determination." The formula African American was integrated into Hollywood's army years before he was admitted into the real one—a case of Hollywood's dream factory functioning as a social avant-garde. The dark-skinned members of the platoon frequently had the good grace to make the ultimate sacrifice for the good of the whole unit, expressing supreme loyalty in the process of expressing their nearly mandatory expendability. Similarly, the presence of the Pima Indian Ira Hayes among the flag-planting Marines of Iwo Jima certified the democratic significance of the war. The war against fascism became a war of liberation in behalf of what was distinctly American: the diversity of the *demos* fused into a single, solid phalanx.

Not that xenophobia vanished. Anti-Semitic attitudes and practices (restrictive covenants, university quotas, and job discrimination) thrived through the 1940s. Of all discriminations, phobic reactions to skin color proved the least meltable, and fierce racism not only remained but, in one respect, intensified during the national mobilization as Japanese Americans were interned and their property expropriated. In anti-Japanese propaganda, the buck-toothed, dementedly grinning "Japs" signified subhumanity. Restrictions on Chinese and Filipinos, our allies, persisted through the war and beyond. Still, the Japanese Americans—and, for a time, the rare Italian and German Americans suspected of fascist sympathies—were the exceptions to an assimilationist impulse. America understood itself mainly as a nation that gathered peoples and fused them into a singular people.

But victories lead to dissension. Once the pressure for unity subsides, quarrels of interpretation break out. Hence the triumph of 1945 might have spurred a round of centrifugal cultural motion—an upsurge of class, race, and political tensions—but for the coupling of an extraordinary economic boom and the onset of the Cold War, two potent forces that between them offered quick and emotionally compelling answers to the perennial predicament of American culture, or at least ways of suppressing lingering doubts and staving off crisis. First, the Cold War: Who were we? *We* were what *they* were not, what *they* were trying to crush. *They* were slavery; *we* were freedom. *They* were faceless hordes ruled by secret police; *we* were middle-class individualists ruled, in principle, by ourselves. The time-honored riddle of American identity evidently had a solution: we Americans were all of *us* who lined up against *them*. We were, in fact, the very proof of the commonality of mankind, an *omnium gatherum* of immigrants who had the great gift of absorbing differences into a common crusade—a veritable popular front against Communism. Defined most firmly by what we were not, declaring ourselves to be in our deepest spirit the negation of what we rose so vigorously to fight, Americans could sustain an appearance, even a conviction, of unity. If any more proof were needed, former Vice President Henry Wallace's disastrous presidential campaign against the Cold War in 1948 proved that the new consensus reached far beyond elites; it was a popular cause, *the* popular cause, a rock-bottom conviction that marked the boundary of all legitimate political discourse.

To a considerable degree, the principle of unity through antagonism continued the fused Americanism of World War II. The sociologist Nathan Glazer has written that even at the end of the Fifties, the intellectual mood was still "shaped by the aftermath of the war against Hitler, and part of our propaganda effort in that war—one in which social scientists as well as publicists and politicians were engaged—was to argue that there were no meaningful differences among groups." Ideology crowded out difference. The ideological bedrock of unity was anti-Communism. Liberals and conservatives disagreed on whether the enemy was principally without or within, but all could agree on the evils of Communism. So flagrantly brutal was its Stalinist incarnation that Communism in the Soviet Union and its satellites mobilized a countertotalist reaction that was almost as bracing and embracing for its partisans as Communism had been for its own adherents. Still, the many crimes of Communism could not explain the paranoid energy of anti-Communism. Communism was a gift to Americans who, without it, would have lacked a sustaining cause.

With Communism in foul odor, the Popular Front Americanism of the 1930s quickly crumbled. The common man had a new cause: stop the Red Army. During the Depression, such popular figures as Will Rogers, John Steinbeck, and, for that matter, Franklin Delano Roosevelt had crystallized sentiment about the virtue of the common man into a rhetoric aimed against economic royalists and Republican skinflints. Now these were no longer the favored enemies. When President Harry Truman proposed a crusade against the commercial control of medicine, he was beaten back by the medical profession's counterattack against "socialized medicine." McCarthyism, a populism of fools, arose out of the Midwest to transform class and regional resentments into a single iron conviction. The common man was now encouraged to express his hostility to striped-pants Eastern Establishment types by sniffing out Communists in the State Department.

Still, for the purpose of shaping popular identity, McCarthyism was of limited value. For several years a successful political crusade, it was still not a source of social location and ultimate meaning for most Americans. Hence the importance of the second adhesive force working against centrifugal cultural motion: the rising standard of living. The prospect of an unceasing improvement in private life became a decisive foundation of American political identity during the quarter century after the end of World War II. For if the common man was, in fact, making a good deal of progress, as measured by the sole criterion for progress that was alive in the culture—namely, economic advancement—then Americanism *worked.* Government policies were mobilized to deliver a postwar cornucopia. From the Servicemen's Readjustment Act of 1944, guaranteeing low-interest home loans to the sixteen million servicemen who would return from the war, and insuring builders' investments, to the road-building laws culminating in the Federal-Aid Highway Act of 1956, government action created the material base for a culture of affordable acquisition. In the suburban home, the family commanded an array of technical services that not so long before had been available only to the very rich: central heating, indoor plumbing, telephones, automatic stoves, refrigerators, and washing machines. The dream of the common man materialized in the common home. Thanks to government subsidies, private utopia was readily affordable: in 1948, Levittown's tract houses could be bought so cheaply that mortgage, interest, principle, and taxes combined amounted to less than sixty dollars a month. The sense of having arrived (in the suburbs, in a car) was extraordinary. The majority felt comfortable. Who needed a Popular Front? The demobilized troops could disperse to the suburbs, to be middle class with the rest of the lonely crowd.

The salient identity, the one that mattered, was: middle class. The term "middle class" has a long lineage in America, and a different one than in Europe, where in the Marxist tradition it signified *bourgeois* prosperity. As early as the 1820s, the term was used in the United States to mark out a distinct social group with something of its own self-awareness. In 1858, none other than Walt Whitman, the poet of the brawny lumberjack and the wind-burned sailor, editorialized: "The most valuable class in any community is the middle class, the man of moderate means." By 1900, American cities were already surrounded by rather homogeneous "middle-class" suburbs, joined to the city by streetcars. The boom in clerical and sales white-collar jobs made the term "middle class," even "the great middle class," steadily more common. Increasingly, an American was someone who wished to join that middle class—this was the meaning of the "Dream," the "Way of Life." By the mid–twentieth century, "middle class" had become a catch-all label of choice beloved by pollsters and politicians and editorial writers, and a brilliantly flexible one it was, enabling office and technical workers to share status with doctors and corporate managers. To identify oneself as part of that great blur was an affirmation of normality—the averageness that Americans cultivate as an ideal while loudly proclaiming their individualism. To say you were middle class was to say that you were a regular person, an ordinary Joe or Jane—and eventually, that you belonged to the majority. For by the 1980s, more Americans identified themselves (to pollsters, at least) as middle class (43.3 percent) than as working-class (36.6 percent), and the self-professed middle, supplemented by the self-professed upper-middle (8.2 percent), added up to a majority. Among voters, the middle-class majority would be still greater.

The middle-class ideal took on a special allure in the suburbs. The free-standing home was now integral to American identity. It was the present-day extension of the homestead, the marker of yeoman liberty. Men readily described themselves as *home*owners; the majority of women were *house*wives. You were where you lived. To say *home* was to say *family,* and to say either was to say *goodness*—moral goodness as well as a good way of life. The family home was a place to make babies and rear children, to display the luster and powers of income, to make the grass grow and the car glow and the television set radiate images of carefree people mowing their grass and burnishing their cars to a fine gloss.

The small screen was far more than a machine for perpetual entertainment. Television was an amusement bank, a national bulletin board, a repertory of images, an engine for ideas, a classification index, a faithful pet, and a tranquilizer. Perhaps most of all, the television networks were crucial dispensers of America's master idea of itself. The dream of normality was incarnate in *The Adventures of Ozzie & Harriet, Father Knows Best, The Donna Reed Show,* and comparable rituals of cheerfully intact white families living the good life within their white picket fences and solving their silly problems. The boundaries of morality were marked by the likes of *Dragnet* and *The F.B.I.* policing transgressions. *The Lone Ranger* and *Gunsmoke* gave the moral law roots in a mythological history. For exotica, Americans could turn to *Disneyland,* hosted by folksy Walt Disney of Kansas City, certifying that we were a fun-loving, innocent people who deserved to be on top of the world.

All in all, television flattered Americans that they had never had it so good—and that they had a common destiny. According to programs and commercials alike, they had no regions, no accents, no divergent histories. Television was a school for manners, mores, and styles; for repertories of speech and feeling; even for personality. Television helped teach Americans how to talk, look, and behave—which meant, in some measure, teaching them how they should think, how they should feel, and how, perchance, they should dream. And so, while certifying the high-consumption way of life, network television also served as an instrument for the nationalization of culture—and in the end, therefore, helped further a certain bland tolerance while eroding ethnocentrism and other forms of parochialism. It was no small blow against white supremacy, in the 1950s and 1960s, to bring into American living rooms images of the brutality meted out by Southern segregationists against noble civil rights campaigners demanding their rights.

During the first two postwar decades, then, television helped crystallize a sense of the privileges to which a majority of Americans were to feel entitled. The privilege included upward mobility—not only for one's children, but for oneself. If one's own house, one's home, looked meager, there was a solution to that, too: work harder, earn more, and trade up. If the ladder upward was real, then opportunity could compensate for envy, which Tocqueville rightly considered the democratic sentiment par excellence. What did the inequality of income and the far greater inequality of wealth matter? The majority of Americans were willing to overlook inequality as long as opportunities for improvement abounded. Through the 1960s, enough upward mobility took place among a middle-class person's middle-class acquaintances and relations that those who failed to ascend apparently had only themselves or their spouses to blame for not being up to snuff.

Whatever the failures and false promises of the past, America *would* be, was *coming* to be, was on its way. So the combination of postwar boom and Cold War made palpable a new basis for national unity. Together they formed a Grand Creed. For the majority, any class resentment yielded to gratitude for a system that delivered the goods, or enough of the goods to warrant the gratitude. The common man had a double cause: to achieve home and family and to defend the community of homes and families against the Communists. You did not have to be a McCarthyite to share this sentiment of the Fifties. In fact, it was in the name of the common condition of Americanness that McCarthyism was eventually brought low, tarnished as divisive, anti-individualist, and therefore, in a certain respect, un-American. Thus, the significance of two symbolic confrontations of the 1950s. The first came during the televised Army-McCarthy hearings of 1954, when McCarthy not only had the gall to attack the military but also cast aspersions on the left-wing past of a junior lawyer on Joseph Welch's team. Welch brilliantly counterthrust, casting McCarthy as the bully who would deny a man the opportunity to remake himself into a respectable middle-class American. Five years later, during an American exposition in Moscow, Vice President Nixon asserted that most American families could afford the panoply of kitchen goods on display. Khrushchev, waving a finger in Nixon's face, denied it. Nixon, however, was on the mark, and his audience back home knew it. Anti-Communism and suburban pride converged. Freedom *worked*.

For four decades, anti-Communism remained a binder in the American cement. Amalgamated with economic expansion, it could accommodate several versions. In the right-wing version, racial equality, socialized medicine, and militant unions alike were the immoral prologues to Communism; they led to disunity and therefore, by definition, aided the enemy. In the liberal version, equality—especially racial equality—was the opposite: a form of fortification against Communism, necessary to woo postcolonial Africa. Either way, anti-Communism defined the periphery of the debate. The Cold War propped up America, and in any event, what were the alternatives? No other popular and compelling idea was available with which to express the unity of America. To put it symbolically: During the war against fascism, Germany was the enemy that helped unite our states. After the war, the Iron Curtain that tore Germany asunder helped hold America together.

Yet even in the frozen 1950s there were certain intimations that the potent combination of Cold War and prosperity was not an all-purpose answer to the question of what America had in common. Race was a centrifugal pressure, especially at the time of the *Brown v. Board of Education* decision, the Montgomery, Alabama, bus boycott, and the Little Rock school integration crisis. And there were other signs of discomfort as well. At the height of the Cold War, the American establishment wondered aloud what was the common national purpose. Such insecurity led President Eisenhower to appoint, with much hoopla, a Commission on National Goals—the sort of enterprise one cannot imagine in Great Britain, or France, or Mexico. In the final report, released in 1960, NBC mogul David Sarnoff answered the question of purpose with official cant: "Our message to humankind must be that America has decided, irrevocably, to win the cold war." But the editor of the report, a *Life* magazine editor, approvingly quoted Walter Lippmann, America's premier pundit, who had no clarion call to sound:

> The critical weakness of our society is that for the time being our people do not have great purposes which they are united in wanting to achieve. The public mood of the country is defensive, to hold on and to conserve, not to push forward and to create. We talk about ourselves these days as if we were a completed society, one which has achieved its purposes, and has no further great business to transact.

Not that African Americans were speaking of themselves as part of a completed society. But outside the South, the rest of the nation could take pleasure in the fact that it was, after all, not the South, and that eventually the South would be brought—would be integrated—kicking and screaming into the whole.

3. The Vietnam Crackup and the "Anti-American" Left

The Cold War unified only as long as it played well. If, in America, nothing succeeds like success, by the same token, nothing fails like failure; and when the Cold War went hot in Vietnam, the result was a shattering failure on a scale that the architects of postwar American identity could not have imagined. Therefore, Vietnam proved not only a bad war and a failed war but a wedge in the binding idea of America.

For their part, the elites who embraced the war regarded it—and promoted it—as more than a policy. During the decisive years of escalation, 1960–68, whatever their policy differences, they presented it as a manifestation of moral excellence, a test of the Grand Creed, and (they believed) *the* logical extension of the Cold War. "Limited war" anywhere was to be a decisive test of indivisible national will. One breach in the wall and containment was doomed. Vietnam was a Station of the American Cross, a decisive battle in the endless war to "defend free peoples," the reincarnation of Tripoli, Fort Defiance, San Juan Hill, the beaches of Normandy and Iwo Jima: the testing ground of the hour, the newest frontier where "freedom" would be defended by "guardians at the gate." America's war policy was more restrained than many hawks wished, but the weaponry was sufficiently monstrous and the rhetoric sufficiently bellicose and sweeping to make of Vietnam not *a* war but *the* war.

At the mythic level, Vietnam was more than a place or a policy. It was engraved in the national soul as the exposed salient point in an unending line of demarcation. The nation's security *and* honor were at stake, declared the partisans of the war. Since the war is the deed that stands for America's word, said the party of war, those who oppose the war are enemies of the nation. Such beliefs had their logic. If America's nature was to be an ideological bastion, then opposition to policy *was* tantamount to heresy. But this identification of the nation with the war held a potential for backfire, for the Americanness that Cold War and economic boom held together was more fragile than it appeared. A critical mass of the young middle classes slowly followed an emotional logic of their own to the conclusion that "affluence" was hollow, boring, and stupid, and that nuclear-tipped anti-Communism was too dangerous to justify patriotic surrender and meltdown in the caldron of unity. A critical mass of blacks had their own reasons for staying out of that caldron. In backlash, a movement of whites surged up from the Right, expressing outrage and dispossession.

The seams of American identity began to give way. Growing numbers in the civil rights and antiwar movements began by rejecting American practices, went on to reject American ideals, and soon, since America *was* its ideals, rejected the conventional versions of American identity altogether. The early New Left rejected the American political consensus as hypocritical: the country was in default on its promise to recognize equal rights. The later New Left and the black liberation movement rejected the promise as well: the American political consensus was cursed by original sin, it was and had ever been racist and imperial, it had long been making its way to napalm in the defense of freedom; the very idea of a common America came to feel like a pernicious defense of unwarranted and injurious privilege. Revisionist history arose to support what the New

Left already suspected: that Vietnam was only the latest battlefield in the Indian wars. The war gave rebirth to a Left, but the Left it spawned was moved by a negative passion that matched the warmakers' own negative passion: their commitment to stamp out Communism in Vietnam by destroying the country.

As the war burned on, the problem of what to say about it turned into the problem of how to feel about America as a civilization. With an eerie suddenness, virtually before anyone noticed how drastically the terms had changed, American identity was at stake. On the Left, the first impulse of militants in the antiwar movement was to deploy their own patriotic imagery in an attempt to capture the flag. In November 1965, for example, Carl Oglesby stole the show at a mild rally against the Vietnam War (the official signs reading "Negotiate Now") by treating the war as the product of an imperial history. Oglesby refused to let "the bitter ugliness of Czechoslovakia, Poland, those infamous Russian tanks in the streets of Budapest" justify the war: "My anger only rises to hear some say that sorrow cancels sorrow, or that *this* one's shame deposits in *that one's* account the right to shamefulness." But Oglesby, the son of an Akron rubber worker, also self-consciously invoked "our dead revolutionaries" Jefferson and Paine against the likes of Lyndon Johnson and McGeorge Bundy. He romantically summoned up a once-democratic America against the "colossus of . . . our American corporate system." He wanted to rescue the good name and promise of "American humanism" from an "anti-Communist corporate liberalism" responsible for imperial expeditions in Iran, Guatemala, Cuba, and elsewhere during the Cold War. He chastised chastisers who might say "that I sound mighty anti-American. To these, I say: Don't blame *me* for *that!* Blame those who mouthed my liberal values and broke my American heart."

In the summer of 1966, the Berkeley antiwar leader Jerry Rubin, subpoenaed by the House Un-American Activities Committee, was persuaded by the head of the San Francisco Mime Troupe, R. G. Davis, to dress up in an Uncle Sam Revolutionary War costume—to convey, as Davis told me later, "the straight image of America." Some elders also promoted the idea that opposing the war was, in fact, the height of patriotism. "I don't like the sight of young people burning the flag of my country, the country I love," thundered the old-time socialist leader Norman Thomas in 1967. "If they want an appropriate symbol they should be washing the flag, not burning it." By the fall of 1968, though, Jerry Rubin was dressing up for the cameras in a pastiche of Indian war paint, hippie beads, Vietnamese sandals, and a toy machine gun. With hellfire raining on the land and people of Vietnam, Norman Thomas's fusion of Protestant patriotism and cautious politics looked less and less impressive to the growing ranks of the militant antiwar young.

But if the war incited the New Left to detest patriotic symbols, there were other causes as well. To start with, those young radicals moving leftward were already prone to a deep and passionate alienation from the whole ensemble of American normality, its racism and suburbs, its sexual hypocrisy and cultural fatuousness alike; the patriotic, Victorian, suit-and-tie attachments of a Norman Thomas were not for them. Worse, in the case at hand many a prominent left-of-center patriot, including Thomas himself, was equivocal about leaving the war. As late as 1967, liberals like Victor Reuther of the United Automobile Workers, Joseph Rauh, Jr., of Americans for Democratic Action, John Kenneth Galbraith, and Arthur Schlesinger, Jr., were unwilling to support American withdrawal. Martin Luther King, Jr., tried to uphold the constitutional faith while opposing the war. But his murder in 1968, followed by that of Robert F. Kennedy, refuted the hope that America could make itself safe for democracy. The anti-American outrage of Malcolm X and the Black Panthers became far more appealing. Increasingly, in the later Sixties, when the advocates of the war plastered their bumpers with *America, love it or leave it!* antiwar militants responded, *So be it! and to hell with you, we have left it and its napalm. Good riddance.*

In an effort to reclaim a patriotic aura, moderates arose in vast numbers, waving American flags, dressing respectably, working in political campaigns "within the system." But militants also reproduced, fueled by disgust at this apparently endless war, and often by rage against its supporters as well. Among the militants was a minority ready and eager to offend the majority, and able to command the attention of TV cameras by carrying North Vietnam's banners. Later, antiwar Vietnam veterans would try to recapture symbols of American history, naming their 1972 hearings on war crimes after the "winter soldiers" celebrated by Thomas Paine— the true (as opposed to "sunshine") patriots who defend their nation's honor during its bleakest hours. But efforts of this sort were too few and too late. The symbols of patriotism were firmly in the hands of Richard Nixon. Democratic Americanism, an Americanism of constitutional faith strong enough to override the racism of American history, an Americanism despite everything, was throttled.

It is important to be clear about what this anti-Americanism of the time was and was not. It was a sentiment more than a commitment, a loathing more than a theory, a yelp of anguish more than an ideology. It was built on disappointment—the crashing of a liberal faith in American goodness, and, as a result, the turning of that faith upside down. The result was that as the war ground on, any lingering New Left belief in a redemptive American dream to be held in common bled away. The climate became so inflamed, the disbelief in constructive change so fierce, and the despair over the course of American policy so pervasive, that even a critical-minded figure like the journalist Paul Cowan could call his 1970 memoir *The Making of an Un-American.* From the early nineteenth century onward, nativists and immigrants alike had each proclaimed that they were the *real* Americans, as opposed to those Others. Now, for the first time in American history, there were groupings who had no stomach to be included, and wanted out.

A sympathetic though critical onlooker, someone possessed of a large and not punitive vision, might have discerned the rage of the rejected child pleading to be let in and loved—a plea that America be refashioned, in fact, so an outsider might find an honorable place. But the populace who recoiled were not large of vision. Their Americanness was too narrow, too resentful, too negative itself to permit commiseration with rebels. Attacks on American symbols they took at face value, and personally. If they were immigrants (especially from the Communist bloc) or the children of immigrants, their own need to prove themselves loyal was too great. Anti-Americanism seemed indiscriminate, a slap not only at established elites but at their hard-won privileges and achievements, at the myths they wished to believe.

The New Left proved, for several reasons, largely uninterested in celebrating or proposing a common American identity. With the eclipse of Martin Luther King, Jr., followed by his murder, the most energetic and conspicuous African-American leaders could not summon up any romance in behalf of a concept from which they had been excluded for so long, or to which they had been appended as an afterthought. From the start, by contrast with earlier American Lefts, the New Left had been unimpressed with the common man. Many student radicals insisted on being *un*common. Despite attempts to plant roots in a historical soil of slave revolts, abolitionism, labor and feminist organizing, the movement found it hard to summon up faith in American redemption. A common American identity, if there had ever been one, was either a hoax or a menace. There was to be no revived Popular Front.

True enough, during the 1960s many white activists collected every scrap of evidence they could scour up that common men and women could be wooed to a radical movement. They celebrated salt-of-the-earth commoners who had been found friendly. Some tried to organize soldiers and draft-eligible working-class youth, hoping to cross the class barrier, and in the case of antiwar soldiers, succeeded to a considerable extent— though after the student movement had crested, and at a time when antiwar activists had been discredited in the eyes of many GIs. Other- wise, the gestures were frequently forced, the projects usually less than brilliantly successful. On the whole, the New Left could not deeply imag- ine a populism in which it might take part. Often it defied popularity altogether. It was suspicious of majorities. Majorities were, after all, sus- picious of *it*. Majorities could turn genocidal. White majorities in particu- lar were connoisseurs of the privileges of skin. Common men (and women) lined up at draft board demonstrations and glared at comfortably raised youth chanting "Power to the people!"

It was left to the imagination to conjure a majority force that might be coaxed into existence. Imagination responded with fantasy. Some activists leapt out of the American frame altogether and conjured images of a new Popular Front on a global scale: a Third World hypothetically unified in revolution against the white world (excepting white "mother country brothers and sisters"). Here was one root of the multicultural impetus of later decades. Outside the New Left properly speaking, but sharing its bravado, was the counterculture's claim to be, in Abbie Hoffman's memo- rably wrong-headed phrase, Woodstock Nation. (A slice of a generation is never a nation.) The Third World and Woodstock Nation images looked, in effect, like exits from the expressway of straight America's common dreams.

Thus did young insurgents imagine themselves storming away from the overstuffed American way of life. In the process, the idea of a common America, if there was to be one at all, was ceded, by default, to the Right.

4. The Reagan Restoration

When prowar demonstrators laid claim to the American flag and with it the national legacy, they were asserting that there was a single national identity with a single mission, and that they embodied both. But during the bitter days of the late 1960s and early 1970s, the Right had its own sizable problems formulating the terms of American unity. The Grand Creed had been profoundly shaken. Hawkish anti-Communists were reduced to waving about the symbols of their Americanness at just the time flesh-and-blood Americans were deserting their cause en masse. Americans may not have been prepared to admit that they had lost their war, but they certainly had no doubt that they had failed to win it—and failed to hold together, to boot. If Vietnam was what happened when the Cold War ceased being theoretical, what was to be said about this Cold War itself as a righteous cause and a source of national identity? If war passions were unavailing, then what *was* the collective mission?

At the very least, not to be—in Richard Nixon's phrase—a "pitiful, helpless giant." But a pitiful giant the nation did seem. Certainly, nobody danced in the streets as the soldiers straggled home from their impossible mission in Vietnam. To the contrary: those streets were soon to be filled with cars waiting in line for gasoline. The postwar boom was fading on terms as humiliating, in their own way, as the Vietnam War. In 1971, the United States ran its first trade deficit since 1893. The inflation kindled by Johnson's refusal to raise taxes to pay for the war began to eat away at the savings of the elderly population—precisely those who had until then gained most from the postwar bargain. During the gasoline shortage of 1973, Americans even discovered that the automobile, insolent chariot of American freedom, was dependent on the goodwill of oil sheiks. The air was thick with signs that America was no longer Number One, and the Germans and Japanese were back, too. If we were not born to win, who were we?

The consensus on Cold War and prosperity was rubble. By the time the Americans evacuated Saigon, Nixon himself was a pitiful (although thanks to Gerald Ford's pardon, not exactly helpless) ex-president. The long, twilight humiliation of Watergate left the Right with a sense of betrayal and the nation with a sense of broken authority. Vietnam, Watergate, and the unraveling of the economic order virtually all at once: triumphalism shuddered.

Was a rebirth of aggressive nationalism the inescapable outcome, then? Blows to national pride are, in principle, excellent fodder for a nationalist politics of resentment, but there was nothing inevitable about the Right's subsequent victory. To restore a sense of national mission was the political and ideological achievement of Ronald Reagan and his handlers. They had to find an enemy and cheerfully launch into battle, but more: they had to forge a political majority. The traditional imperial motif of Manifest Destiny came to the fore. What more unifying emotion than popular truculence about the decline in America's fortunes? In his 1976 campaign against Gerald Ford's status quo, Reagan denounced an impending Panama Canal treaty as a "giveaway" and insisted on the need "to halt and reverse the diplomatic and military decline of the United States." The security of Panamanian waterways was not a sufficiently urgent concern for Republicans to carry him to nomination over an incumbent of their party, but on the strength of his rousing nationalist appeals, Reagan won more than 47 percent of his party's delegate's votes.

Four years later, Reagan was able to rekindle the nationalist passion and propel the Right into power. To do so, he could not blow on the ideological embers of the Vietnam War.* He needed to confront America with conspicuous enemies in the present tense. These readily presented themselves in the one-two combination of Ayatollah Khomeini and Leonid

---

* Indeed, the Vietnam War set a trap for him. Reagan's dubbing the war a "noble cause" in a 1980 speech to the Veterans of Foreign Wars turned out to be, according to his own pollster, the greatest mistake of his campaign against President Carter. To profit from the nationalist potential in American political culture, Reagan needed, in fact, to *avoid* the subject of Vietnam, for the memory was living proof of the perils of indiscriminate nationalism.

Brezhnev. The Shah of Iran fell, Khomeini rose to power, OPEC boosted the price of gasoline again, and Revolutionary Guards chanting "Death to the Great Satan" took over the American Embassy in Teheran. If that weren't enough, Brezhnev's invasion of Afghanistan in 1979 restored the roar of the Soviet bear and revived the Cold War. America's rock-bottom Cold War purpose had been, after all, to contain the military power of the Soviet Union—and here were Red tanks taking advantage of détente and rolling across a national border.

What gripped Americans most was the psychological humiliation in Iran, raised to the *nth* power by a nonstop media barrage. The long-running hostage crisis launched "America Held Hostage," a nightly crisis report on ABC News, and seemed to demonstrate, in living color, that America was indeed a pitiful, helpless giant. For the second time in a decade, Americans were branded losers. Conspicuous defeat was getting to be a habit—even an identity. All over the globe, revolutions were hollowing out what was supposed to be the American Century. From the vantage of the embattled American, it mattered little whether the revolutions were Communist or Islamic; all that mattered was that they were fervent and unremitting. Nightly, relentlessly, as the weeks turned into months and the months piled up into a year and more, Walter Cronkite closed his CBS News broadcast by ticking off "the *nth* day of the captivity of the American hostages in Iran."

At least as important, Reagan profited from the substantial economic travail of stagflation, easily pinned on the maladroit Jimmy Carter. The economic troubles appeared to be largely a consequence of America's loss of global hegemony. How could it have turned out that America, God's country, the Free World giant, proved dependent on foreign lubrication? Carter's economic and foreign policy defeats dovetailed in the gas lines of 1979. Americans did not suffer a shortage of affordable gasoline with equanimity. Such an infringement on the American way of mobility was a symbolic wound of major proportions. Double damage was done: to a dream of absolute freedom, and to the most egalitarian thing about that dream—the fact that the vast majority could afford to take an engine out on the open road. It was the hapless Carter's fate to preside over the shriveling of the cornucopia.

As the prosperity that had bound American identity against its centrifugal tendencies wore thin, conditions for a nationalist revival were ripe. But necessary conditions are not sufficient, and the revival was not automatic. One of the ingenuities of the American constitutional system is that it furnishes an institutional means of symbolic unification for a nation whose identity is frequently under pressure: the presidency, in principle standing above the nation's diversities and transcending them. As a result, no one should underestimate the latitude of a popular president to federate a majority and overcome centrifugal tendencies, assuming only that he begins with the elements of a promising coalition. In his person—or his persona, which in practical terms amounted to the same thing—Reagan *was* the nation that its voting majority wished to exist. Never mind his lackadaisical, frequently somnolent "management style," the fumbling and ignorance easily mocked by the likes of the liberal cartoonist Garry Trudeau ("In Search of Reagan's Brain"). It was neither "management style" nor incisiveness that spoke to the symbolic expectations of a majority of the voters. Reagan's mission was to preside over the in-gathering of a majority and the invocation of a unity, and this he did with extraordinary aplomb.

To start, he enfolded conservative differences. The Right was, like the populace as a whole, an assemblage. Social and economic conservatives had to be brought together. Indeed, early in the twentieth century, many of the former, personified by William Jennings Bryan, had been Democrats, detesting Wall Street as much as the teaching of evolution. No, the new Republican majority was not born; it had to be made. "The time has come," Reagan told a banquet of the American Conservative Union less than a month into Jimmy Carter's term, "to see if it is possible to present a program of action based on political principle that can attract those interested in the so-called 'social' issues and those interested in 'economic' issues." Reagan brought together the old probusiness, antiregulatory right of small-town chambers of commerce, "Reagan Democrats," principally white workers, weary of feeling that it was they who had been compelled to pay the price for black progress, Protestant fundamentalists, and antiabortionists alongside mainly Jewish, ex-leftist and ex-liberal neoconservative intellectuals, and the paleoconservatives personified by William F. Buckley, Jr., and his *National Review*. There were enough whites in this mixed bag to compose a majority impressed by common identity as well as common enough interests. There were, in particular, enough white men—Reagan received 59 percent of their votes. Academic leftists like to talk about "Gramscian intellectuals" who fuse diverse interests, or "class fractions," into functioning "historic blocs" by enunciating their common cause. In this light, no American in the latter half of the twentieth century has been half so Gramscian an intellectual as Ronald Reagan. He invoked a most historic bloc indeed.

But Reagan spoke for more than concerted conservatism. His images brought him front and center as the stand-in for the common man: the man of football and movies, of small-town Illinois and Iowa, of Hollywood and the Sacramento statehouse and the Santa Barbara ranch; the loyal son of an alcoholic father; the good husband and (on camera) good father and grandfather all at once. He was the reigning master of the ensemble of American myths: the man who could kick off his campaign in Philadelphia, Mississippi, without mentioning the civil rights workers buried there by their murderers in 1964, and still chop wood like the rail-splitter Abe Lincoln himself; the ex-Democrat who could invoke John Wayne and Franklin Delano Roosevelt without fear of self-contradiction. With his solid and twinkly face, his broad shoulders and manly frame, his perfectly delivered colloquial lines, his husky whispers of reassurance, his plain-spoken anecdotes and hometown rhetoric, he embodied some imperishable idea of the common America, the America of the common people— an America that was, at once, his audience, parish, and platform. He was the folk incarnate, presiding over the Puritans' city upon a hill.

Can there be any doubt that Reagan, Central Casting's idea of the common man, owed his achievement in good measure to his personal aura? In the wake of the 444-day hostage drama in Teheran, his buoyant and grandfatherly persona lifted spirits. After Carter's hard-luck term in office, Reagan seemed the very incarnation of victory. As long as the top one-fifth of the population experienced some measure of economic improvement, and a majority could bask in the return of the hostages and then in the military boom that Reagan delivered, his personal triumph played as a national triumph. He punctuated his policies with ceremonies meant to evoke triumphs over adversity, surrounding himself with heroes, teachers, and rescuers, hitherto unsung savers of lives, ordinary people who rose to the occasion, like Ronald Reagan himself. "Morning in America" was a reincarnation of "The People, Yes." With this vision of an America perennially reborn innocent, its tensions and hungers dissolved into a modest and cheerful Main Street, Reagan rekindled the most utopian American rhetoric. Accepting his nomination in 1980, he declared that Americans are "the kind of men and women Tom Paine had in mind when he wrote, during the darkest days of the American Revolution, 'We have it within our power to begin the world over again.' "

In the eyes of followers and pundits alike, Reagan promised to be the one-man antidote to identity crises. In his spectacular public relations effort, he started out as a premium product, benefited from skilled handlers, and played to a popular will to believe. It was the press, bedazzled by his aura, that sprayed that famous Teflon on him—because, disproportionately Democrats themselves, they were bending over backward to seem fair; because they were charmed and flattered by him; because they had loathed Carter, whom they saw as a bumpkin who had the ill grace to come on moralistic; because they were patriots who couldn't help thinking that Reagan was toughening up the "pitiful, helpless giant"; because they thought he did genuinely represent an America poorer and more provincial and less articulate than themselves, and they were eager to circumvent the charge of undermining national self-esteem. It was the press that attributed to Reagan an aura of invincibility, claiming that he was far more popular than their own polls testified. Whatever their on-camera insouciance, they were pleased to see, and say, that "America is back."

In Reagan's iconography, America was back in considerable part because the common man was confronted yet again by an uncommon foe. Social disputes, especially over abortion, could be postponed, internal disputes on the right muted by the more urgent task of confronting the Soviet bear. Reagan's grandiloquent and yet festive views of America's mission harked back to John F. Kennedy's inaugural speech. Reagan varied his Cold War tones at times, but always deplored the Soviet Union as the principal obstacle to the realization of America's mission: freedom. The imposition of martial law in Poland on December 13, 1981, lent at least superficial credence to the all-or-nothing rhetoric of a revived Cold War. Speaking to British Members of Parliament at the Palace of Westminster on June 8, 1982, in what he later called "probably one of the most important speeches I gave as president," Reagan harked to the memory of Winston Churchill in calling for "a crusade for freedom," and decried "the shyness of some of us in the West about standing for these ideals that have done so much to ease the plight of man and the hardships of our imperfect world." Speaking to the National Association of Evangelicals in Orlando on March 8, 1983, he famously denounced the Soviet Union as "an evil empire," called it "the focus of evil in the modern world," and proclaimed the Cold War a "struggle between right and wrong and good and evil." The way Reagan wanted to "begin the world over again" was to erase a good deal of the past—but in this, too, he was the quintessentially American common man.

By contrast to the revitalization Reagan seemed to offer, the Democrats offered no commonality, no alternative crucible, no compelling rhetoric, no political culture—only a heap of demands piled on demands. Reagan told Americans, especially whites, who they were, and equally important, who they were against; Democrats told Americans, especially women and minorities, about their interests. The lackluster Walter Mondale advanced no unifying symbol to overcome race and class tensions within the Democratic base, and not surprisingly, two out of three white men voted for Reagan in 1984. Michael Dukakis offered himself as a son-of-immigrants American success story, but his famously ill-fitting tank helmet symbolized the apparent mismatch that resulted when a Democrat now tried to convince the country that he had the right stuff to tough it out as commander in chief. Not surprisingly, now that Vietnam had discredited Democratic muscularity abroad, it was the Right that did best with jaunty toughness, the Ramboesque and Schwarzeneggerian masculinity that had become the measure of national guardianship, while the Democrats offered no other image of national unity, no ringing answer to the question, "Who Are We?"

5. Nothing Fails Like Success

With the collapse of the evil empire, the triumphalist note trumpeted forth: we were winners again. But when Germans demolished the Berlin Wall in November 1989, the rubble fell on our side of the Atlantic, too.

What would a nation that required a raison d'être do without one? If the old saga culminated in victory, what was the new saga? For all the self-congratulation, the collapse of Communism rattled America—not just the consciously held ideas of what America had won and why we had won it, but also deeper, barely articulated ideas of what America was and how Americans were attached to each other. It was as if for half a century the nation had been a tug-of-war team, held together largely by the force of the adversary pulling against us. When the other team dropped their end of the rope and fled the field, what was there to hold us up?

Initially, pundits and politicians, especially on the Right, flattered us that, having prevailed in a titanic contest, we were entitled to coast to glory. The nation was unmatched in its power; the free market—such was the misleading slogan with which the corporate economy was adver-tised—ruled unopposed. Who or what could stand in our way? But such self-congratulation ran tinny. There was an unsatisfying sense of anticli-max. The peace, it turned out, was even more abstract than the war had been. As there had been no great, final battles, so there were no rites of victory—no ceremonial surrenders, no victory parades, no tearful re-unions. Indeed, the collapse of Communism left America with an enemy crisis.* The 1991 Gulf War did, it is true, produce a righteous mobiliza-tion, but the yellow-beribboned uproar in behalf of the Desert Storm troops, intense as it was, came and went within months. Once the troops were out of harm's way, national political culture returned to its frag-mented status quo ante, and the media spotlight moved on. America the centrifugal was left to itself (or its selves). We fell, and what we fell into were culture wars.

It was, moreover, evident that as America's Cold War cement cracked, the economic side of the postwar bargain was also falling apart. The world's largest creditor nation in rapid order became the world's largest debtor nation. Hell-bent on profit, companies "downsized" and capital

---

* The final phase of the Cold War had already proved emotionally too flat to capture the collective imagination long enough to dampen domestic strife and restore a political sense of national union. Neither Colonel Gaddafi nor General Noriega could produce long-lasting thrills. Nor could the Sandinistas, nor the obscure Grenadans. All were too local, too puny, too unthreatening to the homeland, just as in the years to come neither Saddam Hussein nor Kim Il Sung, neither Colombian drug lords nor Japanese investors nor Mexican immigrants quite fit the bill.

fled. Inequality mounted, and the public sector crumbled. The jolt was felt most acutely by the Americans who had least expected to lose momentum and were least equipped to manage a jolt to their expectations: precisely the middle—or would-be middle—classes who had drawn the most advantage from the truncated American century of 1945–73. Undoubtedly, nobody is comfortable with a decline in living standards, but Americans may have been uniquely vulnerable because such things were not supposed to be possible here. If America *is* the dream, then in a certain sense, the end of the dream portended the end of the nation.

'Twas a famous victory, then, the end of the Cold War, but with victories like this, who could abide defeats? Without the enemy, what united the states? The formula for American commonality would have to be worked up and fought over anew. Absent the Cold War, both Right and Left were in need, first, of cement for their own coalitions, and second, of compelling ideas to take to the rest of the country about what Americans had in common. What would pick us up, restore our morale, hold us together? Ideologues of the Right, now in short supply of external barbarians to help federate their economic and social conservatives, began to search for domestic ones obstructing the people's will: Dan Quayle's "cultural elite," the "liberal media," the universities, the National Endowments for the Humanities and the Arts, public television and radio, and later, Newt Gingrich's "counterculture McGoverniks." These defenders of civilization were at times fully aware that they longed for the moral equivalent of the Cold War. The influential neoconservative Irving Kristol wrote in 1993: "There is no 'after the Cold War' for me. So far from having ended, my cold war has increased in intensity, as sector after sector has been ruthlessly corrupted by the liberal ethos. . . . Now that the other 'Cold War' is over, the real cold war has begun. We are far less prepared for this cold war, far more vulnerable to our enemy, than was the case with our victorious war against a global Communist threat." Authentic American identity would draw a line in the sand against "the liberal ethos." In this spirit, Patrick Buchanan's declaration of "war for the soul of America" in 1992 was succeeded by Gingrich's denunciation of Bill Clinton as "the enemy of normal Americans" during the run-up to the midterm elections of 1994.

The problem of finding a basis for commonality was still more grave for Democrats, and for the Left at their flank. The Democrats were a loose, baggy party, the Left an aggregation of movements, grouplets, and ideological tendencies, both suffering from a disproportion of margins to center. Both now amounted to collections of interest groups and little more, and lacked a vocabulary for the common good. Both had shed the custom of affirming the whole people. Not only were they ethnically and racially diverse, and so especially vulnerable to centrifugal tendencies, but, in the New Deal tradition, they had believed in government spending as a social binder, an instrument of justice, a means to reduce inequality and a defense of the middle class all at once. Without the Cold War, growing numbers of Americans now asked, what was the positive point of the government? It was seen as an instrument of division, a plaything of "special interests," a broken machinery—or an ogre.

The Democrats, though frequently distancing themselves from the Left, had also borrowed its energies and, in return, often reluctantly, legitimized and absorbed some of its institutions and projects—its unions in the 1930s, its civil rights movement in the early 1960s, its antiwar and feminist concerns in the early 1970s. One could argue about whether, in the process, the Left was depleted or nourished, but in any event, the Left and the Democrats had risen and fallen together. Since the McGovern convention of 1972, raggedly and selectively, the Democrats had taken much of their poetry from a Left that had no conviction that commonality was possible. As prosperity seeped away, so did the unions and the Democrats' white working-class base, while the party's very successes during the postwar boom reduced the numbers of white poor and of Democrats, especially in the suburbs. The civil rights movement and its white backlash cost them the South, and then some. The Democrats lost the ability and the will to mobilize the government without antagonizing the Thirties side of their coalition to benefit the Sixties side. Facing their most intractable issue, race, they trapped themselves in zero-sum programs—busing, affirmative action—that split their base.

The travail of the Democrats was more serious than a shortage of policies; it was symbolic. In the metaphor wars of the post-Reagan period, the Democrats could not agree on a common story. They did not march onward together toward an extension of rights or a rally of the whole people; they did not march onward together, period. While the Republicans upheld "freedom," "the nation," or "the family," the Democrats had no America to affirm against "the interests." As much as George Bush, they lacked "the vision thing." Instead of a melting pot, they intermittently offered a "gorgeous mosaic" (without cement), or a "salad bowl" (with cracks), or a disorderly "rainbow" (whose distinct bands were constantly pulling apart). The images themselves were fragile, makeshift, evanescent. The Democrats stared uncomprehending into America's post–Cold War identity crisis, barely aware that they lacked even the terms of unification. In 1992, Bill Clinton's "forgotten middle class" was quite a comedown from "the people."

As for the outriders on the Democrats' left, rarely did they amount to more than loose collections, nor did they seem to care. Like the opponents of the Houghton Mifflin history textbooks—*and even like the books' defenders,* with their broken narratives and MTV juxtapositions of separate group chronicles—they didn't add up. They were, in theory and practice, less than the sum of their parts. Rarely did the segments recognize that, even to win what each of them wanted, they needed a whole that was more than a heap. But their incapacity was a chapter in a longer ordeal: the breakdown of the idea of a common Left.

3

The Fragmentation of the
Idea of the Left

1. United Humanity and United States

Between Left and Right there has taken place a curious reversal. Throughout the nineteenth and twentieth centuries, the Left believed in a common human condition, the Right in fundamental differences among classes, nations, races. The Left wanted collective acts of renewal, the Right endorsed primordial ties of tradition and community against all disruptions. The main line of the Left stood for the equality of all persons; the main line of the Right for distinctions and privileges of birth, position, nationality. Thus, the royalist Joseph de Maistre in 1797: "In the course of my life I have seen Frenchmen, Italians, Russians; I even know, thanks to Montesquieu, that one can be a Persian; but *man* I have never met." Today it is the Right that speaks a language of commonalities. Its rhetoric of global markets and global freedoms has something of the old universalist ring. To be on the Left, meanwhile, is to doubt that one can speak of humanity at all. So Oakland's dubious textbook battle is more than a sign of the loosening of consensus about American identity. It is a sign of the thinning out of the Left as a live political and intellectual force.

Our secular twentieth century has known two great universalizing passions: universalizing in the sense of maintaining that humanity has a common nature and a common destiny; passions in the sense of worldviews affirmed with a depth of conviction that led millions of people to sacrifice their lives in their names. On the one side, liberal democratic Americanism; on the other, socialism. Both agreed that anyone from anywhere could affiliate. Both fused the modern Western faith in the active molding of history with a conviction that progress was already unfolding. Born in rebellion, both were captured by establishments. Today, both are damaged—one fatally, the other perhaps not. The visions of humanity that once stressed a common condition, that understood difference against a backdrop of what was not different, are feeble. The problem much of the world wrestles with is how to imagine a common world without their vigor.

For two centuries in the West, if there was no conviction that deliverance for all was at hand, there was at least a conviction that the commonality of mankind was a noble and imaginable project. Whether the common bond was inalienable rights, reason, man's creative nature, or membership in the working class, the premise was that human capacities were the foundation of an improvable society. Today, we witness an exhaustion of that core belief shared by Americanism and by the historic ideals of the Left: a belief in progress through the unfolding of a humanity present—at least potentially—in every human being. What proliferates in the West is the "post" mood. We belong to a time of aftermaths: we are after Auschwitz, after Hiroshima, after the Gulag. And if this much was already clear in 1945 to anyone who wished to see, today one must add: after Vietnam, after Cambodia, after Sarajevo, after Rwanda. After such knowledge, what faith? Universalism has a bad name. Reason seems frail—or worse, its claim to progress through understanding is billed as the instrument of white, Western, male domination, and hence of the pollution and destruction of the earth.

The "post" mood may appear as exhilaration or weariness, but both celebrants and disputants of the new disorder are partly right: a sense of

ending is irresistible. Certainly, there remain vigorous ideas and sentiments of a universal humanity, perhaps best expressed in the Universal
Declaration of Human Rights, in organizations like Amnesty International and Médécins sans Frontières, in campaigns for the defense of
Salman Rushdie and against genital mutilation. There remain cosmopolitan spirits who live in urban zones where identities mix and multiplicities
thrive, where the pleasures of coexistence and the adhesive forces of
solidarity outweigh the arrogance of elites, the impositions of millennial
religion or imperial power, and the tensions and distentions of difference.
There remain, not least, universal predicaments—we live under one
ozone layer, in one single greenhouse, though certainly the view from the
penthouse is not the view from the basement.

In much of the world, however, the universalist initiative has passed
back to religious faith, with its longing for transcendence and otherworld-
liness. In Islam and Christianity, under the scrutiny of the All-Knowing,
the faithful aim to unify the world into the order of the Prophet or Savior.
They imagine that they are already unifying the world—or would be doing
so, were it not for the infidel, the secularist, the modernist blasphemer.
Meanwhile, in recent decades, all kinds of secular commonality ideas
have lost much of their cogency and power. The Enlightenment belief in
progress rooted in the onward march of reason seems reserved for scientists, or students of society who fancy themselves scientists; it is not a
popular faith. The liberalism of individual rights is under fire for cultivating systematic irresponsibility and failing to offer a sense of community.
The secularist, cosmopolitan young who wish to feel part of a global
community turn to the disposable imagery of popular culture—the
Madonnas, Michael Jacksons, Arnold Schwarzeneggers, and Disney crea-
tures who seem to inhabit a world without locality and to speak some
primitive language without depth. The weightless, spurious universalism
of commercial culture, the thrill of new technologies for wiring together
the world, the all-consuming blankness of Generation X—such attachments and detachments are alluring substitutes for deep belief in the
whole human project. The consumerist utopia of the Mall Without Borders offers endless enticements, but hopes only to heighten the pleasures
of the ephemeral. It offers no commonality but the lightest, no vision of
the future but more fun. There are pleasures and addictions and evanes-

cent communities galore to be found under the big tent of popular culture, but what there is not is a sense of common citizenship. Instead, people seek solidarity among those who resemble themselves.

The loss of the vision of a common future is most striking for the Left, where the faith in eventual progress was once so strong. Here lies the largest meaning of the little frictions, dubious battles, and culture crusades of our moment. At the root of the many meanings of what we call the Enlightenment was a conviction that there is a common human condition on the basis of which progress, if not perfection, is at least possible—if not imminent. The Enlightenment was a secular version of Christian ideas about human destiny. How fusty these hopes sound today! Marxism, the principal theology of the Left, has barely any supporters anywhere, even in Central Europe or Central Asia, where voters return former Communist bureaucrats to office. The collapse of Communism and the Cold War balance of terror did not clear the slate for a renewed commitment to egalitarian values, but revealed European social democracy to be in a crisis of its own, unable to rally popular enthusiasm against the pressures of the global economic convulsion and a declining belief in the efficacy of the public realm. Defenders of some Platonic ideal of a Left have only a tattered flag to wave, and are today, like their counterparts on the Right, more adept at vituperation against their enemies than at reflecting upon, let alone practicing, human arrangements that would make life more supportable and dignified for humanity at large. But it will not do to raise the trumpet for a restoration of the grand old unities. An abiding faith in the human future is not summoned up by an act of will.

For two centuries after 1776 and 1789 believers in a common humanity everywhere clustered around two great progressive ideals: a liberal one enshrined in the Declaration of Independence, the U.S. Constitution, and the French Declaration of the Rights of Man and Citizen; and a radical or socialist one that crystallized as Marxism. Here was launched the very language of contemporary politics. Even the political metaphor of Left and Right, however much knocked around, has survived on the strength of an assumption that history is a single story proceeding along a single time line. The idea of a Left derives, strictly speaking, from the seating arrangements of the French National Assembly, but two-sided political symmetry has another intuitive appeal. Like the Christian division of history into before and after, the language of Left and Right stems from the idea of a universal history. Revolution, like the story of Christ, splits history down the middle. Past and future are the essential categories. Old regimes want to conserve, new regimes want to change. This is the melodrama the Left has always been partial to—casting itself as action thrusting into the Future while the Right represents reaction, the dead hand of the past.

Such legitimacy as the Left enjoyed in the West rested on its claim to a place in the grand story of universal human emancipation. The Left addressed itself not to particular men and women but to all, in the name of their common standing. If the population at large was incapable, by itself, of seeing the world whole and acting in the general interest, then some enlightened group would take it upon itself to be the collective conscience, the Founding Fathers, the vanguard party. Even Marx, lyricist of the proletariat, ingeniously claimed that his favored class was destined to stand in for, or become, all humanity. Whether reformers or revolutionaries, the men and women of the Left invited their listeners to see their common interest amply, as citizens of the largest world imaginable. All men were supposed to have been created equal, workingmen of all countries were supposed to unite. The respective founding fathers left at least half the species out of account, yet the logic of their language implied the eventual defeat of their prejudices.

Even the nationalist revolutions that were the nineteenth century's principal passion understood themselves as tributaries joining a common torrent, a grand surge of self-determination justified, in the end, by a general need for peoplehood and the equivalent worth of all national expressions. Difference was universal; only autocrats could deny it. The resulting "politics of recognition," building on the writings of Rousseau and Herder, was predicated on a *general* human need for the dignity of persons, a dignity inseparable from their right to distinct attachments. When universalist ideals lined up behind national flags—as they did during most of the nineteenth century—what they paraded was this interesting paradox: nationalism with a universalist rationale. Even Mazzini, the guiding spirit of Italian nationalism, told his followers: "You are *men* before you are *citizens*."

2. From a Theory to End All Classes to a Theology Without God

Not even its fiercest critics can underestimate the ingenuity of the Marxist intellectual system, which linked the *is* and the *ought,* the material and the philosophical, the empirical and the theological so compellingly as to make history for more than a century. Leave aside the abundance of colorations under the Marxist flag, many famously renounced by Marx with the cry: "I am not a Marxist!" Big intellectual movements are bound to elude the grasp of their founders. Still, Marxism's martyrs, hypocrites, and antagonists alike shared a core idea of what this Marxism was that deserved their sacrifice, lies, and passions. Marxism—nothing if not audacious—became the heir of all the other socialisms, solidarities, and *fraternités.*

Marx's pride and joy was to have "brought philosophy down to earth." In the nineteenth century, his thinking gained plausibility and urgency from the convulsive growth of industrial capitalism in Europe. Had Marxism been nothing, however, but an economic theory of how capitalism works, Marx would have accomplished little more than to give capitalists a name and a notion of what they were up to. He would have belonged to the history of economics as a proponent of an oversimplified labor theory of value, a questionable "law" of the falling rate of profit, a prediction of sharpening class polarization and immiseration. As a founder of sociology, he would have been seen as a pioneer theorist of the dynamics of productive systems and social classes. As a socialist, he would have been one among many. But Marxism has been an enormous force in the world not for its economic claims, its sociological insights, or its values. Marx mattered because he stood for an overarching worldview and a vision. Central to the appeal of his intellectual system was its prophetic ambition: to frame the meaning of history and announce the universal destiny of humankind.

Like the idea of Christ's coming, and the idea of America, the whole intellectual and emotional system of Marxism was predicated on a messianic faith—a good faith to unmask bad faiths. In many a tract and letter, Marx dripped scorn for his contemporaries' ideas about the common good. These he saw as nothing more than masks for particular interests—

ideologies, not truths. In the *Communist Manifesto*, he sneered at such naïfs as Germany's "True" Socialists for claiming to represent "not the interests of the proletariat, but the interests of Human Nature, of Man in general." Generations of Marxists would go on to consider tenderminded-ness about universal humanity premature, obscurantist, and (curse of curses!) "idealist." But Marx objected only to shallow universalisms. He was offering the real thing, unflinchingly acknowledging the most antago-nistic social differences, boldly recognizing the ferocious struggles be-tween classes, asserting, indeed, that they were the engine of history, but proclaiming that, in the end, the war to come was only the prologue to ultimate peace in the commons.

In the face of social upheaval, what a trump this was! Marx's brilliance was to argue that the imagined future was already in process, that all humanity was already represented by a class destined to overcome all differences by ending all classes. The Left was to be the marriage of body and soul, muscularity and brains—proletariat and party—prefiguring a world in which the limits imposed by the division of labor would break down entirely. There exists, Marx asserted in his early writings, a univer-sal identity: the human being as maker, realizing his "species being" in the course of transforming nature. With the audacity of a German idealist primed to think in first principles, Marx adopted from Hegel the idea that there was a "universal class" that would give meaning to history. Begin-ning with people uprooted from the land, his universal class was bound for classlessness. As capitalism inexorably simplified the class structure, the proletariat would swell into the majority. As the world market spread, "entire sections of the ruling classes [were], by the advance of industry, precipitated into the proletariat," many an astute bourgeois changed sides, and "the other classes decay[ed] and finally disappear[ed]," only a shrinking minority of exploiters would remain to be expropriated. The proletariat was not only the embodiment of right but the embodiment of might. No utopian wish, no moralist sermon, it was a dynamo. It was already the future in embryo.

An elegant intellectual system! The universal class destined to redeem history would follow in the footsteps of the universal class that had al-ready appropriated and transformed history: the "constantly revolution-izing" bourgeoisie, whose "need of a constantly expanding market for its products chase[d] [it] over the whole surface of the globe . . . nestl[ing] everywhere, settl[ing] everywhere, establish[ing] connections every-where, . . . giv[ing] a cosmopolitan character to production and con-sumption in every country," destroying "all old-established national industries," generating "universal interdependence of nations," making "national one-sidedness and narrow-mindedness . . . more and more impossible," in sum, "creat[ing] a world after its own image." The univer-sality of capital was the crucible for the universality of labor.

But not without assistance. To accomplish its transcendent mission, the class to end all classes required a universal midwife: the revolution-ary Communist. No matter where he originated, this agent of history overcame his particular class and nation. Taking a cue from the interna-tional bourgeoisie, the revolutionary Communist prefigured the working men of the future, who "have no country." To every particular circum-stance and cause, the universal priesthood of Communists was charged with bringing the glad tidings that History was the unfolding of Reason. The Communist party, like God, had its center everywhere and nowhere. Like the church of Jesus, it was charged with inserting ultimate meaning into everyday life. The proletariat was the Communist's nation. Like the émigré Marx, he was a denationalized world citizen, prefigured by Lafay-ette and Thomas Paine, liberated to teach people of all nations that their destinies were intertwined; for all the world was becoming one, "national differences and antagonisms between peoples [were] daily more and more vanishing."

Marx's emissary possessed the key to the future: the overwhelming majority of human beings were united by their participation in labor. That was their "identity." But unlike the race, gender, sexual, and other birth-right identities of today, this membership was ecumenical, open to any-one who migrated, or fell, into the proletariat. So the task of Communists was, in the midst of national and particular struggles, to "point out and bring to the front the common interests of the entire proletariat, indepen-dently of all nationality." However thwarted by local interests, the Com-munist universalist belonged to the Left, the one true international church, where the Englishman and the German, the Indian and the Chi-nese, met to prefigure the borderless world to come.

With this lyric, Marxism hoped to rescue the universalist passion from the liberationist cause that absorbed most of the energies of idealists during the first half of the nineteenth century—nationalism. Marx's rhetoric, not the particulars of his theoretical framework, imparted to revolutionaries a sense of common cause for a century after the death of the founding father. Social democratic, syndicalist, and other variants, all claiming to be the true heirs, were crushed when they failed to prevent World War I. Leninism won the contest of the heirs—in no small measure because one nation, the German, found Lenin a useful instrument to wield against another nation, the Russian, and transported him across the country in 1917.

Lenin ushered into the twentieth century a fusion of thought and action that brilliantly, and dangerously, updated Marx. Under Lenin, the Party and the International purported to see all, know all, and act in the general interest. They claimed to embody the Enlightenment's faith in the knowability of the human situation. The Bolsheviks would rescue the working class from its parochial identities and superficial attachments. Without the Party's high-minded theorizing and planning, Lenin argued, the working class was doomed to bog down in "trade-union consciousness"—the defense of its own particularist interests. Lenin made intellectuals universalists with a secret police.

What Lenin developed in theory the October Revolution of 1917 accomplished in action. The Party proved an instrument infinitely adaptable to circumstance as long as one condition was met—absolute power. When the Russian detonator failed to set off the larger European bomb, Lenin devised a theory for leaping from *a* to *the* Revolution. Just as imperialism was "the highest stage of capitalism," so anti-imperialism would be the highest form of anti-capitalism, the passion that united the world proletariat. On a world scale, Lenin argued, it was imperialism that now constituted "radical chains"—*the* form of oppression so fundamental that when the oppressed united against their appointed place in the global system they would bring down the whole structure. The road to Paris, Lenin said, led through Beijing.

Marxism retained the grandeur of a universalist dynamic, and neither Leninism nor Stalinism did much if anything to weaken it. In Europe, Marxism took strength from the abundant miseries produced by capitalism, and Leninism acquired the prestige of an achievement. Nothing secures the longevity of a faith better than institutionalization, even a cynical one. As a faith, Marxism held onto its universalizing spirit partly because of its moral authority as a critique of capitalism, but at least as much because of the peculiar prestige that accrues to existence. Whatever one knew of or made of Soviet crimes, the Soviet Union—and, from 1949 on, Mao's China—was an enormous fact. However pointed the criticisms of Trotskyists and anarchists, whatever the utopian alternatives advanced by anti-Soviet socialists, the Soviet Union existed. Existence, the real "propaganda of the deed," apparently clinched the argument. Wasn't Marxism supposed to be practical? Under the stress of circumstance, it was not difficult for reasonable men and women to persuade themselves that Moscow was the closest approximation to the Jerusalem of the Church Militant—the prerequisite for an eventual triumph of justice and reason.

In the hearts and minds of Communists and their fellow travelers, the prestige of existence was yoked to the will to believe. Once one accepted the either/or logic that decreed that capitalism and socialism were the only two choices, and concluded that the command economy of the Soviet Union was as close to socialism as it was possible to get in a harsh world, then Marxism could easily be blamed for Stalin's inferno. Democratic socialists were superb moral critics of the Stalinists, but the command economy was the only economy socialists offered. While a few "market socialists" did try to imagine combining free pricing with the order and justice that could be organized by limiting the freedoms of capital, they commanded no divisions.

Above all, the command economy gained plausibility because the capitalist economy was devastated. It was the combination of global economic catastrophe in the 1930s and the rise of fascism over much of Europe that prolonged the life of the Marxist framework and its Leninist machinery in the West. Was it not manifest that capitalism manufactured suffering, and that ruling groups in the democracies had no compunctions about coming to terms with grotesque police states? In this setting, many an egalitarian was willing to overlook the worst of what he knew, or might have learned, about the Soviet Union in the interest of holding open the door to a decent universal future. From 1935 to 1939 and again after the Nazi invasion of the USSR, the Popular Front could even conjure a new commonality—a cobbled-together anti-Fascist alliance. In the end, Marxists asked rhetorically, what was the alternative that promised a universal transformation, universal justice, a single humanity? Partly, then, by default, partly by blindness, partly by despair, from one revision to the next, Marxism haunted all left-wing thought.

Ideologies end with whimpers, not bangs. In the history of latter-day Marxism, one disillusion followed another, and yet each time an intellectual generation emerged to reinvent the promise. Each generation wrestled with the system's failings, picked up some pieces, and launched into a not-so-fresh beginning. But it is clear fifty years later that once the anti-Fascist alliance of World War II was broken, so were the prestige and the universalist promise of Marxism, and correspondingly its appeal—at least outside university circles—in the United States. It wasn't simply the Cold War and McCarthyism that wrecked the Marxist prospect in America. It was the unignorable evidence that "actually existing" "state socialism" was, to put it mildly, hostile to universalist prospects—except perhaps to the prospect of a Gulag stretching across borders. The Prague putsch of 1948, the Berlin guns of 1953, and, most of all, the Soviet tanks rolling through Budapest in 1956 made obvious even to unreconstructed sentimentalists that Soviet Marxism amounted mainly to *raison d'état*. Each reinvention rallied a smaller number of adepts, only to be set reeling again—by Solzhenitsyn on the Gulag, by news of the Khmer Rouge atrocities, by the bitter truth about Chinese and Cuban tyranny. It required ever more blindness to miss the pattern. In the face of such crimes, reason wept.

The Marxist cycle of eschatology and disillusion is finished now. The collapse of European Communism wiped out the *état,* leaving Marxist (and indeed non-Marxist) socialists in thin air, whatever their protestations. They point out, accurately, that the breakdown of a theology does not erase the conditions God was supposed to address; that unbridled markets may generate economic growth, but also exacerbate grotesque inequalities; that capitalism's "creative destruction," in the economist Joseph Schumpeter's words, fuels fundamentalist retrenchments. Nevertheless, Marxism after Communism lies in ruins, and the disturbances of capitalism are unlikely to resurrect it.

Socialism is reduced to a sketch of an ethical ideal, or a goad to social democracy, or what Émile Durkheim once called "a cry of grief, sometimes of anger, uttered by men who feel most keenly our collective malaise." Some of the salvage efforts have been ingenious, to be sure. Academics have tried to stretch the definition of "the working class" in such a way as to obscure its evident fissures. Gramsci's vocabulary has been deployed to sanctify a loose assemblage of fragmentary identity movements as a "historic bloc." Watching these efforts at "reconstruction" and "reinvention," one is reminded of Ptolemy's seventeenth-century followers, whose geocentric view of the universe rested on the belief that celestial bodies rotated around the earth along curves they called "epicycles." As more information was gathered and anomalies piled up, the Ptolemists spun off a profusion of new epicycles—seventy-nine, eventually—as they strained to hold onto their antiquated cosmology against the Copernican challenge. *Mirabile dictu,* the model "worked," actually rendering predictions more efficiently than the Copernican paradigm for decades. But it "worked" at the cost of an absurd cumbersomeness, and so was doomed.

In the academy, Marxists can only anxiously clutch at the remnants of the true faith. What results is, for example, the broken and desiccated "Marxism" described in this passage by Michael Bérubé, a talented and prominent radical professor of English at the University of Illinois:

> The current Marxism of cultural studies, it turns out, is a Marxism that stopped believing in historical inevitability long before the Wall came down; it is a Marxism that denies the primacy or unity of "class" (and emphasizes the relevance of race, gender, sexuality, subjectivity), no longer believes in an intellectual vanguard, no longer believes in the centrality of Europe, no longer believes that the base "determines" the superstructure, that the ruling class owns the ruling ideas, that class struggle is inevitable, or that ideology is just "false consciousness."

The shapeless mélange that results remains Marxist only sentimentally. Instead of a brief for unification, it descends to a list of subcultures.

In short, Marxism without a revolutionary proletariat has all the pathos of a theology without God. Failing to take its poetry from the future, as Marx recommended, this gestural Marxism dresses up in a wardrobe from the past. From a history that is either failed or catastrophic, it salvages icons. The good father is to be protected from the depredations of bad brothers and sons—the "authentic" (or "early") Marx unblemished by Engels; or the one read by Luxemburg, not Lenin; or by Lenin and Trotsky, not Stalin. Perhaps there is, after all, a global working class in embryo, but it has been unfortunately misled, or its hour has not yet come round—give it time! Even at its best, this shapeless "Marxism," lacking a labor theory of value, lacking the transcendent homogenization of a universal class, lacking a universalizing agency, shrinks into a set of analytic tools with which to grasp the globalization of capital and offer a moral critique of exploitation—a valuable angle from which to criticize some social arrangements, but hardly a mission or a politics, let alone the invocation of a universal spirit.

3. The New Left and the Search for Surrogate Universals

The gross defects of Marxism did not go unnoticed by the early New Left. Most of the leadership dismissed Marxism for what C. Wright Mills called its "labor metaphysic." While prone to a romance with Cuba and opposed to the American obsession with the Cold War, the movement still felt no attachment to the promise of the "socialist" camp. The energy for radical social change and a new universalist creed came from other sources, particularly the redemptive spirit of the civil rights movement. On the surface, the civil rights movement sought an extension of traditional civil and political rights in accordance with the Declaration of Independence, the Constitution, and the Bill of Rights. To oppose racial oppression was to affirm that everyone had the right to sit at the same lunch counter, to vote at the same voting booth, to sit in the same seats on the bus, and swim in the same pool. But civil rights actions embodied another objective as well: the experience of community and solidarity. Ostensibly a means to secure equal rights, solidarity also turned out to be an end in itself. In the experience of the mass meeting, the organization of the boycott of buses and stores, *fraternité* manifested itself alongside *liberté*. Civil rights activists spoke unabashedly of the "beloved community," as did their student radical allies in the largely white New Left.

Much of the intellectual work in the New Left, especially the 1962 *Port Huron Statement* of Students for a Democratic Society (SDS), aimed to present more than reform proposals: it wanted to find a theoretical underpinning for such movement experiences. What was in fact distinctive about the *Port Huron Statement*, what excited student activists around the country, was neither the document's proposals nor the adversaries it named. Rather, it was its rhetoric of total transfiguration. In a revival of the Enlightenment language of Jean-Jacques Rousseau, SDS spoke self-consciously, with no sense of immodesty, about the entire human condition: "Human brotherhood," it said, "must be willed . . . as the most appropriate form of social relations." The universal solvent for difference would be the principle that "decision-making of basic social consequence be carried on by public groupings." "People Should Make the Decisions that Affect Their Lives"—reduced to a slogan on a button, this was "participatory democracy," an idea about the power inherent in all human beings. Participatory democracy was a single standard against which to judge all existing social arrangements. To the limited engagements of representative democracy, it opposed the unlimited commitments of direct democracy—enshrined, half-satirically, in the slogan, "Freedom is an endless meeting." In practice, the principle was tailored to students (students who didn't have jobs, at that) collected in "knowledge factories" as the industrial proletariat had once been collected in mills and mines; young people who had grown up in relatively democratic families or, if not, had been uprooted from their communities of origin and were now being encouraged to think of themselves as practitioners of reason. They were skilled talkers and writers and had plenty of time on their hands. They knew how to write and mimeograph leaflets and how to organize meetings. It seemed to them that they didn't need authorities, or even their own leaders, to get things done.

In effect, the students of the New Left were syndicalists who knew they were not sufficient unto themselves. So these radical democrats set out to level themselves, arguing against the very qualifications that were theirs by virtue of middle-class birth and education. When the early New Left set out to find common ground with a like-minded constituency, they reached out to the impoverished—the Student Nonviolent Coordinating Committee (SNCC) to sharecroppers and SDS to the urban poor, all of whom seemed to have little to lose, were free of the compromises of middle-class life and therefore, in theory, might commit themselves to democratic participation.

On campuses, student radicals extrapolated from the civil rights insurgency. The decisive innovation was Berkeley's Free Speech Movement, heavily influenced by students who had tasted the spirit and danger of the Mississippi Freedom Summer of 1964 and gone back to school wishing for a deeper politics of their own. The movement began with a demand for elementary political rights—mainly, the right to recruit and rally for off-campus civil rights demonstrations. Fearful of recriminations from influential Republicans like former Senator William Knowland, whose reactionary paper, the *Oakland Tribune*, had been picketed by student activists, University of California administrators cracked down. When they sent campus police to arrest a political recruiter, they shocked the campus and exposed the bureaucratic heavy-handedness and impersonality of the university as a whole. These themes were manifest in radical individualist slogans like: "I am a human being. Do not fold, spindle, or mutilate." The ensuing experience of free-form mass rallies and endless meetings gave participatory democracy a footing in experience.

But for most of the New Left, most of the time, the ideal of participatory democracy proved only a secondary force. In the early 1960s, the passion that drove most activists was civil rights for black Americans, not the transformation of everyday life or even of political institutions. The New Left was mainly a movement of solidarity with the oppressed, though at times it searched for an ideology to transform itself into a movement for self-liberation. Demands for student power swelled into ideological absurdities like a widely distributed pamphlet called "The Student as Nigger." In any case, the principle of participatory democracy was too demanding for even a relatively small movement, no less a whole campus, let alone an entire society. After a while, freedom as an endless meeting proved alluring only to those with the time and taste to go to meetings endlessly—less and less even to devotees. Eventually, participatory democracy would be weakened into a more modest though still forceful tendency, a movement for citizen involvement. Citizens would succeed in prying open faculty councils and government bodies. Outraged stockholders and consumers would mobilize against corporate policies. But the strong form of the idea would crash into the objection attributed to Oscar Wilde: that socialism would take too many evenings.

Where, then, were students and ex-students to turn for a useful theory of general social transformation? Reenter Marxism. In the latter half of the 1960s, New Left intellectuals worked up a host of Marxist variants, imports, and revivals, each promoting a different surrogate proletariat. There was French theory, according to which students themselves prefigured a "new working class." There were Leninist retreads, in which students would go to the factories, or working-class neighborhoods, and lead young workers into revolt. But most influential were notions of a Third World Revolution. Latter-day ex-student radicals, first inspired by the Cuban revolution, now found further inspiration in the writings of Frantz Fanon, a Caribbean native who had become a psychiatrist in Paris, worked with insurgent Algerians, and theorized, often brilliantly, about anticolonial wars. Other New Leftists turned eagerly to the Chinese Cultural Revolution, which they saw as a congenial exercise in radical democracy, and to the Maoist notion that the Third World, the global "countryside," would someday overpower the First World, the rich "cities." The most urgent and compelling invitation to a new internationalism came from Vietnamese exemplars of revolutionary redemption. The more atrocious the American assault on their country, the more moral force was attributed to the enemy. The most accessible single hero was the ascetic yet romantic, indeed sexy, finally martyred Argentine-turned-Cuban, doctor-turned-professional-revolutionary Che Guevara, at home (yet homeless) everywhere, calling for "two, three, many Vietnams," rekindling Marx's ideal of the revolutionary who is no respecter of borders.

For all the photogenic qualities that boosted their visibility, the revolutionists were always outnumbered by proponents of more concrete reforms—equality of condition between blacks and whites, an end to the Vietnam War, and more democratic institutions. But however straightforward and this-worldly these goals may have seemed, expectations were rising fast—much faster than conditions were changing. There was a sea change in political culture. If society as a whole seemed unbudgeable, perhaps it was time for specialized subsocieties to rise and flourish. For this reason if no other, the universalist impulse fractured again and again. In the late 1960s, the principle of separate organization on behalf of distinct interests raged through "the movement" with amazing speed. On the model of black demands came those of feminists, Chicanos, American Indians, gays, lesbians. One grouping after another insisted on the recognition of difference and the protection of their separate and distinct spheres.

What was going on? Was this separatist urge the result of rational choices made by activists convinced that ecumenical movements were futile? Or was it a return of the repressed, of long-deferred dreams now bursting to the surface? From the speed with which separatism multiplied, the furies it tapped, it is reasonable to assume that deep impulses were stirred up. What took place was one of those convulsions in culture that cannot be reduced to the sum of its immediate causes. Certainly, separatism was more than an idea, because it was more than strictly intellectual; it was a structure of feeling, a whole way of experiencing the world. Difference was now felt—perhaps had long been felt—more acutely than commonality. Initiative, energy, intellectual ingenuity went into the elevation of differences. The very language of commonality came to be perceived by the new movements as a colonialist smothering—an ideology to rationalize white male domination. The time for reunification would come later, so it was said—much later, at some unspecified time.

As the political scientist Donald L. Horowitz has observed: "There seems to be a kind of 'Parkinson's Law' at work, by which group identity tends to expand or contract to fill the political space available for its expression." If, in the early 1960s, the civil rights movement had breathed life into commonality politics, in the latter part of the decade the only thing that kept up the appearance of one big movement was the fact that there was one big war. In retrospect, it is blindingly clear that New Left universalism was fragile from the outset, that the category of citizen, or even human being, had long felt like a weightless abstraction. It was as members of a specific category—as a black person, a woman, or later as a Jew or a lesbian—that people increasingly insisted on being represented in "the decisions that affected their lives." People lived, felt, desired, revolted as members of identity categories—not as citizens, let alone as human beings. The student movement and the Third World revolutions had briefly revivified the Marxist faith, but the infusion proved evanescent except among university adepts, which, however much they stressed the category of class, still could not find an actual proletariat. For the most part, divisions of race, then gender, then sexual orientation proved far too deep to be overcome by universalist rhetoric.

From the 1970s on, left-wing universalism was profoundly demoralized. It was an airy notion without a program, a longing without a constituency. It was scorned as nonexistent, hypothetical, nostalgic, or, worse, deceptive—a mask assumed by straight white males as they tried to restore their lost dominion. Feminists would argue that their politics were rightly understood as commonality politics: that their preoccupations deserved to be those of all humanity, and that men, too, would (ultimately!) benefit from a feminist transformation. At times, feminists promoted an androgynous ideal. Thus, too, did many gay activists speak of liberating the universal bisexual. But to most men and many women, these claims seemed rhetorical fillips, pious afterthoughts. Feminist and gay communities organized separately, often enough antagonistically. The emphasis in the new movements veered toward a conception that men and women, gays and straights, were fundamentally, irreducibly different—a tendency so common as to be outfitted with the academic shorthand, "essentialism."

In fact, only environmentalists, who had taken a different route out of the 1960s, still thought about a common human condition—endangered, like the earth. But elsewhere, separatism was automatic, a politics built on identity taken for granted. One belonged to a caucus, cultivated a separate culture, and dismissed the idea of the human condition, or the republic, or the common good, or citizenship, as hopelessly pre-postmodernist.

Look for theory, said the academy. But theory did not help much. The fragility of universals extended far beyond Marxism. Throughout the West, social theorists had strained for decades to produce ideas of a common human condition. In psychology, there had been Jean Piaget's universal model of child development. There had been the posthistorical structural anthropology of Claude Lévi-Strauss, declaring that human cognition was organized into fixed "binary oppositions" wired into the human mind. Or, if humans were not essentially labor, perhaps they were essentially language. In America, there was Noam Chomsky's rationalist linguistics, proposing a uniform cross-cultural capacity for grammar. Annexing Freud to Marx, there was Herbert Marcuse's utopian tribute to the free-floating refugees from one-dimensional society. Or, to replace Freud's universal Oedipus complex, there were new and recycled psychologies propounding a uniform human nature: Abraham Maslow's hierarchy of needs and, rediscovered in the late 1960s, Wilhelm Reich's effort to smash up "character armor" with orgasmic release. In an attempt at a synthesis of Marxism and language theory there was Jürgen Habermas's objective of undistorted communication.

By the late 1970s, however, universalists were passé, even if, with a new generation of leftist intellectuals slogging along on the long march to tenure, the universities were soon churning out vast numbers of theoretical trainees. The allure of their theory seeped beyond the campuses—to periodicals like the *Village Voice,* to art schools, to feminist and gay scenes. Attention turned to the dazzling French historian-philosopher, Michel Foucault, renowned for his studies of power and discourse in institutions like mental asylums, clinics, and prisons. Foucault, like Marx, presented himself as an "archeologist" of intellectual systems, but was himself an unintentional universalist, for his own intellectual system was predicated on the centrality of one invariant all-consuming human project: the Nietzschean will to power. The leftish, the avant-garde, and other would-be transgressors in quest of theoretical comfort and a justification for social marginality were attracted by Foucault's conviction that all knowledge and all social reality were reducible to power relations— that all being was local, all thinking self-interested, all understanding fatally circumscribed by history. The only common condition worth thinking about was the impossibility of commonality.

On many levels, then, the travail of commonality thinking in the 1990s has been long in the making. Many traditional claims that a common condition already existed were in fact lies, or screens for domination. Interest groups sprang up to defend the excluded, to recover their dignity, to study their history and arts. That was the spirit of the time—to decompose false claims that universality was cut to the measure of the West, or of men, or of whites or heterosexuals. But claims about the diversity of the human condition that made much good sense (and wreaked much havoc) in their origins have, over time, hardened into an orthodoxy that, with drearily uniform slogans, elevates diversity—that is, fragmentation—to religious heights. The new identity orthodoxy is more than a cultural tropism encouraged by a passion for community; it is enforced by laws and administrative regulations.

Still, to deplore fragmentation is one thing; to formulate, feel, act on a common human project, quite another. Universalists today look to ideals of ecology and human rights, but even these appeals to humanity unravel into their separate strands. The ensuing debates are bitter. If toxic dumps are not, generally, to be found in the wealthy suburbs, and middle-class environmentalists are not, in general, preoccupied with the pollution that afflicts factory workers, is the ecology movement disinterested, or is it the latest cover for class privilege? If cultures in large parts of the world support genital mutilation, are Western feminists imperialist? If the Marines are dispatched with a human rights rationale, as in Somalia and Haiti, does one support them? On the Left, there are few automatic positions.

A liberating dénouement, perhaps. But the break-up of ideas of a whole Left throws the contest to the Right. On many matters, the Left's ragtag party of commonality sounds the clarion call and then reluctantly swivels to see that the troops are not following. It speaks for no movement. It fails to generate an emotional tide. Many of its public defenders, white males like myself—Robert Hughes in *Culture of Complaint,* Russell Jacoby in *Dogmatic Wisdom*—are accused of nostalgia. Women and people of color who look askance at identity politics are commonly dismissed as interested parties themselves, as fronts for the powerful or as representatives of ethnic groups—Asian Indians and Afro-Caribbeans, for example—who are not officially sanctioned minorities.

As these two chapters should have made clear, there is no golden past to recover. Neither the good society nor the good political movement is out there, intact and timeless. Neither the old home ideas of the Left nor those of America are waiting for prodigals to return to their welcoming portals. If there is to be any transcendence of our present broken condition, it is going to have to be a creation, not a recovery. We know too much to rest on the premise that once, before we were lost, we were found; that once, before we were uprooted, we were firmly planted. In many ways, a centrifuge has taken the place of the whole because the whole had already failed, and the news keeps arriving late, like the light from a dead star.

III.

The Aggrandizement of Difference

Is it that every man believes every other to be a
fatal partialist, & himself a universalist?

—RALPH WALDO EMERSON

4

The Coloring of America?

Were it not for unmistakable changes in the color of American life, *Time* would not have been asking, "Who Are We?" According to the 1990 census, non-Hispanic whites number 75.2 percent of the population. By the early years of the next century, a majority of the nation's children— for whom the textbooks are written—may well be blacks, Latinos, and Asians. At the same time, 57 percent of American adult women work outside the home, including some three-quarters of mothers of school-age children, and while there is evidently, to date, a glass ceiling beyond which female executives do not rise, the height of that ceiling has risen relatively rapidly within a single generation. Gone are the days when the establishments of politics, journalism, the professions, and the academy consisted almost entirely of white males whose interest in fretting that the rest of their establishment consisted of white males was limited. The most cursory inspection of a university campus reveals tremendous racial variety.* No wonder the colors of the faces in the textbooks, on the billboards

---

* But this is perhaps the place to record my uneasiness about the casual and routine use of the term "race." "Race" is not a biological fact but a cultural assumption (and not only in the West). Genetic differences between members of different "races" are far fewer than genetic differences within

and TV shows, in Congress and City Hall, have changed significantly in a generation. American imagery seems to be catching up with demographic arithmetic—not fast enough in the eyes of Oakland's textbook critics, but catching up nevertheless, faster than in any other plural society anywhere.

Time's question was, in the simplest sense, demographic, and without doubt, demographic change is central to America's identity travail. One answer to "Who are we?" is turning out to be: less white than we thought. It would be simplistic to refer in sound-bite fashion to the coloring, or unwhitening, of America, but the truth is that whiteness is not the norm it used to be.

Simply put, the white percentage has been declining for decades, and the rate of decline accelerated after 1970 (though the actual decline was frequently exaggerated in the press and popular lore). Between 1950 and 1970, the white percentage (including those Hispanics classified by the census as "white") declined by 2 percent, from 89.3 percent to 87.6 percent, while the black percentage rose by 12 percent, from 9.9 percent to 11.1 percent. Between 1970 and 1990, the white percentage declined by more than 4 percent, twice the earlier rate, from 87.6 percent to 83.9 percent, while the black percentage rose by a slightly smaller rate of 11 percent, from 11.1 percent to 12.3 percent. Still more striking changes were evident among Americans whose origins were in Latin America, Asia, or the Pacific Islands. Between 1970 and 1990, the Hispanic population almost doubled, from 4.9 percent to 9.0 percent, while Asians and Pacific Islanders more than doubled, from 1.4 percent to 3.0 percent. On campuses, the shift was even more dramatic. In 1960, 94 percent of college students were white, and 34.5 percent were women. In 1990, the white percentage was down to 84.3, and 54.5 percent were women.

The magnitude of these shifts swells when we take into account the upsurge in interracial marriage. For all America's racial antagonisms, the number of interracial couples rose by 535 percent between 1960 and 1980 to nearly 2 percent of all married couples; whereupon, in the follow-

---

"races." There is only one race: the human race. For this reason, Kwame Anthony Appiah, who makes this argument powerfully, uses the term "race" only within quotation marks. For the most part I have not followed him down this punctuation road, not wanting to clutter the text with all those extra marks, but I applaud his impulse to underscore that the category of race is made, not born.

ing decade, according to preliminary analysis of the 1990 census, it rose again, to 2.7 percent. The number of births of mixed-race babies rose at a rate twenty-six times as fast as that of any other racially defined group, increasing from 0.7 percent of all births in 1968 to 3.2 percent in 1990. According to the journalist Lawrence Wright, "The number of children living in families where one parent is white and the other is black, Asian, or American Indian . . . has tripled—from fewer than four hundred thousand in 1970 to one and a half million in 1990—and this doesn't count the children of single parents or children whose parents are divorced. Blacks are conspicuously less likely to marry outside their group, and yet marriages between blacks and whites have tripled in the last thirty years."

Astonishingly, in 1986, outside the South, more than 10 percent of black men who married were marrying white women, up from 3.9 percent in 1968. (The respective rates for black women outside the South marrying white men were 3.7 percent and 1.2 percent.) In the South, the rate for black men jumped from 0.24 percent to 4.2 percent. While Jews outmarry at a rate of 52 percent, up from 10 percent in 1960, Japanese Americans are outmarrying at an astonishing 65 percent, Native Americans at an even more astonishing 70 percent. (Many of the latter especially, of course, are of "mixed blood" to start with.) Where there was a parent in either of the latter two categories, more children were born interracial than not. Interracial births are still relatively rare, but their growing numbers may influence the future of racial categorization. Some of these statistics were reported in a special issue of *Time* called "The New Face of America," featuring a cover portrait of a strikingly beautiful computerized hybrid representative of the "new Eve," her features derived from Anglo-Saxon, Middle Eastern, African, Asian, Southern European, and Hispanic types.

Since Americans live in the future, projections—the sense of the direction of change—also matter. By the year 2000, non-Hispanic whites are likely to compose only 66 percent of the under-35 population. According to the Census Bureau, between 1990 and 2020, the aggregate white percentage is expected to fall to 78.1 percent, or an additional 6.9 percent—a substantial decline, though at an annual rate smaller than the rate of decline between 1970 and 1990. Between 1990 and 2020, the black population is expected to rise by 13 percent, to 13.9 percent, a smaller rate of growth than during the previous two decades, but the Hispanic population is expected to rise by almost three-quarters, to 15.7 percent, and the Asian/Pacific Island group to grow by 233 percent, to 7 percent. (See table.) The Hispanic population should surpass the black population in 2013.

Indeed, the coloring of America—or to put it more clumsily, though more accurately, the relative decline of the non-Hispanic whites—may be expected to continue apace through the middle of the twenty-first century. According to census projections, by 2050 the Hispanic population is likely to increase to 21.1 percent, the black population to 16.2 percent, and the Asian/Pacific Islander population to 10.7 percent. The non-Hispanic white population is expected to stop growing, in absolute numbers, by the year 2029, and to decline, by 2050, to 52.7 percent. Contrary to popular mystique, differential birth rates are expected to account for more than twice as much of the change in racial and Hispanic proportions as new immigration. Still, during the years between 1990 and 2050 the descendants of new immigrants will outnumber the descendants of people who already lived in America in 1990.

Changes in U.S. Racial and Ethnic Distribution, 1950–2050
(percent)

	WHITE	BLACK	ASIAN/ PACIFIC ISLANDER	HISPANIC
1950	89.3	9.9	—	—
1970	87.6	11.1	—	4.9
1990	83.9	12.3	3.0	9.0
2020 (projected)	78.1	13.9	7.0	15.7
2050 (projected)	72.8	16.2	10.7	21.1

Moreover, these real and expected changes are magnified because minority populations are concentrated in big cities and are disproportionately young. Whites are already a minority in New York, Los Angeles, Chicago, Detroit, Atlanta, and other major cities. Still, a great deal of America remains extremely white. In almost half the counties of the

United States, the black population is less than 1 percent. California and Texas between them have more than half the Hispanics, while in the Midwest, fewer than one person in thirty is Hispanic. California is by far the most multiracial state in the union, with only 57.2 percent of its population composed of non-Hispanic whites in 1990.

The numbers sound crisp, but it is dangerous to prophesy about the racial and ethnic future with much confidence. Racial and ethnic categories are scarcely natural or fixed. They are matters of convention, and conventions change. On census forms, Americans are told to choose racial and ethnic identifications *from among the categories given;* but the answers depend, in part, on the alternatives proposed. And these categories are, to some extent, built on British slavery codes, which were more rigid than the Spanish or Portuguese and generated traditional white American paranoia about blacks, which in turn produced an either/or classification system quite different from, say, those that prevail in much of Latin America. For decades, in the either/or spirit, nine of America's southern and border states imposed a "one drop of blood" rule, declaring that a person with one black great-grandparent was legally "black" (in three other states, one great-great-grandparent would suffice) and therefore banned from marrying a "white." Africans make innumerable distinctions among themselves, by color, tribe, and so on. "Blackness" is highly relative, indeed arbitrary. In the United States, in the wake of the civil rights movement, "one drop of blood" laws were overturned, but the legacy of the either/or mentality has left us with a system of categorization that is rigid to a degree that astounds (and horrifies) many people outside the United States, especially in countries like Canada, Mexico, and France, which have banned the collecting of racial statistics. What these critics often fail to understand, however, is that in the United States, the categories are not simply imposed from on high; they are internalized. Whites tend to think "black" on meeting a person with African features; so do blacks. In defense and in self-assertion, increasingly, new categories are demanded. Racial and ethnic categories were inserted into the census—"Hispanic" in 1970, "Asian/Pacific Islander" in 1990—as a result of political pressures from groups seeking to maximize their representation in public life. So much rides on how people name themselves in America! For many, it is a matter of recognition as well as a tactic for garnering resources. In any event, even if slavery codes are at the root of our categories, the future is not the past, and the categories are subject to flux.

To make matters more complicated still, the Census Bureau's projections presume no procreation across race and ethnic lines. With the curious flexibility that shapes ethnic and racial "options" in the United States today, people not only name their own "identities," they can declare their children's, at least for statistical purposes, and their choices may alter population projections that are brandished today as if firmly established. If the next generation procreates in significant numbers across race and ethnic lines, the choices that parents make about how to identify their children, as well as their children's own intermarriage rates and self-definitions, will determine the "race" and "ethnicity" of their descendants. Research shows that members of different ethnic groups assign ethnic memberships differently. Because Hispanics, especially those of Mexican origin, are more likely than others to intermarry and to identify their children as Hispanic, the Hispanic proportion of the population might be expected to grow even more than census figures anticipate. The sociologists William Alonso and Mary C. Waters performed a statistical experiment in which they assumed that couples in the United States continue to intermarry and apportion group identities to their children in the proportions that prevailed in 1980. Statistically, they "grew" these children and "married them off" in the same proportions for five generations, roughly 125 years. They assumed zero immigration and a fixed fertility rate across groups. The result was that the percentage of Hispanics in their hypothetical population grew by more than 25 percent. But then again, whether "Hispanic" will have the same meaning thirty or fifty years hence is debatable. In 1980, 40 million Americans claimed Irish origin, many more than could have descended from Irish immigration alone, partly because of high rates of intermarriage and partly because of sentimental choices—yet the significance of the badge (probably at the expense of the numbers claiming Scottish "blood") is questionable.

And what is to say that intermarriage rates and the assignment of "identities" to children will not change as well, as a result of shifts in culture or social policy or for other unpredictable reasons? As Alonso and Waters point out, "Had there been population projections by groups during the period of peak European immigration (1880–1920), trying to guess what the nation would 'look like' in the year 1950 or 1980 or 2000, those predictions would almost certainly have been wrong in more ways than one. They would have seriously overestimated the proportions of some European origin groups and underestimated others." In the words of the demographer Paul R. Spickard, "Almost no White American extended family exists today without at least one member who has married across what two generations ago would have been thought an unbridgeable gap." O brave new world, where ethnic categories are chosen and malleable, yet flourish as if they were firm, and are made the basis for important social decisions as if they were as self-evident as the colors of the leaves of the trees!

Whites and minorities alike observe the coloring of America, but they frequently exaggerate the magnitude, speed, and significance of the change. Unfortunately, no one seems to have studied systematically the estimates people make of demographic reality. But it seems only reasonable to surmise that because racial minorities are confined to narrow worlds where they look like majorities, they are prone to magnify their percentages and minimize the size of the white population. Folklore magnifies the evidence of the senses, sometimes absurdly. Paul Rogat Loeb reports a 1990 student meeting at Emory University where "black students kept repeating that America would soon be two thirds people of color." So astute a critic as Henry Louis Gates, Jr., has declared without warrant that "a majority of our citizens will be people of color by the year 2020." Deborah Meier, for many years the principal of the Central Park East School in New York, asked her largely minority students what the racial makeup of New York City is and was told that the city is 60 to 70 percent black, perhaps 20 percent Latino, and the rest white. (The actual figures from the 1990 census are 29 percent black, 24 percent Latino, 52 percent white.) Meier adds that these young people tend to believe that the country at large must have similar proportions.

Such factual errors can lead easily enough to the disastrous conclusion that if only minorities were more militant, they could wrest the country away from the controlling minority, whites. Inaccurate knowledge of this sort, as Deborah Meier says, "shapes the way people imagine the world," leading in turn to skewed political strategies. It should go without saying that the exaggeration, however understandable, of such a fundamental fact as numerical strength is a poor foundation for politics. Generals could be court-martialed for errors so drastic. To base a worldview on an overestimation of strength leads to overreaching—and almost certain defeat.

Realists have made this point for decades. Roy Wilkins, longtime head of the NAACP, deplored the Black Power militancy of the late 1960s in these terms: "I knew that anyone who was not cautious in leading a one-tenth minority into conflict with an overwhelming majority was a fool." In the heated atmosphere of the late 1960s, only a moderate like Wilkins was willing to stare demographic reality in the face. While radicals were going for broke, Wilkins seemed the very personification of outdistanced, outorganized moderation. That the one-tenth minority of 1966 has grown into the one-eighth minority of 1994 does not alter his point, nor does the invocation of an ideological category, "people of color," clinch what is now a common assumption that African Americans can afford to discard the chance of alliances with whites and other minorities. Politics in a multiracial society is alliance-making, and the work of alliance-making is not accomplished by adding up numbers. There is nothing automatic about it.

Neither is it clear just what automatically follows from the mushrooming category "Hispanic." The label was an administrative convenience manufactured for the census. Its usefulness for describing reality is something else again. Of Americans whose origin was given as Hispanic in 1990, 61 percent were Mexican, the second largest number (22 percent) being Puerto Rican. The category eclipses generational differences, which, as in the case of all immigrants, are culturally immense. This jerry-built name ropes together second-generation South Texas Chicanos and first-generation Los Angeles Chicanos, New York Puerto Ricans and Florida Cubans, among others. The people thereby affiliated by administrative fiat do not even share common music or food, and frequently not even language, for by the third generation many so-called Hispanics do not speak Spanish. Why presume, then, that "Hispanics" form a functional bloc with a common world view, a "culture"? Because of language and skin color, they frequently suffer discrimination in employment and housing, but while such injustices may dispose them to a solidarity they might not otherwise feel, it does not produce anything so hard and fast as an "identity." Unlike Italians and Poles, but more like Greeks and Palestinians, "Hispanics"—especially of Mexican origin—are likely to sustain connections to "the old country." They visit, they send money, they frequently cross the border. But this fact in itself does not make them live, think, or even dance like "Hispanics." The identity "Hispanic" is made, not born. It has even been spurned by radicals who claim that the word foregoes the Indian side of the heritage for the Spanish.

In their way of life, for that matter, what do the Spanish-surnamed have in common but a variable relationship to the Spanish language and often a slightly darker skin than many "whites"—although not, perhaps, than many Greeks, Italians, or Palestinians? The second-generation Mexican-American assistant principal of a Los Angeles area school reads *The Economist,* votes Republican, and is married to a woman of German ancestry. A few miles away, during the 1992 Los Angeles riots, Chicanos criticized Salvadorans for rioting. During the 1994 midterm election, 23 percent of Hispanic voters supported Proposition 187, which deprived the children of (largely Hispanic) illegal immigrants of schooling and all but emergency medical care.

As citizens, leaving aside tastes in food and music, many if not most second- and especially third-generation Hispanics are indistinguishable from the grandchildren of Italian, Irish, or Polish immigrants. Most likely, with time, their attachment to their nations of origin will dwindle. In any event, it is something that they will choose to sustain or not—which is to say, it is not primordial, not that ineradicable fact of birth that the term "ethnos" denotes. Their ethnicity is, as Mary Waters says of most whites, an "option." It may change in the course of an individual life. Indeed, it may change more than once. In important respects many "non-Hispanic whites" and "Hispanic whites" will share life experiences, will agree on political and cultural and economic matters more than they disagree, certainly more than the Cuban-American banker in Miami will agree with the Dominican welfare recipient in Manhattan or, for that matter, than either can be presumed to agree with the black fireman in Chicago. If they agree in thinking that the children of illegal immigrants should be punished, that may indeed be "ethnicity" speaking; but if they disagree over welfare stipends or foreign aid, it will be their class position speaking louder than the language of their parents.

Moreover, even the physical qualities associated with Hispanic whiteness (or nonwhiteness) are dubious. Every census table that breaks the population into "racial" and "ethnic" proportions carries (for good reason) the obligatory note: "Hispanics may be of any race." That is why the numbers frequently add up to more than 100 percent—as in the table on page 110 above.

All in all, given the many uncertainties of those baggy categories "race" and "ethnicity," to assume any distinct commonality, any automatic or easy alliance among "people of color," the descendants of Africans, Puerto Ricans, Koreans, Salvadorans, Cubans, and Chinese, say, is far-fetched—especially on the strength of the experiences of New York, Los Angeles, Miami, or San Francisco, where conflicts of interest and perception among nonwhites range from striking to harsh. The antagonism between African Americans and Korean shopkeepers in New York and Los Angeles is well known. Everyone has seen footage of the Los Angeles Koreans defending their stores with rifles against black attackers, though black rage against the Korean-American shopkeeper who shot and killed a black teenager for alleged shoplifting was certainly not so well-publicized as the beating of Rodney King. (The storekeeper was found guilty of voluntary manslaughter six months before the Rodney King verdict. Although this crime carried a penalty of up to sixteen years in prison, the failure to convict her of murder was frequently cited by African Americans explaining the targeting of Koreans during the riots.) In the wake of the riots, moreover, fights over resources to rebuild the damaged city were legion. In San Francisco, beginning with a 1982 court-ordered desegregation settlement with the NAACP, the student bodies of all schools were restricted to 40 percent from any single ethnic group. In 1993 the elite Lowell High School was found to have enrolled 42.9 percent Chinese Americans, even after turning away many other qualified Chinese Americans, and was ordered to return to the 40 percent limit. When, in 1994, Chinese-American groups announced they were going to try to overturn the court pact, they were again opposed by the NAACP.

Similar tensions developed at the University of California, Berkeley, in the early 1990s between Asians on the one hand, and blacks and Hispanics admitted on the basis of affirmative action on the other, with many Asians convinced that they were the victims of racial quotas that worked to the advantage of favored groups. (The actual situation was more complex, as we shall see in chapter 5.) In 1994, Latinos in the Los Angeles–area city of Compton charged police brutality by black police and demanded affirmative action in city employment—against what they regarded as an African-American establishment—while at the local high school, Chicano and black teenagers were squaring off against one another. Anecdotes are not conclusive, but in California, they are always undermining fantasies about the solidarity of "people of color." In Berkeley in 1992, during some minor local rioting triggered by the Rodney King verdict, a blonde student told me how frightened she had been when some black youths surrounded the car in which she was riding, rocked it back and forth, and screamed and cursed her before letting her and her passengers move on. Her surname is Lopez. Somewhere there are rhetoricians and political strategists grouping her and her assailants together as "people of color." The assumption among identity politics militants that natural alliances exist on the basis of nonwhiteness is purely sentimental.

Much demographic misrecognition stems from the wish for a collective movement against the white majority. There is also a white misrecognition stemming from fear. For generations, white racial fears have magnified estimates of immigrant "waves" or "tides" of immigrants. The "Yellow Peril" has a large place in the history of white American paranoia. In his inaugural address, Theodore Roosevelt warned against "the suicide of the race." Tom Buchanan, the boorish bond dealer of Fitzgerald's *The Great Gatsby,* broods that "civilization's going to pieces" on the strength of a book he is reading, *The Rise of the Colored Empires,* which argues "scientifically" that "if we don't look out the white race will be—will be utterly submerged."

Submerged, that is, in an ocean of danger. Whites translate fear of crime into fear of blacks, although whites are less than half as likely as blacks to be victimized by violent crime. On television news, black criminal defendants are more likely than whites to be shown in mug shots or still photos, unnamed, anonymous, presumably representative of a great undifferentiated menace. They are significantly more likely to appear in the physical custody of law enforcement officials, so that, even when accused of similar crimes, they appear more dangerous. But even without media exaggeration, the fear of black criminals has a certain basis in fact, because—there is no way to deny it—those who are arrested, charged, convicted, and jailed are disproportionately black. The fact that blacks suffer more than whites from black criminals is faint consolation to whites who have themselves been mugged, or whose children have been robbed or beaten, by blacks. Any rational fear is, in turn, compounded by a welter of sex fears, darkness fears, death fears that have for centuries been buried deep within whites' own heart of darkness. The terror of Willie Horton was one episode in a long-standing white panic: what the rap group Public Enemy called "Fear of a Black Planet."

Today, white panic over nonwhite engulfment is fueled by competition for jobs, promotions, university admissions, and other practicalities. On campuses, many students and their parents think that minorities are "taking over." Since superachieving Asian Americans are generally admitted by color-blind criteria, and cannot be rationally faulted for white insufficiency, it is affirmative action for blacks that many whites blame for taking slots that should, they think, be allocated strictly by merit. This is true even on campuses where the percentage of minority enrollment has, in fact, declined in recent years. Black and Hispanic enrollments on college campuses, measured against high school graduation rates, declined by about 15 percent between 1976 and 1988, and then began to rise again, though by 1991 they had still not returned to the levels of 1976.

Whatever the facts, large numbers of white males in particular see themselves losing ground. Just how much ground they have actually lost, in the aggregate, is more than a little questionable. Statistically, it is blacks whose unemployment rates have risen, relative to whites, since the late 1970s—until, in 1990, a black person's chances of being unemployed were 2.76 times those of a white person. In 1990, 12.1 percent of white men earned more than $50,000 a year, compared to 3.4 percent of black men. In actuality, blacks are 0.1 percent (one in a thousand!) of top corporate CEOs, 4.5 percent of college teachers, 3.2 percent of lawyers, 3.0 percent of doctors, and 3.6 percent of engineers. Statistics about promotions are harder to come by, or to assess. But whereas in 1983 the median white family possessed eleven times the wealth of the median nonwhite family, in 1989 the ratio was twenty to one.

And more to the point, people do not live in a statistical universe. When whites, especially males, feel blocked, in a culture that tells them they have only themselves to thank for success and only themselves to blame for failure, they look for culprits. Why not blame racial minorities and immigrants? The corporate boards who can profit just splendidly without them, the savings and loan executives whose perquisites everyone's taxes continue to subsidize, are usually anonymous. They seem abstract, beyond reach. By contrast, minorities stand out. They are more convenient targets than women, although in all likelihood, white men's sense of embattlement stems less from competition with racial minorities than from a relative loss of power vis-à-vis women in daily life. In bedrooms, barrooms, locker rooms, boardrooms, staff and faculty meetings, the white men have lost many of their male preserves. They have been targeted as harassers and date rapists. They have had to concede language—"chairperson," not "chairman," and so on. They feel dispossessed. But misogyny, that hardy perennial, is hard to express in everyday life. Forthright loathing is usually frowned on. Most men, after all, love women and rely on them—and, increasingly, on their paychecks.

But minorities? They are something else. More than ever before in the United States, despite low numbers in most professions, minorities are visible in conspicuous places: members of Congress, mayors, city council members. They are celebrities, sports figures, faces on television news. They are prize-winning authors and film directors, deans at elite universities. Stories of whites who lose government contracts or jobs to minorities are easily amplified and radiate everywhere. Since the traditional lock of white men has been broken in the name of diversity, if some white men don't get jobs or promotions to which they are arguably—or in any case feel—entitled, they scream from loss and find their culprits in dark skins. Here they can compete for victim status. In a world of racial and gender definitions, are they not a race and a gender too?

"White male" is, of course, a statistical category that has always been with us, but in recent years the category has crystallized. It looms large in popular consciousness. The common sense of relative dispossession is a major reason. Another is that white males have been challenged, even routinely demonized, by identity groups. The demonized tend to reinforce the identities that are singled out by the demonizers. But also important is that, in recent years, the media have singled out white males as a bloc, united by this most salient characteristic, white maleness.

Consider, for example, *Newsweek*'s March 29, 1993, cover story featuring Michael Douglas's fierce face, his thin lips, his pores, the right lens shattered in his glasses, with the headline: "WHITE MALE PARANOIA." Why frame the image that way? The popularity of the movie in which Douglas was starring, *Falling Down,* could have been interpreted as evidence that urban angst had reached a boiling point. It could have been interpreted as the return of the Western, this time set amid the breakdown of Los Angeles. But *Newsweek* decreed that the wretched Douglas character, a laid-off defense worker who began his photogenic violent crack-up by picking a fight with a Korean grocer whose English he could not understand, stood for white malehood, and that the question of the week was "New Victims or Just Bad Sports?" The main article inside, by David Gates, did sensibly note: "White male paranoia isn't old-fashioned white liberal guilt: it's atavistic racial and sexual dread, and it achieves critical mass when a rapidly contracting economy becomes overcrowded." But the cover said something else. So did the sidebar by Ellis Cose, which referred to a generic "white male ego" and "white male pique," as if Secretary of the Interior Bruce Babbitt, President Bill Clinton, singer Boy George, President Boris Yeltsin, President John F. Kennedy, Senator Robert Packwood, Woody Allen, magnate Abe Hirschfeld, the CEOs of General Motors and Lotus, and the sexual marauders of Glen Ridge, N.J.—to name some of the white men pictured throughout the magazine—had something significant in common. In the light they—we—were presumably all the same.

In one of the sloppy locutions that have become the norm, the *Newsweek* writers use "white male" to mean, more or less, prosperous, straight, white North American. Thus, in the sidebar, Ellis Cose asked: "Why would white men feel they are being pushed to the wall when they hold most of the top jobs?" *They* hold most of the top jobs. The checkout clerk, the investment banker, Slobodan Milosevich, and the Caucasian holding a VIETNAM VET WILL WORK FOR FOOD sign were grouped together. When *Newsweek* featured paranoia as a characteristic of the generic white male—even as, in places, it declared the paranoia unwarranted—it stood in the front ranks of the terrible simplifiers. It joined the makers of *Falling Down* in one of America's few growth industries: the exploitation of rancor.

Newsweek was scarcely alone. Around the same time, *Business Week* devoted a cover story to the complaints of white males who feel passed over in business. (The magazine had never run a cover story on job discrimination against blacks, women, Hispanics, or homosexuals.) In earlier decades, it is far from true that all white men thought they were powerful; still, there was always some lingering sense of caste solidarity, some privilege that even the poorest of white men could feel; and the change that has had to register on white men in recent decades is extraordinary and often perturbing to them. No small thing, and not to be easily assuaged by pointing out that men, or whites, have slipped somewhat from the once-commanding heights they did not deserve to occupy unchallenged—for it is not a group's absolute position but its relative slippage, or the perception of such, that fuels the reactions of reactionary movements.

For many whites on campus, the sense of relative decline is compounded from several directions: by a fear of the declining economic value of a college degree; by a sense of having been unfairly targeted; by resentment over (frequently misunderstood) affirmative action policies; by envy of others felt (often in an exaggerated manner) to be better organized; by peer pressure; by the anonymity of campus life (though this is hardly a decisive factor, since some of the most fervent crusades of identity politics have taken place at small liberal arts colleges); and by the desire to mimic the identity consciousness of others. In 1985, a white Berkeley freshman in a huge undergraduate lecture class approached me during my office hours to talk about a quandary. He was timid, soft-spoken. Unlike many Berkeley students, he came from the Central Valley. He had no distinct ethnicity in which to find refuge, being neither Jewish, nor Italian, nor Irish. All around him, students of color were organizing in separate groups, expressing pride in their races and some antagonism toward his. He was embarrassed to ask, but some of his acquaintances were organizing a white student association, and he wanted advice about whether to join. The group was not white supremacist, he insisted. He did not have the swagger or truculence of a white supremacist. Had this young man of seventeen or eighteen been deeply prejudiced, he would not have cared about my opinion; he had heard me lecture on the abominations of American racism. Another lecture was not what he wanted or needed. No, what he wanted was an identity group; and yet he felt troubled about what he found himself wanting. I told him that I sympathized with his desire to have a group to feel comfortable in, but that given the grim history of what happens in America when whites proclaim their whiteness, a group defining themselves by membership in the dominant race had to be wrong. He went away unhappy—possibly less lonely, having gotten his professor's attention, but no better equipped with a hard-and-fast identity.

How representative is such a young man? Representative enough to take seriously, even before the media megaphone goes to work. In 1991 students at a high school in Anaheim, home of Disneyland, organized a European American Club, claiming that they felt no racial animus but wanted to have an identity group to join. The head of the group was a girl who was half Lebanese and half Irish, but no matter—she wanted a group she could call her own. Her group and the Berkeley student belong to a demographic obsession already swelling into an identity panic. To their eyes, the entire society is apparently grouped into exclusive "communities." Such is their experience, and so the media insistently remind them. Why shouldn't they, too, demand affirmative attention?

With no single racial or ethnic group constituting a racial majority (in fall 1990, whites were 42 percent of registered students), the Berkeley campus is scarcely representative of America or even of campuses. But even where minorities are few in number, white males who are not wealthy and not secure—that is to say, most of them—are frequently less than enthusiastic about the coloring of America. Very few of them, it is safe to say, are skinheads, rapists, or gay-bashers. As well as survey researchers can detect, a minority—it would sound complacent to say "only a minority"—are willing to deprecate blacks outright, at least to a stranger. Straightforward discrimination and bigoted speech have certainly waned since the 1960s. Yet there remains plenty of bigotry, more than enough to indicate how far whites are from the color blindness commended as a value—even presumed as a fact—by those who think that the nation has done enough, or more than enough, to remedy the situation of blacks. In a 1990 survey, 29 percent of a national sample of whites grouped blacks as unintelligent—four years before a best-selling book lent this notion a certain respectability with full pseudoscientific trappings. Whites who said they supported antidiscrimination laws in home sales increased from 34 percent in 1973 to 51 percent in 1990, an improvement of 50 percent; but this means that almost half were still not willing to support open housing.

And yet white attitudes may be more ambivalent and flexible than these disturbing results convey. In 1989 Paul M. Sniderman of Stanford University and Thomas Piazza of the University of California, Berkeley, asked a random sample of whites their opinions of blacks (they could choose more than one description). Twenty-six percent said blacks were "irresponsible"; 20 percent, that they were "lazy." An equal number of randomly sampled whites were asked their opinions of blacks only after they had been asked a question about affirmative action: "In a nearby state, an effort is being made to increase dramatically the number of blacks working in state government. This means that a large number of jobs will be reserved for blacks, even if their scores on merit exams are lower than those of whites who are turned down for the job. Do you favor or oppose this policy?" In this population, the number who said blacks were "irresponsible" rose to 43 percent; those who said blacks were "lazy" rose to 31 percent. In other words, the mere mention of affirmative action, albeit attributed to "a nearby state," triggered an increase of more than 50 percent in the number of whites willing to express outright denigration.

One may suspect that the "mere mention" of affirmative action signaled to veiled bigots that the researchers might be receptive to otherwise tabooed expressions of racial hostility. It is well known that survey interviewees are reluctant to own up to bigotry. But when Sniderman and Piazza's interviewers argued with their interviewees in either direction, even in a rudimentary way, they could easily sway them, or at least influence the words they were willing to express. The fact that people are flexible on these questions is chilling. But flexibility is preferable to dyed-in-the-wool prejudice. It creates latitude for political leadership. For "mere mentions" are not confined to survey experiments. "Mere mentions" circulate through the media and in everyday talk. In political campaigns, Republicans need "merely mention" jobs, taxes, and welfare to get the attention of white males—the bloc accountable for their sweep in the midterm elections of 1994.

Not so long ago—and before then, in his father's time, and his father's father's, and so on—the straight white male was the American norm. Everyone else was measured, and usually found wanting, by virtue, or vice, of deviance from that norm. If he was born without many advantages, still, his whiteness and maleness protected him to a certain degree. He took his insulation for granted. If life dissatisfied him, he was apt to conclude that he had no one to blame but himself. Today, the straight white male frequently finds himself on the defensive. He is, like everyone else, a member of a category, the oppressor category at that, scrambling for cultural space while his own prospects seem less than luminous. His intentions with respect to minorities and women may or may not be noble, but he is tempted to declare himself a victim like the victims he deplores.

University culture in particular encourages this sort of rivalry for the crown of thorns. From minorities, the finger of accusation readily points at the white male close at hand, presumed guilty ipso facto of discrimination, or at least of profiting from an institutional bias based on the discrimination practiced by his forebears or somebody else's. In the eyes of many women's studies professors and students, he may be a "potential rapist." Although racist and sexist abuse is sometimes exaggerated, many outbreaks of verbal viciousness and violence do take place. So the well-meaning white male may try to go out of his way to be sensitive. He learns that if he finds himself walking down the street behind a woman, she may well cringe at his footsteps, wheel, check him out—even if she will feel relieved to discover he is not a badly dressed black. He may well know that she has reason to fear, and therefore not begrudge her the scrutiny. Still, he carries with him the knowledge that he is suspect—not because of who he is, but because of what he looks like. He is weary of having to live on sufferance, weary of having to suppress his resentment. Weren't we supposed to be done with labels, he demands, tempted (to say the least) to make the most of his own label? He wants to know why fairness should stop before it gets to him.

"If you want to go with the stereotypes," one white student told the

Berkeley Diversity Project, which studied racial typecasting between 1989 and 1991, "Asians are the smart people, the blacks are great athletes, what is white? We're just here. We're the oppressors of the nation. At Berkeley being white is having to constantly be on my toes about not offending other races, not saying something to be construed as, 'I am continuing to be the oppressor of America.'" If not an oppressor, the white male is a blank, made to feel he lacks roots, culture, substance. "Being white," as one student put it, "means having no box to check on admission forms"—and means being available to vote against benefits for the children of illegal immigrants, against affirmative action, and, not least, against Democrats.

5

Marching on the English Department While the Right Took the White House

1. The Cant of Identity

The more vociferously a term is trumpeted in public, the more contestable it is under scrutiny. The automatic recourse to a slogan, as if it were tantamount to a value or an argument, is frequently a measure of the need to suppress a difficulty or a vagueness underneath. Cant is the hardening of the aura around a concept. Cant automates thought, substitutes for deeper assessments, creates the illusion of firmness where there are only intricacies, freezes a fluid reality. Cant is sincere, usually, and its sincerity also protects against scrutiny. Cant comforts. And cant tends to corrupt its opposition into countercant. There is the cant of identity and the cant that rises with righteous and selective indignation against the "political correctness" of the Left, though not against that of the Right.

The cant of identity underlies identity politics, which proposes to deduce a position, a tradition, a deep truth, or a way of life from a fact of birth, physiognomy, national origin, sex, or physical disability. The hardening of one of these categories into cant begins with binary thinking—

things are either raw or cooked, male or female, this or that—a propensity that may indeed be, as Lévi-Strauss maintained, universal. Anxiety generated by difference may well be embedded in the human condition; so may be the animosity that accompanies anxiety. Perhaps the capacity quickly to classify "the other" as same or different, friend or enemy, once conferred a benefit for survival. But whether or not it was originally a means of natural selection, this sort of binary thinking certainly helps clans, elites, and nations maintain themselves. From binary thinking follows a propensity for identity thinking, which categorizes strangers—this is a person of Type X, not Type Y. The identity thinking of the powerful reassures them that they deserve to rule; the identity thinking of the oppressed affirms that they are not who the rulers think they are. If the identity affirmation of the oppressed begins as a defense against claims of superiority, it can swerve into its own sense of superiority. All forms of identity politics are overly clear about who the insiders are—*"normal* Americans," *"the* people," *"la* Raza,"—and overly dismissive of outsiders. In either case, cant makes for efficient simplifications, but only at the price of rigidity. Cant is what we have when we think we know more than we do. Its opposite is curiosity.

Today, it is the cant of identity that many Americans espouse, and the question is why. The beginning of an answer is that identity does more than exclude. It transcends the self, affirms a connection with others. Erik H. Erikson, whose writings in the 1960s did a lot to popularize the notion of identity, put the matter this way: "The functioning ego, while guarding individuality, is far from isolated, for a kind of communality links egos in a mutual activation." Identity extends through space, binding a person to fellow travelers in the human project. But identity also extends through time, linking the individual with past and future, extending beyond the mortal body. As Erikson wrote, "Psychosocial identity is necessary as the anchoring of man's transient existence in the here and now." Erikson warned against fossilizing identity, which, he said, "is never 'established' as an 'achievement' in the form of a personality armor, or of anything static and unchangeable." But the cant retailed from his thinking spread rapidly throughout vertiginous America, a society founded on rootlessness, devoted to self-creation, worshipping evanescence, stuffing its spiritual voids with the latest gadgets.

Americans are obsessed today with their racial, ethnic, religious, and sexual identities. What is supposed to be universal is, above all, difference. And yet there is a peculiar blindness. Beneath the rhetoric, the functional assumption shared by virtually all Americans is that the market is the place to look for values, that what matters is "the bottom line." While Americans busily dig for roots, their economy is built on the steady replacement of old things with new things. The hypertrophy of difference, at least at the level of rhetoric, masks disrespect for the real thing.

2. The Beauty and Power of Blackness

For much of American history, "Americanism" was the belief that there was a correct way to be American—despite the palpable looseness of national definitions. The insistence on the virtues of "native Americans" at a time when this term referred to native-born whites was an attempt to shore up groups who worried about their prospects in new and unsettling circumstances. Racial classification, in particular, is in the American grain, beginning with the obsessive concern over maintaining the purity of the category "white." Racism is labeling made invidious, in fact. Throughout most of American history, the law ratified community bigotry by assigning and affirming racial identities, from slavery codes and laws against interracial marriage to the Chinese Exclusion Act. By contrast, "ethnicity" had social more than legal significance. "Ethnicity" was crystallized in group life: in regions and neighborhoods, in common occupations, in foreign-language newspapers and urban politics. Even the Left was rooted disproportionately in particular ethnic groups—Socialist Germans through World War I, Italian anarchists in the 1920s, Socialist and Communist Jews during the Great Depression. Later, under the label "national origins," ethnicity was enshrined in immigration quotas. To identify as Mexican, German, Irish, Italian, Greek, or Jewish was partly embraced, partly imposed: a matter of affirming "what one already was."

The longer white ethnics lived in the United States, the more "American"—assimilated, acculturated—they became. Inevitably, ethnic identities slackened—or seemed to. But racial identity came roaring to the fore in the late 1960s. The trigger, of course, was the civil rights movement, or rather, the liberationist impulse that came to the fore as the movement succeeded. The civil rights revolt against racial oppression exploded with a pent-up force that no partial legislative reforms could adequately assuage. The momentum of the movement outran legislative redress. The civil rights movement, after all, meant to redress *three centuries* of racial oppression—slavery followed by the semi-serfdom of sharecropping and other inequalities. The mass immigration from the South to northern and western cities met with discrimination, producing steadily denser, younger, poorer, and angrier ghettos. Were young blacks, ill-paid, ill-housed, ill-treated, now supposed to feel tranquil because Congress had finally seen fit to ban white-only drinking fountains? Neither the Civil Rights Act of 1964 nor the Voting Rights Act of 1965, nor even Lyndon Johnson's endorsement of affirmative action, could placate all of them. Growing numbers did not want to "look white" anymore. They did not want to take a back seat in American culture. There was no more patience for humiliation. White riots in the Chicago area against Martin Luther King Jr.'s marches for open housing in the summer of 1966 only confirmed that the prospects for social integration were not impressive.

But it did not take Malcolm X or Chicago's white rioters to goad a group of black students in Oakland, California, during the fall of 1963 to threaten to stop reciting the pledge of allegiance. (The president of the Oakland Youth Council declared that, for a Negro, the notion of "liberty and justice for all is so naive that it is almost facetious.") There is a nationalist streak that has surfaced periodically in African-American history since the Civil War, uniting the otherwise disparate Martin Delany, Marcus Garvey, and Elijah Muhammad, and again it swelled. Encouraged by African anticolonialist successes, significant American black leaders now looked abroad for allies, and then for names, for clothing, and, indeed, for identity. "I'm from America," Malcolm X said at the University of Ghana on May 13, 1964, "but I'm not an American. I didn't go there of my own free choice. . . . [I] come to this meeting as one of the victims of America, one of the victims of Americanism, one of the victims of democracy." "We need allies," he told a rally on December 13, 1964, "and as long as you and I think that we can only get allies from . . . up on the Grand Concourse [where Jewish liberals lived] . . . our source of allies is limited. But when we realize how large this earth is, and how many different people there are on it, and how closely they resemble us, then when we turn to them for some sort of aid, or to form alliances, then we'll make a little faster progress." In his final phase, after breaking with the Black Muslims and working his way toward some sort of transracial idea, Malcolm X founded a grandly titled Organization for Afro-American Unity whose significance lay not in its size—at his death, it was little more than a hope—but in its hyphenation. To call yourself "Afro-American," Malcolm wrote, was to reject both "American" and "Negro" —though interestingly, it was not to escape "American" altogether.

This was a time when cross-racial alliances for civil rights were proving unmanageable. In 1964, civil rights workers from the Student Nonviolent Coordinating Committee (SNCC) and other groups brought an elected Mississippi Freedom Democratic Party (MFDP) delegation to the Democratic Convention in Atlantic City and demanded to be seated as the official delegation in place of the official white supremacist regulars, who had been chosen without the slightest participation by blacks, and who would not even promise to support the Democratic nominee. (In the end, they endorsed Barry Goldwater.) President Johnson orchestrated a compromise, supported by liberals, labor unions, and moderate civil rights leaders, offering the MFDP a token two votes for its leaders, retaining the official delegation, while pledging to change the rules by 1968. The MFDP refused the compromise. The radical position was immortalized in Fannie Lou Hamer's famous statement that it would be wrong for the leaders to take seats because "all of us [in the MFDP delegation] are tired."

Among black activists, the thrust was toward the spirit of go-it-alone. The militants of the Student Nonviolent Coordinating Committee felt betrayed by mainstream liberals, lost interest in alliances with whites, and ended up expelling even radical white organizers. After Malcolm X was cut down by an assassin's bullet in February 1965, the pressure toward a visceral rejection of American identity grew—and grew even more furiously with that August's Watts riot, as mainstream opinion called it, or the Watts rebellion, as it was known to the Left. In this climate, the "Black Power" proclaimed by SNCC's Stokely Carmichael in June 1966 was, beneath the militant sound, an ambiguous slogan, partly advocating a black role in a hypothetically unified Third World revolution, partly advocating cultural and political pluralism on the model of America's white ethnic groups. The high boil of the northern and western black ghettos after Watts intensified both tendencies. And yet, coiled within the pluralist version, there remained the hope to redeem America. Representative of militant writing was this 1968 passage from Julius Lester, then a close associate of Carmichael:

> Those who advocate Black Power today . . . are the inheritors of a proud tradition of resistance to America. Blacks can see very clearly that America is a nation built upon inhumanity. The signers of the Declaration of Independence put down their quills to go home and beat their slaves. . . . To die in the attempt to humanize America is preferable to being an American as America is now constituted.

America had to be *resisted,* something done by outsiders; but it also had to be *humanized,* something done by those who belong.

Like many in SNCC after the whites were expelled, Lester aligned himself with the new black-is-beautiful culture of music and natural hair and political insurgency, all of which he identified with "another language . . . rhythm . . . 'soul.' In Africa they speak of negritude. . . . It is the recognition of those things uniquely ours which separate us from the white man." More than a "recognition," it was an intoxication, the seeming realization of a dream endlessly deferred. The joy of kicking away from a white-imposed definition of beauty, of order, of conduct, was intense. What could be more exultant than Lester's title, *Look Out, Whitey! Black Power's Gon' Get Your Mama!*? It was inflammatory in the manner of a cartoon. Despite the earlier reference to "humanizing" America, Lester claimed it was pointless to "stir . . . the moral conscience of America," because, indeed, "America has no moral conscience." "It is clear that America as it now exists must be destroyed. There is no other way. It is impossible to live within this country and not become a thief or a murderer." As Stokely Carmichael told a Berkeley crowd in October 1966: "I do not want to be a part of the American pie. The American pie means raping South Africa, beating Viet Nam, beating South America, raping the Philippines, raping every country you've been in. I don't want any of your blood money."

If not to America, then to what could blacks belong? To un- or anti-America: the wretched of the earth, the global army of destroyer-redeemers. Lester ends his book by invoking anti-imperialist identity: "The struggle of blacks in America is inseparable from the struggle of the Third World." He affirms the brotherhood of blacks—unlike white Americans, he points out, blacks refer to each other as brothers. The other theme is rebirth through uprising. We *were* exploited, therefore we *are*. This was the spirit of the most conspicuous black militants from 1967 on. In 1967, the same year Lester wrote his manifesto, the openly armed Black Panther Party seized the media spotlight by flaunting guns in a protest (against a law banning the carrying of weapons) at the California state capitol in Sacramento. The Black Panther Party, in particular, affirmed a revolutionary identity (variously Cuban, Vietnamese, Algerian, North Korean) without any root in American history. Racially, the Panthers were not separatist—they wanted white allies and devoted a good deal of energy to cultivating them—but they had no interest in the radical streaks of American tradition, even in slave revolts, abolitionism, and Reconstruction. Politically, they were separatist. To affirm the global revolution was a sort of spiritual secession, and an ecstasy as well.

Another way to affirm a distinct identity was to substitute African-based customs for those of a white-dominated society and turn color consciousness from a stigma to a badge of pride. For centuries, white society had imposed notions of black inferiority—ideas that most blacks had internalized. To shake off that burden was immensely hard—wrenching, but often exhilarating, like a slave revolt or a prison break. Inspired by African anticolonial leaders and by celebrities like Miriam Makeba, Odetta, Lorraine Hansberry, Abbey Lincoln, and Nina Simone, all featured on *Ebony* magazine covers with the kinky hair they had been born with, a few black women at Howard University as early as 1962 put down the straightening comb and started wearing their hair naturally. The new cultural nationalists did not have to read Frantz Fanon's *The Wretched of the Earth,* first published in English in 1963, to feel the thrill of breaking from white standards. Men in civil rights also came to prefer these kinky "Afros." Black Muslims had already sundered themselves from their family names, calling them slave names, and taken up the indeterminate X instead, as if to say that, having been stripped of identity, they were reinventing themselves. Soon enough, the X was in turn replaced. In Los Angeles in 1966, Ronald McKinley Everett became Maulana Ron Karenga, assumed African robes, took up the Swahili language, and in December organized the first Kwanzaa celebration, an invention based on African festivals. Around that time, Americans of African descent put on African clothes and declared that they were no longer Negroes but rather blacks or Afro-Americans, a race with a history and a wide world to identify with.

Note that all these varieties of militancy and identity refashioning preceded the assassination of Martin Luther King, Jr. At the moment when the life of the unsurpassable orator was snuffed out, his hold on the black youth of the ghettos was already weak. Any hope of a mass integrated nonviolent movement was already fading fast. The militants of SNCC had long mocked him as "De Lawd." Yet he was there to mock, to oppose, to love. While King lived, he embodied the possibility of a redemptive struggle across racial lines. He journeyed to Memphis to support a strike by black garbage workers—a solidarity that had class as well as race dimensions. The Poor People's Campaign to which King committed himself before he died was unabashedly, deliberately transracial. Even in eclipse, King was the personification of faith and possibility: the incarnation of a black leadership that might build bridges from the movement against segregation to a successor movement against poverty and the inequality of wealth.

His murder snuffed out whatever leftover belief there was among blacks that a new America might ever be reborn. The outpouring of desperate rage was a measure of just how immense, how irreplaceable a figure King was. He was all of thirty-nine at the time he came down from the mountain to Memphis. Whatever defeats he would have been dealt over the next decades—and they would have been many—whatever weariness and despair he would have felt—and he would have felt much—he would still have lingered as a unifying presence, as goad and conscience, as a living link with the America of Paine, Thoreau, Douglass, and Lincoln. After King, there was only the smoke of *what if* rising from burned-out cities. King alive was the refutation of separatism; King murdered was its rationale. James Baldwin had already asked rhetorically: "Do I really *want* to be integrated into a burning house?"

3. The Ethnic Multiplication

The spirit of black cultural assertion deserves credit for tremendous achievements. "Black is beautiful," never the path of least resistance, left an irreversible mark of pride in the lives of black people in the United States and elsewhere. The growth of African-American politics, arts, and intellectual life since the 1960s is indisputable. Whether more could have been done to overcome the unequal conditions of blacks and whites if the civil rights coalition had been sustained against all odds cannot be known.

But the consequences of the black move toward separate organization after civil rights were profound and multiple in unintended ways. For one thing, black revolutionism spurred the white Left into its own go-for-broke trajectory. It would be hard to overestimate the impact of black rage and estrangement on white radical rage and estrangement in the later 1960s—when "America" came to seem synonymous with the devastation of Vietnam. But more, the black identity movement became the template for ethnic multiplication. Especially among intellectuals of all stripes, distinctness became a new principle of organization while integration became passé. By 1969, with Robert Kennedy dead and Richard Nixon in office, the question of poverty, no less how to redistribute wealth or how to compose a majority with that in mind, had melted off everyone's agenda. Radical organizers of the New Left who had not so long before hoped to inspire "an interracial movement of the poor" were moving on to antiwar projects. Community organizations ceased to be of interest to them because the project was not to make a common America but to break up the one that existed. Identity groups were where the action was.

America spawned identities in abundance. The American Indian Movement seized the former prison island of Alcatraz in San Francisco Bay on Thanksgiving Day 1969. In Northern cities, Puerto Rican groups organized. In the West and Southwest, Chicanos were doing the same— César Chavez's farm workers in California, Reies Tijerina's land grant movement in northern New Mexico, an antiwar Chicano Moratorium in Los Angeles, Chicano intellectuals launching the journal *Aztlán*. In California, young Chinese Americans insisted on their distinct needs as an interest group. "Third World Liberation Fronts" began to organize at state universities late in 1968 and were instrumental in militant student strikes at San Francisco State College and the University of California, Berkeley.

Some of the new identity groups took their shape and impetus from the immigration law of 1965, which eliminated the old Eurocentric quotas, guaranteeing that Latin Americans, Asians, and Africans would become the vast majority of the newest ethnics in the years to come. In some respects, the new ethnicity of color resembled the traditional urban ethnicity of the white working class. The new immigrants and their children also concentrated in particular neighborhoods. They tended to marry within the group. They clustered in particular occupations. Family networks helped family members immigrate, find jobs, start businesses. What was new was the belief in ethnic militancy, the attack on assimilation, the assertion of pride, the stripping away of deference to the majority.

Whites en masse were slower to spring to ethnic consciousness. As late as the fall of 1965, Nathan Glazer was writing: "For the moment, ethnic self-assertiveness is in eclipse and even in bad odor." This was, he wrote, largely because of the national preoccupation with black rights and poverty. Until 1969 or 1970, wrote Andrew Greeley, "practically no survey questionnaires had an ethnic question. Even [in 1971], the Gallup organization [did] not routinely ask about ethnicity." But during the mid-1960s, the black secession from integrated (if black-led) organizations proved traumatic for white liberals. It undermined their raison d'être. (What, after all, was liberalism without grateful lower classes to be liberal for?) Meanwhile, in cities and working-class suburbs, where New Deal liberalism was based on the alliance between the ethnic (largely Catholic and Jewish) and black votes, black action was prompting a white counterreaction. Many of these whites felt pinched, their economic position tenuous, their neighborhoods declining, crime on the rise. They were not getting attention from top officials. Television did not recognize them— except perhaps as "the backlash." Envious and vengeful, many retreated to the redoubt of whiteness.

At first this resentment was not delivered in ethnic terms. It had other political channels—remnant urban machines like Mayor Daley's in Chicago or the Wallace vote of 1968. But within a very few years, ethnic claims mushroomed. How deep they ran is a difficult question to answer. Gunnar Myrdal's impression in 1974 was that the "craving for historical identity" was not so much "a people's movement" as the product of "a few well established intellectuals, professors, writers—mostly, I gather, of a third generation." There was survey evidence, for what it was worth, that ethnic whites were no more racist than any others—perhaps less. In any event, white ethnic groups, fueled by more than a few intellectuals, did proliferate. Certainly, ethnic assertion spread among the educated, the professionals, and the clergy—with a not-inconsiderable assist from the mass media, which amplified the sense of a collision between ethnic whites and blacks.

Any combination of white motives was possible. Resentment and fear said: if blacks were "getting theirs," the only way to compete for political and cultural goods—especially in a stagnant or shrinking job market—was to declare fealty to one's own lineage and fight back. Rivalry said: if blacks were combining to demand jobs in previously protected occupations (say, among Italian construction workers or Irish plumbers), whites had to work to define themselves as an oppressed or overlooked group, and the language with which one accomplishes that, in American culture, is the language of ethnicity. Admiration coupled with envy said: blacks are becoming adept at feeling whole. They are ceasing to look outside themselves for confirmation that they matter. We can learn from them. All these feelings combined to say: look at the pride that comes from ethnic assertion; and anyway, to be strictly an unhyphenated American is not enough. Certainly, the shine had worn off the old undifferentiated American identity. America's political, racial, and cultural seams showed so evidently. At times, resentment and admiration of blacks were hard to disentangle.

The ethnic whites were choosing to be ethnic. They embraced what Herbert J. Gans called "symbolic ethnicity." Ethnicity was legitimate when whiteness as such was not. If American blacks were identifying with Africa, why shouldn't American Italians identify with Italy, American Poles with Poland? Whiteness had been a gift to European immigrants, but it was a check that the second and third generations were reluctant to cash—it reeked of racism. Ethnicity, on the other hand, was becoming the common coin of the realm. It was an approved way to be a special American. At a time when an unmodified American identity was losing its moral and adhesive force, many younger whites insisted that they had ethnicities too; even that they were ethnic before they were anything else. They looked to discarded or superseded values of ethnic solidarity to oppose the fatuities of suburban and television culture. Jews whose fathers had changed their names proudly resumed the names of the grandfathers—the son of the popular novelist Irving Wallace becoming David Wallechinsky, for example. If they had spent part of their childhoods in urban ethnic enclaves, they stamped those old stomping grounds, after the fact, with sepia virtue. If they had grown up de-ethnicized in the suburbs, they enjoyed a trip to their grandparents' old neighborhoods, to Little Italy or the Lower East Side, at least for a weekend nosh. They wanted the chicken fat, the kielbasa, the cannoli that Ozzie and Harriet hadn't served. Many wanted even more than the secular signs of ethnicity—they wanted the old-time religion.

In other words, the grandchildren of turn-of-the-century European immigrants by now felt sure enough of their Americanness that they were free to revolt against it—symbolically. Just as a certain affluence purchased the power to revolt against affluence, so did a certain security breed a desire to compound one's identity, to be something other than a generic "American." It was the Jews, among white ethnics, who insisted on their hyphens first. Their motives were complex, but one important element was a recoil—even many radicals recoiled—when black militants with whom they had worked for civil rights sided with the Palestinians in the wake of the Six Day War of 1967 and declared Zionism a central enemy of the "Third World Revolution." Jews felt the shock spurned lovers feel. Then, the Jews of New York City, the largest and most influential single bloc of American Jews, were traumatized by the black anti-Semitism that surfaced during a prolonged and bitter teachers' strike in 1968–69, when Jewish teachers found themselves pitted against black parents. The teachers, major carriers of prestige and achievement for the Jewish community, had only recently unionized after years of subordination by WASP and Irish school officials. They were liberal, in the main. But from the militant black point of view, they stood in the way of "community control." Now they heard black activists tell them to step aside and relinquish the power and legitimacy they had struggled for.

The insult helped galvanize Jewish identity just as anti-Italian slurs helped mobilize Italians. But such ethnic identity was not necessarily, not altogether, defensive. It could also be assertive, an affirmation of peoplehood, a declaration of faith in the virtues of the community. The established Jewish organizations turned to the cause of Soviet Jews. Why, they asked, should Jews cultivate black radicals who were, in any event, rejecting them and damning their national liberation movement, Zionism, when there were Jews in trouble? Then too, many Jewish radicals were already beginning to think and speak of themselves in reverse order, as radical Jews. Radical Jewish Unions began to form at Berkeley and other campuses. The radical activist Arthur Waskow wrote a radical Passover Haggadah just after the assassination of Martin Luther King, Jr., and held the first Freedom Seder in 1969. A national meeting of Jewish-radicals-cum-radical-Jews followed. These Jews, deeply identified with the fight for black rights, now felt the need to approach that fight as representatives of their own community. That was the only way to have standing.

Jews in America had long held to a relatively strong sense of cultural separateness; what was striking, during the late 1960s and early 1970s, was that considerable numbers of other whites felt comparable impulses. "I think those of us in the ethnic bag can learn from the blacks about the importance of cultural identity," wrote the prominent Monsignor Geno Baroni in 1970. "We are beginning to celebrate our differences instead of insisting that everybody has to be the same." Emulation was a tangled impulse: it sublimated a widespread white resentment at being blamed for the racial oppression of blacks. But emulation was not the only motive. A host of white ethnic Americans found it insufficiently clarifying, insufficiently forceful, insufficiently "meaningful" to be white. However much they or their families might have benefited from being white, they felt enough sympathy with blacks not to want to pride themselves simply on being members of the ruling race. Many also felt a marginality that was scarcely grasped by the label "white." They longed to belong to more distinct, better-defined and -defended tribes. They wanted to recover the histories of their peoples, wanted their children to be transfixed by those stories, wanted them taught in the schools. Bumper stickers and lapel buttons proclaimed the virtues of Polishness or declared: "Kiss Me, I'm Italian." Ethnicity offered pride and victimization, assertion without the need for defensiveness.

The new white ethnicity was not a simple resumption of the traditional urban American, largely working class alignments of the late nineteenth and early twentieth centuries. It did not have many links with the "old country." The new ethnicity was articulated by upwardly mobile intellectuals who did not reside in homogeneous neighborhoods. It did not require marriage or friendship within the tribe, or work within the family trade. It did not accompany political machines. It was not passed down from the parents but borrowed from the grandparents. It was not so much inherited as chosen; not so much taken for granted as flaunted. And no small difference, the new ethnicity was modeled on—even if at odds with—that of blacks.

"I want to have a history," declared Michael Novak, an antiwar intellectual and theologian of Slovakian origin, in his pivotal manifesto, *The Rise of the Unmeltable Ethnics,* published in 1972. "I am born of PIGS— those Poles, Italians, Greeks, and Slavs, those non-English-speaking immigrants numbered so heavily among the workingmen of this nation." "In recent months," he wrote in a self-dramatizing chapter called "Confessions of a White Ethnic," "I have experienced . . . a willingness to think about feelings heretofore shepherded out of sight," a sentiment he likened to the liberation of women "to give tongue to their pain. . . . The PIGS are not silent willingly. The silence burns like hidden coals in the chest." "Where in America," he asked, "is there anywhere a language for voicing what a Christian Pole in this nation feels?" "The recent increase in Black, Chicano, and Indian consciousness," Novak added, "left other ethnic groups in a psychologically confused state. They are unable to be WASPS; they have lost confidence in being themselves." Black demands, moreover, burdened the white ethnics far in excess of the likely rewards. The children bused to remote schools for the sake of integration were not the children of the lawyers who won the lawsuits but the children of hard-hats. Why pick on them? *Their* ancestors were not slaveowners, though they may have been serfs.

Novak was on his way to a neoconservative backlash, but had not yet arrived. He lamented the fact that the Left was making a mistake "conced[ing] the [white] ethnic voter to the conservative movement," and leaped to the assumption that "we are, in a word, ineffably ethnic in our values and our actions." Left-wing intellectuals, WASPS and Jews, deprived him and his coethnicists of their dignity. "Why do the educated classes find it so difficult to want to understand the man who drives a beer truck, or the fellow with a helmet working on a site across the street with plumbers and electricians, while their sensitivities race easily to Mississippi or even Bedford-Stuyvesant?"

There was, however, little proof that the truck driver was brimming with ethnic sentiment. In the climate of the early 1970s, he was probably more likely to be feeling his whiteness—an issue Novak skirted. He was also, as Novak did note, feeling his patriotism. "To ethnics, America is almost a religion. The flag alone proves that they are not stupid, cloddish, dull, but capable of the greatest act men can make: to die for others. The flag is not a patriotic symbol only. It is the symbol of poor and wretched people who now have jobs and homes and liberties. It is a symbol of transcendence. Many millions proved that they were men, not PIGS, by expressing a willingness to die beneath those colors. . . . 'I AM AN AMERICAN!' How many humiliations were endured until one could say those words and not be laughed at by nativists." They wrapped themselves in the flag, in Novak's view, because without it they were naked and cold.

Novak overlooked evidence that, for all their patriotism, the less educated were more likely to oppose the war than the more educated. But even if his "unmeltable ethnics" were more complex than he said, he did see how unnerving it was for many white ethnics to watch their flag disgraced—right there on television—on the streets of their own cities. No wonder these people were bitter. No wonder that, in the 1970s, they were ready to contemplate voting Republican, something their parents and grandparents could scarcely have imagined. No wonder they reviled the McCarthy-McGovern side of the Democratic party, which represented, in their eyes, the alliance of the overeducated and the undereducated (meaning blacks) against the middle, the plain folks, the meat-and-potatoes, no-nonsense Americans. Many of these men felt that the muscle and bone of their political party was going soft, deserting the sturdy likes of Hubert Humphrey and Henry (Scoop) Jackson. And if their party had made a mistake committing their glory and treasure in the cause of a bad war, well, that was a bad *policy,* a policy to be changed, which is how Americans did things, and since they were nothing if not loyal, since their families had scratched and clawed to get them as far as they had gotten, just because their flag had been carried into the wrong action didn't mean that they were going to turn their backs on that flag.

In his exaggerations, Novak observed—and furthered—the central paradox of the so-called ethnic revival: the more ethnic the children of Slovakian and Hungarian and Italian and Irish immigrants purported to be, the more American they felt. Claiming to be unmeltable, they would melt, they hoped, into the American majority. An American was someone who arrived on these shores and worked feverishly to *become* an American. In this view, not old-line Mayflower WASPS but immigrants were the true carriers of Americanism. What Americans melted into was a country that knew itself to be touched by God *because* of the ordeal of melting into it. Nationalism through difference, difference through nationalism: this was yet more fuel for the romance of identities.

4. The Separatist Impulse

Identity politics based on race spawned identity politics based on ethnicity. The same model was adopted by the women's and gay liberation movements in 1968–69. The spirit of the New Left released long dammed-up forces of revolt. Subordination on the basis of sex and sexuality became the basis for a liberationist sequence: first, the discovery of common experience and interests; next, an uprising against a society that had imposed inferior status; finally, the inversion of that status, so that distinct qualities once pointed to as proof of inferiority were transvalued into the basis for positive distinction. It is only this third stage—where the group searches for and cultivates distinctive customs, qualities, lineages, ways of seeing, or, as they came to be known, "cultures"—that deserves to be called identity politics. The motif of participatory democracy had been: Citizenship requires direct decisionmaking. This was not practical. What was practical was identity politics, which affirmed that the basis for public life is membership in a group that has been stigmatized, a trustworthy group sufficiently compact for comfort. In the view from the universalist rearview mirror, the result was fragmentation and the sense of an ending. To forward-looking partisans, it was a new departure, a route to liberation.

The women's movement that spun away from the New Left was fueled by ample and legitimate grievances against discrimination. Women who were at first rebels within the larger movement soon went their separate way under the banner of "women's liberation"—in part because many men dismissed their grievances as laughable or diversionary. But the separatist dynamic at work was more than strictly reactive. It started with women's pent-up grievances but soon discovered the rapture of declaring psychic independence from men. In the revolutionist mood, they met in "consciousness-raising" groups, felt the exhilaration of developing a common vocabulary, justified their rage with analogies to black liberation. The early activists prided themselves on being young, despising the conventional family, and bearing a generational animus against the mothers of the 1950s, whom they saw as victims of men, of the housewife role, and indeed of "the family" as an institution. The young women of the "second wave" burned to transform life in the bedroom, the kitchen, the nursery, the classroom. In a time of apocalyptic ideas about total transformation, they moved their revolutionary animus from capitalism and imperialism to patriarchy. In the revolt against a liberalism they experienced as paternalistic—perhaps even maternalistic—these radical women also arrayed themselves against the feminists of their mothers' generation, who were preoccupied with equality on the job and in wages.

Quickly, gay liberation welled up along similar lines—first, in self-defense, against the brutalities of the police and the humiliations of the closet, then as claimant to a distinct culture founded precisely on the category, homosexuality, that had been crystallized, demonized, and repressed. The closet was full of fear, guilt, and self-loathing, and the joy of leaving it became the core of a new sensibility. The new identity was: gay. In bohemian neighborhoods, gays developed a territorial base, with a matrix of bars, associations, publications, theaters, churches, writers, comedians, professional services, and eventually political representatives. Gayness became a sort of ethnicity with its own codes of recognition, rituals, parades, sacred days, even its own flag with a rainbow motif. As with women, the generational divide was reproduced. So was the tension between reformers, who opposed discrimination, and liberationists, who multiplied theories and practices of sexual identity. So was separate organization by sex. So was the appropriation and inversion of the language of abuse, so that a term like "flaming faggot" could be repossessed, turned into an affirmation of pride.

The dynamism and pride of the gay and lesbian worlds were matched, and then some, by the women's movement. Just as blacks had seceded from white society, so did many women try to create a world apart from men. The point was to become a "woman-identified" woman. If some of the early women's liberation theorists sometimes spoke of separatism as a stage of self-development that would precede the resumption of a politics with men, this proved little more than a sentimental wish. The truth was that there was, in the rhetoric of the time, "no going back" from a separatism of spirit. For some women, willed "political lesbianism" was the logical consequence of going it alone; for others, there was the more diffuse "women's culture," institutionalized in journals and newsletters, in popular music and writing, in networks of bookstores and bars—and eventually in battered women's shelters, "women's spaces," and university women's studies programs. Even before the women's movement settled into the academy, the search was on for a distinct women's sensibility to catch the electricity that was in the air. The search for heretics was also on, with an unflattering psychology fastened onto those who broke ranks. It was important not to be a "queen bee," or "male-identified"—the equivalent of the "self-hating" label affixed by conservative Jews on Jews of the Left.

In mainstream politics, women's caucuses and groups proved brilliantly practical. The reformers were able to convert "personal" grievances into "political" issues. They got results. Laws were made, courts became more responsive. Women ascended to leadership in local and state government, in the nonprofit sector, in many Protestant churches, and to some degree in the private economy. With women at work outnumbering women at home, many discriminations fell by the wayside. At schools and universities, women were immensely energized. In the prochoice cause and with respect to other reproductive rights, encapsulated as "women's issues," they were more successful than not. The result has been a vast expansion of rights and a vast change in the social condition of women, especially in the middle classes. Outside the lower depths of poverty—no small exception—American women have been able to bring about more improvements than in any other quarter-century in American, or perhaps any other, history. The global repercussions have likewise been profound. The women's movement—like the gay and physically handicapped movements—has resisted physical abuse and exclusion on every continent, sometimes with great success. It has been no easy thing to go public, to fight against cultural odds, against insults and scorn, often against physical violence. The excluded did not inherit the morale with which to press for the right not to be discriminated against; they had to win it, against indifference and ridicule. They had to acquire the right to speak even against the prejudices of minority communities—thus the title of Marlon Riggs's film about his life as a gay black man, *Tongues Untied.* Interest groups had to organize against discrimination in hiring and housing, to obtain Braille texts for the blind, signing and captions for the deaf, and wheelchair access into public and private spaces. Whatever their rhetorical excesses, these movements for civil rights will long endure. Whatever their particularist rhetoric, they amount to unprecedented triumphs for the universalization of the human right to be different.

The demand for the right to be different opened up space for parallel developments in the university. Within academic professions, the civil rights generation revolted against a scholarship that consigned the racial caste system to the margins of American history and took male power for granted. The new social history of the 1960s was taken to heart by a new generation of scholars. Struggle, not paternalistic generosity, succeeded to some degree in integrating both faculties and subject matters in established departments. Historians, sociologists, anthropologists, psychologists, and literary scholars of women, as of blacks and other groups, fleshed out the distinct worlds they had to win—establishing that a population had been suppressed and silenced; exhuming buried work and exploring the humanity and resistance of the oppressed; trying to rethink society, history, and culture from the vantage point of the silenced, and showing that the "flaws" in American freedom were, in fact, at its core.

Entering faculties in large numbers, how could women and minorities fail to transform the questions being debated?

From their endeavors flowed—and continue to flow—splendid achievements. Spurious wholes were decomposed, exposed as partial and partisan. Studies of women and labor, of African Americans and Native Americans, of immigrants and racism mushroomed. Two decades on, histories of the world, of culture, and of literature are still shaking. The most cosmopolitan practitioners made serious efforts—no easy matter—to reintegrate the history the new critiques had torn asunder so that the racial caste system, for example, would no longer be a "peculiarity" off to the side of American history, an exceptional sidebar to the main saga of freedom, but a central feature of national life. The Houghton Mifflin textbooks, for all their imperfections, are among the fruits of these efforts.

But years of mainstream recalcitrance also fueled the forces of separatism and fragmentation. The arguments for distinct African-American, Chicano, women's, Asian, and gay—now "queer"—studies programs were considerable. Before these programs existed, their subjects were merrily neglected by mainline departments. Now history, sociology, English, and the rest have learned to be more ecumenical—a net good, not only for the members of minority groups exploring various histories, conditions, and literatures, but also for everyone else. This is the deep value of multiculturalism. The white American is ignorant (of him or herself, not to mention the larger history) without knowing the "people of color"; the man, the woman; the heterosexual, the homosexual; the Western, the non-Western. The student of any color who does not read Douglass or Ellison misses the core of American history and literature as much as the one who omits Hawthorne, Emerson, Melville, Whitman, or Twain. Serious multiculturalism is not a children's party where party favors are passed out to everyone to "celebrate" his or her "contribution"; it is reintegration into superior syntheses.

But alongside such integration, academic cultures of separation began to harden into fortified enclaves. Why? For one thing, there was ample (if often embattled) room for the new programs in sprawling institutions— "multiversities," Clark Kerr called them—that lacked any intellectual center, that were used to appealing to a multitude of constituencies, and whose modus operandi was to accord new space to interest groups. It is convenient to grumble, with Roger Kimball and Richard Bernstein, that the identity politics of the 1980s and 1990s is nothing but the reckless politics of the 1960s left to ferment on campus for twenty years. But the conservatives, still blinded by the traumas of the late 1960s, miss a crucial distinction. The lion's share of the pioneering work of historical reconstruction was done by scholars who had one foot in the Old Left or the civil rights and antiwar movements and therefore came to their specialties bearing something of a universalist or cosmopolitan bent. Historians of slavery like Eugene Genovese, Herbert Gutman, Leon Litwack, Lawrence W. Levine, and Nathan Irvin Huggins; historians of women like Gerda Lerner, Mary Ryan, Katherine Kish Sklar, Linda Gordon, and Ruth Rosen—all had the experience of mass movements before the separatist secessions and the hardening of identity boundaries.

But it was the late New Left politics of separatist rage, not the early New Left politics of universalist hope, that nurtured their recruits, the graduate students and young faculty who subsequently carried what is either harshly or wishfully called "the politics of the Left" into the academy and institutionalized (or interred) it there. Identity politics became an organizing principle among the academic cohorts who followed, whose political experience, if any, began in the late 1960s or thereafter. Politics for them was the politics of interest groups—however laced with revolutionary rhetoric. By the time students born in the late 1950s and 1960s arrived on campuses, identity politics had become the norm of the "Left," *the* tradition of protest. This generation had no direct memory of a unified Left. They had no feeling for a mass movement connecting campuses with off-campus politics. As adults they had never breathed the air of a left-of-center Democratic government. Their experience of active politics was segmented, not unified. By 1975, the universalist Left was thoroughly defeated—pulverized, in fact. Defeat was pervasive, taken for granted.

Cut off from ecumenical political hopes, the partisans of identity politics became preoccupied with what they might control in their immediate surroundings—language and imagery. Thus the singular influence of literary and cultural studies and the virtually self-satirizing obsession with rectifying the language of opponents. Like the rest of American society, the practitioners of identity politics resorted to legalistic regulation to address social problems. They had, by now, many laws and administrative rulings on their side, and a tradition of fighting for more. Campaigning against pornography, they took up Puritan crusades against unholy expression. They promulgated on-campus speech codes and sought to regulate dating. Fights over appropriate language, over symbolic representation in curriculum and cuisine, were to them the core of "politics." Affirmative action substituted for economic reconstruction. The new academic Left tended to mistake strong language for steady, consequential political engagement. They spoke confidently, belligerently, of "disruptions," "subversions," "ruptures," "contestations." The more their political life was confined to the library, the more their language bristled with aggression.

The distinct identity groupings on campus, once institutionalized, found reasons to remain distinct. They radiated savoir faire and solidarity. They seemed to offer the satisfactions of intellectual companionship and political passion at the same time—a heady mixture. Having struggled to overcome silences, they developed their own methods of silencing. They were uncomfortable with self-contradiction and individual difference. They closed ranks and protected turf, for their struggle was never-ending. Identities, however strenuously declared, remained embattled, ever in need of shoring up. Separatism was no longer a stage on the way to some sort of intellectual and political reconciliation; it was an institution and an intellectual given. Difference was vital, commonality moribund. Demands for race and gender blindness and inclusion tipped toward demands for all-consuming race and gender consciousness. Difference was practiced, commonality barely even thought.

For the participants, the benefits of the pursuit of identity were manifold: a sense of community, an experience of solidarity, a prefabricated reservoir of recruits. Identity groups offered ready-made acquaintanceship. From the outside, they seemed bonded. From inside the identity groups, the world looked whole. Try telling someone who feels the hunger for wholeness that this is a totalitarian principle, that he or she had better get used to the overlap and complexity of attachments.

The result on campus was identity politics—the recognition of a collective hurt, followed by the mistaking of a group position for a "culture," followed by the mistaking of a "culture" for a politics. In a world where other people seemed to have chosen sides, and where, worse, they approached you—even menaced you—on the assumption that you were what your identity card proclaimed you to be, it seemed a necessity to find one's strength among one's people. From popular culture to government policy, the world had evidently assigned its memberships. Identity politics aimed to turn necessity to virtue. The demand for the respect for difference—for what came to be called multiculturalism—often swerved into the creation of parallel monocultures. Since the demands of identity politics were far more winnable in the university than elsewhere, the struggles of identity groups flourished there. The damage was both intellectual and political. For the recruits, the fierce pleasures of identity politics outweighed the rigors of cosmopolitanism. A political imperative to cut across academic boundaries and address poverty and inequality in the larger world? Not of interest, not sexy. Identity politics amounted to demobilization into a cloister.

While the Right was occupying the heights of the political system, the assemblage of groups identified with the Left were marching on the English department. They were seizing power in women's studies, African-American studies, ethnic studies. Insurgencies that began in claims to dignity, recoveries from exclusion and denigration, developed a hardening of the boundaries. Isolated, frequently tenuous, scorned by and hostile to the prevailing university culture, these programs sustained a good deal of separatist rancor. The best of these programs were committed to cosmopolitanism and produced excellent scholarship, though most of the best scholars found places among reformed departments in the old-line disciplines. Frequently, however, the separate programs nurtured a "culture" of exultation and victimization (exultation *through* victimization), a victimization the program felt itself, having to fight for funds against the hostility of established departments. They were consumed with factional disputes so bitter that the more cosmopolitan faculty frequently withdrew in sadness or disgust to their home departments.

The appeal of identity politics to an incoming student is easy to understand. Identity politics is already a tradition in its second generation, transmitted, modified, and transmitted again, institutionalized in departments and courses, supported by a critical mass of faculty and a surrounding, permissive ambivalence, embedded in living units, jargons, mentors, gurus, conferences, associations, journals, publishing subfields, bookstore sections, and jokes. By the time they arrive on campus, especially an elite, cosmopolitan, private campus, many students—particularly the political activists—have already absorbed the spirit of hard-edged identity politics from the media, secondary school, or home. Awaiting the perplexed is an identity package—academic studies, perspectivist theory, identity politics, social networks, "diversity" workshops—a whole world organized around identity culture. The newcomer arrives at the university disposed, in a common formulation, "to learn about herself," rather than to learn about the world and herself in it. She finds encouragement. She finds exclusive identity groups for partying, dancing, listening to music in a familiar style. She finds the Black Sociology Association and the Asian Business Association.

Protected by the academic superstructure as a relatively cheap alternative to disruptive protest, the separate programs cultivate a rapture of marginality. "Difference feminism" becomes the order of the day—not so much among feminists in the larger society as in the protected enclaves of the academy. Women's lives are said to be stalked by the fear of rape and sexual harassment; by pornography; by the tyranny of "compulsory heterosexuality"; by the imposition of male-dominated logic over "women's ways of knowing." Single-race or single-ethnicity living units are justified on the basis of the hostility of dominant whites. Black students, whether admitted through affirmative action or not, frequently poorly prepared, feel the glare of white suspicion, and huddle together in separate groups—leading to yet more stigmatization. A fraternity party that turns into a mock "slave auction," a vicious misogynistic campaign against a feminist activist—such disgusting incidents are interpreted as proofs of endangerment. The presumption is that embattled individuals and perspectives need official protection within the walls of exclusive precincts, that otherwise they are weak.

Nourishing separateness, the separatist programs find themselves in turn vulnerable to protests by internal separatists. At the University of Michigan in 1991, a group of women of color walk out of a women's studies course protesting that "only one-third" of the assignments were written by women of color. At the University of California, Davis, a Native

American graduate student in a seminar on women's history complains that a book about Italian-American workers does not discuss Native Americans. A gay English professor at the University of Western Ontario in 1993 creates a course on literature by gays and lesbians, only to have the lesbians walk out, claiming that he as a male has no right to teach "their experience." In private, any honest defender of identity politics acknowledges such "excesses"—an instant before pointing to the ways they are exaggerated by journalists; and anyway, they are anecdotal, and haven't right-wing writers and pundits gone overboard exaggerating their like? Feminists and leftists are loath to wash their dirty linen in public, where the enemy may be out collecting data on their domestic habits. But these incidents of small-mindedness and crude prejudice are legion, whatever the politics of those who report them.

Sectarianism is the worm in the history of every all-or-nothing movement. But this is sectarianism with a distinctive and self-consuming logic. For identity-based movements, the margin is the place to be. Within each margin, there are always more margins to carve out. Postmodernist thought confirms that there is no center; or rather, that those who claim the center—who claim a common truth or even the possibility that a common truth is attainable—are false universalizers, colonizers, hegemonists. The center, if there is one, is the malevolent Other. But this false center—so the argument goes—is only a margin in disguise. The margins are bastions from which to launch intellectual raids on a center that has no right to be central, and has, moreover, lost confidence in itself. Summoning philosophical allies from Paris, the partisans of difference as a supreme principle tack together a ramshackle unity based not so much on a universalist premise or ideal as on a common enemy—the Straight White Male who, trying to obscure his power and interests, disguises himself as the human in "humanism." Within the identity groupings, humanism is dead, a dirty word, a ghost that deserves to be put out of its misery.

The whole edifice of postmodern theorizing is topped by a spire flashing a single slogan: "Objectivity," in the words of a Berkeley activist, "is only another word for white male subjectivity." The reverence for difference ossifies into uniformity.

5. Culture as Surrogate Politics, Campus as Surrogate World

Accused of politicizing everything, identity politics responds that politics is already everywhere; that interests dress up as truth but are only interests; that power is already everywhere and the only question is who is going to have it.

The slogan of choice derives from the late 1960s' women's movement: "The personal is political." In origin, this was a rhetorical masterstroke. That movement's early theorists pointed out that male domination had entrenched itself precisely by excluding from political discussion key questions about women's position. Nobody voted that women should do the lioness's share of the housework; the sexual division of labor was simply taken for granted. In the world of modern capitalism, the segregation of private and public spheres was the master development that consolidated the collective rule of men. To insist that "the personal is political" meant that a man's home was not his exclusive castle, because it was a woman's castle as well. Whatever men did to women, like whatever whites did to blacks, was not private business; it deserved to be brought into the open. The domestic sphere was one of power relations, and so such questions as who took care of the children, who got to have orgasms, who cleaned the house, and who had the right to family property were properly understood as matters of collective power—properly subject to the actions of social movements and, in the case of such issues as abortion and domestic abuse, government policy. This was no mere theoretical flourish; it had great consequence. In subsequent decades, the conversion of sexual harassment into a crime and the growing legal and police sensitivity to spousal abuse followed from the insistence that "the personal is political."

It was this new understanding—not the French thinker Michel Foucault's brilliance or his Gallic and gay aura—that accounts for the post-Sixties academic fascination with the "poststructuralist" theory of which Foucault remains the most influential representative. Americans not normally tempted by the arcana of social or philosophical theory, least of all the thick and erudite French variety, flocked to Foucault's lectures in the

1970s and early 1980s in New York, the San Francisco Bay Area, and elsewhere. Why was he all the rage and why has he remained so? Only partly because he was the Nietzschean lyricist of self-definition, self-revolt, and self-transcendence, with particular reference to sex; not solely because he was the all-knowledgeable master perspectivist on a grand scale.

The other reason why Foucault became a compulsory reference point, if not compulsory reading, was his insistence with great panache that every sphere of life—every profession, indeed, every field of knowledge —was saturated with power. Knowledge was "power/knowledge." So-called private relations were, in effect, ministates. All relations were power relations. Culture was governed—or "constituted"—by discourses that established who and what would be central or marginal, major or minor. The personal was, in short, political—perhaps so much so as to be nothing *but* political. Language was political. Clothing was political. "Lifestyles"—and sexual styles—were political. Whom one slept with, and how, was who one was, which in turn was what one believed. Indeed, for Foucault, "resistance" was merely another aspect of power, the means by which all-embracing power knew itself. In this fundamentally sado-masochistic world, resistance was swallowed up, doomed. In a time of political blockage on the broad scale, this was what the enclaves of the academic Left wanted to hear.

Then university life could come to feel like a consolation prize. If the Right held political power, what did it matter? This bad deal felt even better than compensation. It felt like an opportunity to change life— immediate, lived life—through direct action. And so the blurring of the line between culture and politics perfectly suited the movements that succeeded the New Left. They had vernaculars, turfs, sectoral music, and literature to protect and develop. There were now enough women and minorities at the university to feel like communities unto themselves. There were conferences to attend, journals to scrutinize, theoretical tendencies to compete with. From "the personal is political" it was an easy glide to "only the personal is really political"—that is, only what I and people like me experience ought to be the object of my interest. There was a swerve, in short, toward conventional interest-group politics, paralleling the philosophical swerve from universalism to the denial that any but group-bounded perspectives were possible. The universalism of the early women's movement, which sought for women the rights and powers guaranteed for all by the Enlightenment, yielded to a preoccupation with the inner life of feminism and the distinct needs of feminists.

So, too, with people of color, especially blacks—the swerve from civil rights, emphasizing a universal condition and universalizable rights, to cultural separatism, emphasizing difference and distinct needs. Affirmative action proved just successful enough to create a critical mass of African Americans on campus who felt simultaneously heartened, challenged, marooned, and embittered. Having been told they were nobodies, they were now in a position to insist that they were somebodies. Affirmative action helped propel many of them into the academy, but now they felt intense pressure to justify themselves to institutions that historically had despised them. They were never done proving themselves to a suspicious majority. They were still the lower caste in a caste system. On top of the routine self-doubt stirred up in a competitive culture, they had special rages to bear. They had to strain to prove themselves "the best blacks" when they still couldn't get taxi drivers (including blacks) to stop or storekeepers to open their doors. Whites followed them suspiciously in shops, shot them startled and hostile looks on the street, ran out of elevators to avoid being alone with them, and went out of their way to try to prove that they were inferior. Suspected of receiving "special treatment," they knew that even after graduation they would earn less than whites— considerably less in the case of men. And then whites lectured them about the virtues of color blindness! Whites had the luxury of fancying themselves nonracial because they belonged to the ruling race. Who but blacks could feel what they felt? What was the alternative to exclusive identity groups?

The dynamic of identity politics is self-confirming. A people against whom boundaries were drawn respond by fortifying those very boundaries. The newcomers gain dignity: they are a "culture." Cultures are not to be tampered with. Cultures are entitled to respect, recognition. By insisting on culture, one fights the power. Group secession undercuts whites' (and others) opportunities to demonstrate openness and tolerance, whence they decry balkanization as if shocked, shocked, to discover it was invented yesterday.* In the university even more than in the larger society, prepackaged identities multiply. Group agglomeration comes to feel automatic. When everyone else seems to have found a group to eat with, party with, hang out with, and date, the newcomer feels the pressure to find one as well—or suffer the discomfort of being unmoored. Even students who feel uneasy about the prefabricated categories feel peer pressure to identify with one—for self-defense and self-definition. The group allays what is already an adolescent anxiety about finding a place. But the spread of identity-group culture heightens that anxiety in the first place.

Under these pressures, even the definitive antigroup, the None-of-the-Aboves, are driven to declare themselves a group. As we have seen, for all the profusion of identity politics, interracial liaisons have, since the 1960s, produced a fast-growing population that fits poorly into the standard identity array. So it is that, in the Eighties, at the University of California, Berkeley, students of mixed racial origin founded a Multiracial Intercultural Student Coalition (MISC). They resented having to choose a single race or ethnicity on application forms—yet knew that "Refuse to State" would disqualify them from fellowships earmarked for members of specified minority groups. Regarded with suspicion by the professedly "pure" (although "pure-blooded" racial types are in fact rare), the mixed-race students frequently date each other—becoming, in effect, an identity group, even if the couple are by origins African-Korean or Japanese-Caucasian Americans. There is also a logic of fission. Hyphenations proliferate. Inside the lesbian group, African-American lesbians feel the need for group recognition of their "distinct experience," whereupon those whose lovers are African American decide likewise, and organize separately from African Americans whose lovers are white . . . and so on. What Freud called "the narcissism of small differences" is

---

* Group self-enclosure was apparently acceptable when it was arranged by fraternities, sororities, and exclusive clubs, but in the hands of blacks and other minorities it is suddenly all the rage to denounce balkanization. The term was trundled out by Senator Orrin Hatch (R-Utah), never known for courageous fights against racial segregation in housing, schools, or hiring, when, in 1993, he denounced President Clinton's Justice Department nominee Lani Guinier as "an architect of a theory of racial preference that if enacted would push America down the road of racial balkanization."

relentless. "Diversity" insists that everyone march in lockstep while proclaiming how different they are.

Self-encapsulation develops apace, especially at institutions with large minority populations. At Berkeley in April 1990, a two-day student strike took place for accelerated race-based hiring and admissions. In the days leading up to the strike, the organizers made little effort to explain their demands, let alone defend them. I was teaching an introductory sociology lecture course contrasting the 1960s with the 1980s, and was that day scheduled to screen *The Times of Harvey Milk,* a film about the assassinated gay San Francisco politician. I told the class instead that I would simply meet with any students who showed up to discuss the strike issues. Only about 20 out of some 450 did, though they were of every racial description. A group of strikers strode to the back of the hall and started to shout. I invited them to join the discussion. A black man yelled: "We're dying out there!" This line has echoed in my mind often since. I asked him, "How is admitting more black students and hiring more black faculty going to stop the dying out there?" There was no response.

Most of the violence of the black ghetto is either a historical consequence of slavery and poverty—infant mortality, preventable disease—or the direct result of young black men killing other young black men in the course of criminal activity. The desperate economic condition of the inner cities, exacerbated by the drug trade, bears the stamp of racial oppression, though if it were not blacks bearing the burden of unemployment, it would be some other Americans. Black upward mobility from, or into, the middle class is much to be desired for its own sake. In the meantime, the black poor are left desperate and the residents demoralized. Few political campaigns are launched against the impoverishment of the cities. No off-campus political coalitions are asking for student support. There is little belief that politics can touch, no less bind, the deep wounds of inequality. In the hothouse of the campus, the diversity rhetoric of identity politics short-circuits the necessary discussion of what ought to be done about all the dying out there. Along the way, it is convenient to accuse a liberal professor of racism, to campaign against a campus newspaper that publishes a conservative columnist, to vent anger against a pliant university administration.

In 1992, the sociology department at Berkeley set out to hire an assistant professor to teach race and ethnic relations. The faculty voted to offer the position to Loïc Wacquant, a well-qualified young French scholar who had written several books, published scores of articles, and collaborated with two distinguished sociologists: Pierre Bourdieu of the Collège de France, and William Julius Wilson of the University of Chicago. Himself white—one of his competitors was Japanese American—Wacquant had written his dissertation under Wilson on the world of black boxers. To do so, he had joined a black gym and learned to box. The normally contentious Berkeley faculty voted unanimously in his favor. In doing so, the department overrode strong objections from many outspoken graduate students (a) that the candidate did not specialize in race and ethnic relations (though Wacquant had written a monograph on relations between French colonists and natives in New Caledonia and many articles on the political economy of the American black ghetto); (b) that he had applied fifty-nine days late (true, but the university had never been a stickler for deadlines); (c) that he was arrogant and a bad listener (never an impediment to faculty hiring); and (d) that this particular position had for two decades focused on Chicano studies, and neither of its two previous occupants had gotten tenure, thereby demonstrating the faculty's contempt for that field. The opinion was voiced that the previous holder of the Chicano studies position, a popular teacher whose tenure case had become mired in controversy and who had subsequently accepted a position elsewhere, had run into trouble because he was a self-declared homosexual. In fact, this professor's gayness never played any part in his tenure fight, but the activists, feeling wounded and convinced that the faculty was indifferent to their desires, were not inclined to give the faculty the benefit of the doubt. They were more impressed that the faculty was majority white—and unimpressed that it was the most racially integrated department on campus.

Enraged activist graduate students organized a weeklong boycott of graduate classes. This was the students' deepest political investment in many years. A rhetoric of justice, inflamed by a general sense of neglect, was coupled with a legalistic concern about deadlines and a not very radical preference for academic specialization. That Wacquant would be the only member of the department from abroad, knowledgeable about racial and ethnic relations on several continents, was not a "diversity" that interested them.

I sat down for lunch during the class boycott with two anti-Wacquant graduate student activists and pointed out a flock of factual errors, not to mention tendentious interpretations, in their leaflet. "There is no 'truth,' " one of them, a very intelligent woman, said, "there are only truth effects." "Truth effects": here was postmodernist nihilism come home. She meant that propositions are no more than rhetorical, "discourse all the way down," judged "true" only arbitrarily. But why should there be universities, other than to convey status and take unemployed youth off the streets, if all they do is hurl around transient and arbitrary statements?

The university administration had no official view of truth effects. But it did, of course, hold its procedures to be precious. Although it was not in the habit of rejecting departmental hiring decisions because of late applications, it was afraid of litigation on procedural grounds and eager to cool out the protest. Given racial changes in the student body, the administration feared the prospect of endless volatility: Asian Americans charging discrimination (there had already been litigation and a congressional investigation to this effect), African Americans and Chicano/Latinos angry at their underrepresentation relative to state population, and whites complaining in both directions—each activist group at odds with the others as university funds were shrinking. Conservative administrators from University of California President David Gardner on down were aware that state demographics were ticking away. Sooner or later, they feared, the legislature would abandon the university unless it shed the impression of a white skew. The Berkeley administration ruled that the sociology search had to be reopened.* It was. Wacquant reapplied on

---

* What was at work at Berkeley was routine bureaucratic timidity and politicking rather than the sympathy for identity politics that often plays a part in campus injustice elsewhere. In one egregious 1993 case, two students at Vassar College were, on less than five days' notice, brought up on the charge of harassing a gay activist by leaving a scurrilous message on his answering machine. They were prohibited from bringing their parents or attorneys into the hearing room, and were testified against by the very administrator who had brought the charges. They were refused permission to bring forth evidence that the accuser had previously identified another student as the perpetrator, only to have withdrawn that charge under the threat of legal action. They were refused permission to conduct a voice analysis of a tape that the administration had already played in living units in an effort to identify the offender. One of the students charged, conveniently Arab American, was found guilty of collusion with the other, a white leftist, who was himself found guilty of nothing. Finding

time and the department chose him again. This time the faculty vote was less than unanimous, but still overwhelming. The students, now fatalistic and distracted by a campaign to defend their interests as teaching assistants, did not resume their protest.

The point is this: the Wacquant boycott was the main activity of the activist "Left" during a year when California's state government was savaging the budget for all levels of education. Student fees (the official California euphemism for tuition) had been rising fast, more than doubling within four years. As a result, many eligible students of color, among others, were being deprived of a college education. Against these cuts, there was virtually no public protest from students at Berkeley or at any other California campus. Against cuts in public schools, the same silence prevailed. Not until the Republicans seized the national initiative with the midterm elections of November 1994, slashing welfare, school aid, and other domestic measures, did campus identity groups federate around a program of common opposition on issues reaching off-campus. But the protest against Wacquant—how sweet it was to focus on faculty treachery close at hand! The campaign was overloaded with symbols; it made for confrontation; it might be winnable to boot. The episode was reminiscent of the story of the fool on his hands and knees searching the sidewalk under a streetlight. "What are you looking for?" asks a passerby. "My watch." "Where did you lose it?" "Over there," says the fool, pointing to the other side of the street. "Then why are you looking here?" asks the passerby. "Because it's dark over there," says the fool.

It's dark over there in the world of devastated and desperate neighborhoods. Even on campus, fees rise, courses vanish, jobs for graduates dwindle. The national political scene is forbidding. The public at large has little confidence that problems can be solved by government action. Even Americans unpersuaded by Ronald Reagan that "government is not

---

himself ostracized, however, the latter dropped out of Vassar and transferred elsewhere. In the Vassar case, among others, campus administrators who support the extreme conduct codes, "diversity" workshops, and occasional witch hunts of identity politics frequently draw credentials from the movements of the 1960s, and are therefore assumed to have been activists themselves. But in general, these administrators were peripheral to those far-off campus struggles. More to the point is that insofar as they owe their positions to affirmative action, they are reluctant to offend identity activists.

the solution, government is the problem," lack the faith that anyone knows what to do about cities, jobs, education, or race relations. For all that conservatives argue for good old-fashioned culture, there is no prospect that "traditional family values" can actually heal a broken society. (After all, many blacks believe in parental toughness, and welfare mothers want jobs, to no avail.) What is lacking is not so much values as the means to implement them.

But not until an emergency befell them—not until the Republican offensive of the spring of 1995—did activists mobilize, on campus or off, any attractive political force that cut across identity boundaries. Not that there has been any shortage of students who long to "make a difference" in the world off campus. In vast numbers, probably comparable to the 1960s, volunteers tutor, teach, work in homeless shelters. Their numbers are all the more striking given the high percentage of college students who have to hold down jobs while going to school. "Service" is the unheralded youth movement of the 1990s. But a politics aimed at changing institutions does not appeal to these hands-on activists. The idea of sweeping change seems abstract, futile. They don't want grand designs, they want palpable results. The volunteers have little faith that they, or anyone, can transform the larger social order. Many are politically conservative, or indifferent, and do not look to the government to improve matters. There is a sharp divide between them and the practitioners of identity politics. Yet both camps implicitly accept the belief that nothing much can be done about poverty. Talk about silences!

6. The Profusion of Identities

Identity politics is not an alien excrescence. It is as American as the panoply of pies in the supermarket freezer. The multiplication of ethnicities stems from more than three centuries of human imports, starting with slaves. The campus centrifuge is the result of a long-deferred opening up of the professional classes. So is identity politics on the national scene, the demand that women and minorities be represented as such in government positions. This much excoriated emphasis is, in one sense, an extension of the normal pluralism of American politics—the practice of balancing tickets, for example, between North and South, urban and rural, Protestants and Catholics. On top of such rituals, the 1960s movements popularized identity labels; sociology played a part, too, popularizing the concepts of "identity," "roles," "ethnicity"—describing a sense of social life that many people already intuited, helping make it legitimate and turn it to cant in rapid sequence. Who knows how many people would have told interviewers about their ethnic feelings if the interviewers hadn't asked in the first place?

But the contemporary passion for difference is also the consequence of unsettled psychological states. The American pace of change constantly eats away at identity—and just as reliably kicks up materials for the manufacture, the stitching together, of new possibilities. The search for hard-edged social identities is surely an overcompensation. Americans have gravitated toward racial, ethnic, religious, sexual, and subcultural distinctions partly to build ramparts against confusion. They long to locate what T. S. Eliot called "a fixed point in the turning world." In fact, firmness of identity is hard to come by—so much so that the psychologist Robert Jay Lifton has rightly identified one of today's dominant psychological types as "protean." Shape-shifting is normal. All this diffuseness and flux is unnerving. An intolerance for one's own confusion generates a frantic search for hard-and-fast identity labels. Beneath the flux, America has developed the countertendency toward a fundamentalist identity culture.

None of this is new, but in recent decades the pressures on traditional identities have mounted. The stabilities that cultivate firm (what David Riesman called "inner-directed") character have grown feeble. Old-line churches have lost their hold on religious life, to be replaced by the more up-to-date. Partly to find solid ground to rest on, legions of believers find solace in returning to fundamentals. They are—and what is this if not an identity that refuses identity?—"born-again." At the same time, family ties and gender roles have loosened. Correspondingly, the churn of identity has grown more rapid. Increases in divorce and remarriage, cohabitation and illegitimacy, multiple parentage, and a growing diversity of ethnic and religious attachments make for recombinant families. The forms of personality that develop within the crucible of the family develop in more complicated ways. Children find many—or no—models of adulthood in their vicinity. They belong to several families at a time, each of which makes its demands, requires its negotiations, incites its rebellions, and none of which makes unrivaled claims. The unsettling of American families, in turn, contributes to the disarray of other traditional fixities. One fruit of the feminist revolution is that there are today a larger number of legitimate ways of being female and male. The old strict polarities persist—homemaker versus breadwinner, frail versus muscular, emotional versus rational—but alternatives are visible. Many women and men mix and match the dizzying variants of gender identity.

What is "Americanization" into this churning nation, so multiplicitous, baggy, and overall purposeless? The choices multiply, the vertigo grows, and the market offers an apparently endless array of choices—Identities Lite. The "other-directed" personality, predisposed to rely on peers and the mass media for identity cues, was identified by David Riesman almost half a century ago, but today this radar-driven modern, always in search of cues as to the right thing to feel or think, finds a bewildering variety of others to be directed by. The media rain down a storm of styles. Taste revision is routine. Thanks to remote control devices, niche television, Internet chat groups, and specialized magazines, not only do style choices multiply, so does the ease of knowing what other styles are available and coasting from one to another. Media saturation and the marketing of youth culture institutionalize the cues for self-transformation into a veritable rebellion industry. Today's media, organized by targeted markets and consumption subcultures, capitalize on identity boundaries. Cable television drops black, Spanish-language, and other ethnically distinct programming schedules into more than 60 percent of American homes. Although ethnic marketing campaigns are nothing new, a considerable distance has been traveled from the "You don't have to be Jewish to love Levy's" rye bread ads of the Fifties to Gatorade's "¡Lleno de Gusto!" in the Nineties. Half of the Fortune 1000 companies have ethnic marketing campaigns. Procter & Gamble puts 5 percent of its massive advertising budget into ethnic-specific ads. AT&T advertises in twenty different languages. Today it remains true that immigrants want to assimilate, but the America into which they hope to do so is not the America of white bread. It is an America where the supermarket shelves groan beneath the varieties of bagels, sourdough, rye, seven-grain, and other mass-produced loaves. One belongs by being slightly different, though in a predictable way.

Now, too, there are material incentives for preserving, or claiming, a version (however lite) of ethnic, racial, or religious identity, many of which, today, are paradoxical. Partly because the state legitimizes labels and allocates resources accordingly, people affirm them. "Ethnic pride" develops even where ethnicities have just been invented. "Asian American" is a newly devised category, and can therefore hardly be said to be a "culture" transmitted from generation to generation. What does it describe? Race—a substitute for the widely disliked term "Oriental"? If it describes the continent of national origin, should immigrants from the South Asian subcontinent be classified "Asian American"? If the category is cultural, does it make sense to group third-generation Japanese Americans with Hmong tribesmen, educated Koreans, and the newly arrived Hong Kong poor? People sort and resort themselves, even with respect to claims that, if they are to have any meaning, must logically be matters of fixed inheritance. The number of Americans reporting themselves as "American Indian" or "Native American" in the census grew by 255 percent between 1960 and 1990—from 552,000 to 1,959,000. Most of the growth must be among "new Indians," people choosing—or admitting to—the label. Between 1980 and 1990, the number of Cajuns leaped from 30,000 to 600,000, and the number of French Canadians from 780,000 to 2,200,000, while the number claiming French ancestry fell from 13 million to 10 million.

If "culture" means anything, it is something that persists. But how long must it persist before it qualifies, and who is to say? Only in a fast-food setting, in a society that manufactures novelty, can one speak so casually of "hip-hop culture," "rock culture," "Asian-American" or "European-American culture." The invention of identity is easily mocked for its vagaries and inconsistencies. Yet an insurgent "culture" may succeed in winning the loyalty of large numbers of people, and at the start, who knows just how deeply it will reach, and for how long? The Deaf movement, barely one generation old, is representative of the strengths of post-1960s "ethnicization." The practice of capitalizing Deaf signifies more than a new respect for the those who cannot hear: it has become a sign of activism, with a popular base, with heroes and histories. It includes a commitment to American Sign Language, an active bilingualism, a call for representation (marked in 1988 by the successful demand that the incoming president of Gallaudet University in Washington be a deaf person). It extends as far as the rejection of cochlear implants that are intended to restore a certain degree of hearing. The claim to a Deaf culture is, today, no laughing matter.

Are multiculturalism and identity politics nothing more than the impassioned reinvention of the ethnic- and religion-based local politics of a bygone era? Are universities, art museums, textbooks, and publishers' segmented lists today's equivalents of the working-class cities, with their foreign-language newspapers and specialized cuisines, where political tickets had to be balanced among the Irish, the Italians, and the Jews, and Nelson Rockefeller conspicuously wolfed down his knishes in Brooklyn on his way to the governor's mansion in Albany?

In certain ways, contemporary identity politics does resemble traditional pluralism, but there are crucial differences between today's obsessive elevation of difference and the long-standing ethnic diversity of the northern and midwestern cities. The old mixed-ethnic urban slate was meant to create a working majority in politics; today's cultivation of cultural difference tends to detract from majoritarian thinking. Nothing is more responsible for the current impasse than the black-white divide, which is unlike any other. White Americans may not be frozen in their attachment to white supremacy, but the difference that does not melt is the yawning gulf, in opportunities and neighborhoods, in ways of life and worldviews, between black and white.

In fact, one result of the ethnic revival was to eclipse the uniqueness of the African-American experience. Once ethnicity was everywhere, it was, in a sense, nowhere, and the black experience was rhetorically neutralized. This blur was frequently well-meaning but it was also misleading, even euphemistic. It obscured the special antagonisms and discriminations that whites had imposed on blacks for more than three centuries. Black-white disparities in social condition remained sui generis, and they were likely to prove more intractable than any other racial or ethnic conflicts, past or present. For many blacks, the idea of multiculturalism, then, at first looked like something of a shield. If white racism had victimized many besides blacks, it was more convincingly criticized. The proliferation of "difference" and the rhetoric of multiculturalism permitted blacks to deflect the charge that they sought "special treatment." They could present themselves as one color in the rainbow.

But considering how important "difference" is supposed to be, this notion of "people of color" erased too many differences. In contrast to that of American-born blacks, in many respects the experience of today's Asian and Latin American immigrants—even black immigrants from the Caribbean—is closer to that of European immigrants a century ago. They confront discrimination fueled by economic distress. They cope with deprecation. They fight over scarce resources. But the black-white racial script, throughout its variations, carries a charge that was lacking from nineteenth century tensions between, say, the native-born and the Irish or the Jews. What degree of racial and ethnic integration will take place in America from now on is, of course, unknowable. Because many taboos have broken down since the 1960s, it is even conceivable that the new Asian and Latin American—and Caribbean—immigrants and their descendants, over two or three generations, will succeed in assimilating, promoted socially to the status of "honorary whites," gaining acceptance within a remelted majority. Then the decisive gulf would be black/non-black—not to the advantage of the majority of the native-born black population. At a remove from the desperately poor blacks, a cosmopolitan professional class may be emerging, racially intermarried, ethnically complex, respectful of difference but not obsessed by it, half in the white world, half out, somehow at ease with its self-contradictions—yet a world away from the ghettos and racial furies that preoccupy the American black majority.

On campus, today's obsession with difference is distinguished, too, by the haughtiness of the tribes and the scope of their intellectual claims. Many exponents of identity politics are fundamentalists—in the language of the academy, "essentialists"—and the belief in essential group differences easily swerves toward a belief in superiority. In the hardest version of identity thinking, women are naturally cooperative, Africans naturally inventive, and so on. These pure capacities were once muscled into submission by Western masculine force—so the argument goes—then suppressed by rigged institutions, and now need liberating. Sometimes what is sought is a license to pursue a monoculture. Only the members can (or should) learn the language of the club. Only African Americans should get jobs teaching African-American studies; conversely, African Americans should get jobs teaching *only* African-American studies. Men, likewise, have no place in women's studies. As the T-shirt slogan had it: "It's a Black Thing, You Wouldn't Understand." As Sister Souljah rapped: "If my world's black and yours is white/How the hell could we think alike." Essentialists, when they secede from the commons, dismantle it.

The cultivation of difference is nothing new, but the sheer profusion of identities that claim separate political standing today is unprecedented. And here is perhaps the strangest novelty in the current situation: that the ensemble of group recognitions should take up so much of the energy of what passes for the Left. It is often for good reason that differences have multiplied, making their claims, exposing the fraudulence of the universalist claims of the past. Not everyone is male, white, hearing, heterosexual. Very well. But what is a Left if it is not, plausibly at least, the voice of a whole people? For the Left as for the rest of America, the question is not whether to recognize the multiplicity of American groups, the variety of American communities, the disparity of American experiences. Those exist as long as people think they exist. The question is one of proportion. What is a Left without a commons, even a hypothetical one? If there is no people, but only peoples, there is no Left.

6

The Recoil

1. The Scarlet Letters

If American culture is centrifugal, and things are falling apart, what is the center that is not holding? Presumably some core of principles—individual rights and opportunities—united by the affirmation that America, heartland of the West, is home.

There is, in the end, no more coherence in the defense of the center than in the assertion of essential difference, but there is a common rhetoric. The center under bombardment by barbarians is "Western liberal values," "civilization," "culture," "reason." The tribute to American greatness joins three themes: the embrace of a canonized American (and Western) history and literature, the opposition to group rights, and the affirmation of free speech. The genius of the attack on "political correctness" in the Nineties was to fuse the three, polarize opinion against them, and thereby seize the initiative.

In the polarized view, the center stands for truth long ago arrived at and agreed on by reasonable men. The center is bedrock America, which is a "way of life," a "dream," an avatar of morality. Its history was long ago collectively understood and engraved in granite, where it must remain fixed and available for the reverence of future generations. This history transcends perspectives, particularities, self-interested passions. It affirms that the United States of America is the incarnation of opportunity, transcending gender and race, a guardian of culture, education, and the arts, resplendent in its unmatched human achievement. The mission of cultural institutions is to pass the heritage on, not trade it away for a mess of multicultural pottage.

This tribute affirms that individuals have more than rights. Thanks to this country, Americans have opportunities to realize their powers according to their merits. The idea that people should ever be rewarded (and others, therefore, punished) according to group characteristics flies in the face of a belief that the market, using objective test scores, already adjudicates merit. Individuals are already free to attain what they were meant to attain, and the heavy hand of the State should not interfere. By the same token, America's sturdy individuals need free speech, now under assault from "thought police" decreeing "watch what you say" in ever-widening circles of patrol.

In principle, canon, opportunity, and free speech ought to be mutually detachable. Mixes and matches ought to be eminently debatable. It is logically possible, for example, to support a common curriculum that is both Western and non-Western; to support affirmative action in student admissions but disapprove it for faculties or the Supreme Court; and to oppose restrictions on campus speech but encourage students to conduct themselves with decorum. The charge of "political correctness," however, rests on the presumption that there are only two sides. (So does the standard multiculturalist defense.) Charges of "political correctness" were, and still are, flung about with alacrity, and often enough denied with equally unheeding ferocity. Both sides agree on polarization.

The counteroffensive against the redoubts of the academic Left began in the fall and winter of 1990–91, when magazine and newspaper readers were suddenly regaled with reports of an epidemic raging through academia. Although the academic curriculum and its jargon are not generally of broad journalistic interest, nor admissions schemes, nor restrictions on student life—sexual conduct codes passed without press attention for decades—suddenly these were all of burning interest. The editorial pack, ever eager to sniff out trends by sampling each others' noses, went into full panic. Within a few months, waves of moral alarm were rolling from the *New York Times* ("The Rising Hegemony of the Politically Correct: Academia's New Orthodoxy") to *U.S. News & World Report* and *Time,* and, not least, cover stories in *Newsweek* ("Thought Police"), *New York* ("Are You Politically Correct?"), *The New Republic,* and *The Atlantic,* which featured a long excerpt from Dinesh D'Souza's book *Illiberal Education.* "Tenured radicals are trying to turn campuses into authoritarian ministates," read the pull-quote in a George Will *Newsweek* column. President Bush, not normally concerned with campus trends or the fate of free speech but knowing a no-risk issue when he saw it, contributed a University of Michigan commencement speech on May 4, 1991, deploring "the new intolerance" sweeping the universities and denouncing what he called "the boring politics of division and derision." Ridicule, indignation, and uproar rippled outward through talk shows and news reports, and flowed through millions of eddies and inlets of private conversation into the great sea of opinion and mood where popular sentiment forms. The maxim that the power of the media is not necessarily to tell us what to think but the power to tell us what to think *about,* was thunderously confirmed. PC suddenly stood for something other than Personal Computers. A popular phrase was born.

Among the periodicals in the NEXIS database, the term "politically correct" and its variants appeared 7 times in 1988, 15 times in 1989, 66 times in 1990, 1,553 times in 1991, 2,672 times in 1992, and 4,643 times in 1993. For that matter, no symposium of left-wing academics, especially in literature, history, or cultural studies, lacked its counterattacks on reactionaries who, we were told, cloaked their own orthodoxy (even racism or sexism) by pretending that the textbooks and universities that once excluded people of color and women had, in that more bucolic time, been protected pastures of freedom—at least until barbarians of the 1960s aimed their mortars and bazookas at the ivy-covered ivory tower. In 1993, television's Comedy Central began a weekly series, *Politically Incorrect*; Jackie Mason called his one-man Broadway show *Jackie Mason, Politically Incorrect.* In 1994, a comic Hollywood version of Wesleyan University, *PCU,* was released, and in 1994–95, *Politically Correct*

Bedtime Stories by James Finn Garner was on the best-seller list. Even mockery was, in turn, a move in the accusatory game—fodder for countercharges. Whether the topic was textbooks, museum shows, sexual harassment, hate speech, or racial and sexual representation in Congress, the president's Cabinet, symphony orchestras, or university faculties, the topic of political correctness became an obsession and a maelstrom—easier to enter than to leave.

Properly speaking, the phrase "politically correct" was recycled; the term had been around since the 1930s. *Correct* was a Stalinist relic. In a milieu where certain texts (the "science" of Marxism-Leninism), a certain nation (the Union of Soviet Socialist Republics), and above all a certain man (Stalin) or, for dissenters within the tradition, men (Lenin and Trotsky) were held to have cracked the code of history and to have come into possession of knowledge of how the world was to move forward, *correct* was a certificate. *Correct* transcended *right*. It conveyed historical certitude, arithmetical precision. The term presumed that an entire self-consistent rational system of thought was at stake. To be *correct* was to be stamped with the prestige of that system and assured of victory. Per contra, to be stamped *incorrect* was to be consigned to outer darkness.

Correct and *incorrect* came back into vogue for the New Left of the late 1960s: a sign that smug rigidity, a priori dismissiveness, and metaphysical fantasy had entered a movement that had begun in an exploratory temper, eager to find new language for new circumstances. In the 1970s, the term indicated—according to the user's pleasure—either strict adherence to the political line of one's "tendency" or a certain ironic distance. In the twilight of political certitudes and all-encompassing political visions, the term was ready-made for mockery, even self-mockery, as by the Polish émigré ex- and anti-Communist philosopher Leszek Kolakowski, who once entitled an essay, "My Correct Views About Everything." By the late 1980s, indeed, the term was used mainly tongue-in-cheek. As Richard Bernstein (but not his headline writer) noted in the *New York Times* article that touched off the 1990–91 media frenzy, "the term 'politically correct,' with its suggestion of Stalinist orthodoxy, is spoken more with irony than with reverence . . . the terms ['p.c.' and 'p.c.p.,' or 'politically correct person'] are not used in utter seriousness." Yet the stampede was on.

If the key to the art of demagogy is oversimplification, the crusade against PC was a master exhibit. It suited ideologues of the Right to brandish the term relentlessly, collapsing affirmative action, curriculum revision, and speech regulation codes into a uniform enemy, lumping together nonsensical "Afrocentrism" with serious scholarship, and referring darkly to a "new McCarthyism." The exposés were of uneven merit, but they were brandished indiscriminately, the anecdotes recycled, acquiring instant canonical standing. Ideologues drew the line and demanded to know of wafflers, *Which side are you on?*

The campus climate of the time was, of course, not nearly as suffocating as it was made to sound. Especially at elite institutions, it was frequently arbitrary, fatuous, conformist, and wrong-headed, but rarely punitive. PC did not, in fact, haul miscreants up before congressional committees, fire or flunk nonconformists, pillory them in the press, or take their passports away. It did not force economics departments to hire, or retain, Marxists, nor require of business majors that they study labor history. Conformism there was—unpleasant, stifling, inimical to the high ideal of the free pursuit of knowledge. This climate, where it existed, was well worth criticizing, as it always is when students, professors, or anyone else conforms. Conformism, small-mindedness, abuses of power—these are, indeed, common features of American university life.

In 1960, to take a tiny example, a freshman composition instructor at Harvard assigned his students to write an assessment of a C. S. Lewis essay arguing that pain is an instrument of God's will. Considering this notion outlandish, one student wrote a parody. The instructor, a Jesuit, graded it a D and warned the student that any more of this sort of thing would get him in serious trouble. The student was barely seventeen, and not inclined to explore just what sort of trouble the man in the collar meant. Later on in the 1960s, students were thrown out of universities for refusing to attend chapel or to enroll in compulsory ROTC. In 1965 the president of the University of Tulsa refused permission to a speaker from Students for a Democratic Society to lecture against the war on campus property. I was the freshman who parodied Lewis, and the speaker whose talk in Tulsa had to be moved to a coffeehouse off campus. Newspapers did not fill with denunciations of the tyrannical atmosphere of the universities.

PC was a propaganda slogan from the beginning, a compound of facts and distortions meant to strangle curiosity. By flinging about the scarlet letters, the accuser arranged for a melodramatic confrontation: freedom against slavery. Exuding a love of liberty, he was spared the need to be clear, while pooh-poohing any idea to the left of the current center of gravity of the Republican party, and, moreover, appealing (self-righteously!) to the reasonable person's hatred of self-righteousness. The distinguished English professor Wayne Booth wrote in a February 14, 1994, letter to the editor of the *Chicago Tribune:*

> May I suggest that you reprogram your computers? Instead of supplying the PC expressions when thought fails, program them to ring bells and flash the following whenever any of these expressions is typed in: "PHRASE OUTWORN AND MEANING-LESS! CANNOT CONTINUE UNTIL YOU CHOOSE FROM THE FOLLOWING THE SYNONYM CLOSEST TO THE VIRTUE YOU WANT TO MOCK:
>
> (1) decency; (2) legality; (3) moral or ethical standards; (4) justice, fairness, equality of opportunity; (5) tact, courtesy, concern about hurting people's feelings unnecessarily; (6) generosity; (7) kindness; (8) courage in defending the underdog; (9) anti-bigotry; (10) anti-racism; (11) anti-anti-Semitism; (12) anti-fascism; (13) anti-sexism; (14) refusal to kneel to mammon; (15) sympathetic support for the jobless, the homeless, the impoverished, or the abused; (16) preservation of an environment in which human life might survive; (17) openness to the possibility that certain popular right-wing dogmas just might be erroneous.
>
> PLACE YOUR CURSOR ON THE NUMBER OF THE VIRTUE YOU ARE OPPOSED TO, PRESS THE 'ENTER' KEY AND THEN GIVE YOUR REASONS OR START OVER."

After years of anti-PC blasts and countermobilizations, crusaders might have been expected to take some satisfaction that the worst had been averted. But the *enragés* among the conservatives kept up their insistence that everything of value remained at risk, that the war was total, the stakes absolute. The sense of extremity rivaled that of left-wing absolutists invoking *the* class struggle in the final battle against exploitation. As partisans of identity politics girded their loins for the combat against white men and their works, so did men of flame and brimstone invoke the war against barbarism. Hilton Kramer, a trenchant art critic when he is not *enragé*-in-chief of the right-wing culture monthly *The New Criterion,* warned in 1993 that the "political correctness movement" had achieved "a decisive victory . . . in the realm of education, culture, and the arts." "For a brief moment around 1990," wrote Roger Kimball, managing editor of this same manual of cultural resistance and author of *Tenured Radicals: How Politics Has Corrupted Our Higher Education* (1990), "the 'long march through the institutions' for which sixties radicals agitated seemed to be complete with the more or less total capitulation of most American universities and cultural organizations to the forces of political correctness." Kimball, whose book was one of the first to lend legitimacy to mainstream journalistic exposés of PC, went on to say that "the takeover of the universities and organizations like the Modern Language Association and the American Council of Learned Societies was only the first step."

Pause a moment on these words: *more or less total capitulation; most American universities and cultural organizations; takeover.* It was in 1993 that Kimball published these words, three years after his own book and Dinesh D'Souza's best-seller had sounded their alarms against the PC onslaught. Apparently all opposition was in vain, for according to Kimball, "over the last couple of years political correctness has evolved from a sporadic expression of left-leaning self-righteousness into a dogma of orthodoxy that is widely accepted, and widely enforced, by America's cultural elite." "That was stage one," Kimball added, and as if that were not bad enough, "stage two, the penetration of political correctness into public policy, is now underway." Stage two was inaugurated by the Clinton administration, whose nominations of former University of Wisconsin chancellor Donna Shalala (as secretary of health and human services) and former University of Pennsylvania president Sheldon Hackney (as director of the National Endowment for the Humanities) apparently outweighed his not-very-PC nominations of corporate lawyer Zoë Baird for attorney general and loophole sustainer Lloyd Bentsen for secretary of the treasury. Kimball concluded by invoking the choice between appeasement and military preparedness, citing Churchill's statement in 1938 "that the British people had before them the choice of shame or war. He feared that they would choose shame—and have war nevertheless. He was right."

So, to the sound of martial music, have the exaggerations charged onward. For all their genuflections toward reason, humanism, and liberality in a disinterested search for truth, Roger Kimball, Dinesh D'Souza, and many of their journalistic derivatives were, at the very least, sloppy and amateurish. D'Souza's flying tour of campus atrocities was especially breathless. His polemical method was to gather incendiary quotes and baste them together. The more arrogant the professor and the more ignorant the student, the more typical D'Souza found their quotes. Since arrogant professors and ignorant students are not (and have never been) in short supply, this was not difficult. D'Souza's version of Stanford University's curriculum reform, for example, was woefully wrongheaded. In 1987–88, there had taken place a faculty debate over replacing the required freshman Western Culture course, a proposal declared by Secretary of Education William Bennett to be "a proposal to 'drop the West.' " Like the old requirement, the new one, Culture, Institutions, Values, or CIV, offered students eight alternative choices. In one of the eight, the reading list included *I, Rigoberta Menchú,* by the Guatemalan Indian woman who was shortly to win the Nobel Peace Prize. D'Souza declared arbitrarily that this, one of more than forty assigned texts in the course, was "perhaps the text which best reveals the premises underlying the new Stanford curriculum," and devoted two pages to trashing it. What he devoted no pages to mentioning was that all eight courses assigned the Old and New Testaments, Freud, Marx, Shakespeare, and Aristotle; that seven assigned Augustine, Virginia Woolf, and Rousseau; six, Descartes, Machiavelli, Aquinas, and Plato; five, Euripides, Dante, Luther, Montaigne, and Homer. Nor did D'Souza mention that only about fifty of Stanford's 1,500 freshmen were taking the particular course that inspired his loathing.

One might well want to argue in favor of core curricula—this author would—yet only the tendentious critic would fail to note that these are relatively rare and recent creations in America. Stanford's hoary Western Civ program, begun in the late 1930s, had been dropped in the late 1960s, only to be reinstated (renamed Western Culture) in the late 1970s.

Harvard had only one required course, in composition, when I went there in the early 1960s. (For breadth, students chose, as at Stanford, from among a list of approved courses.) It is not multiculturalism but the shopping mall university, full of electives, ushered in at Harvard in the late nineteenth century, that demoted an earlier generation of classics. One might also argue vociferously—as again this author has—against the instant elevation of popular fiction to classic status, or against the propensity to downgrade literature in favor of "cultural studies" of ephemera. But have the barbarians actually seized the ramparts? D'Souza, to bolster his proclamation that universities are "expelling Homer, Aristotle, Shakespeare, and other 'white males' from their required reading list," quoted the chairman of the English department at Pennsylvania State University to the effect that "Alice Walker's *The Color Purple* is taught in more English departments today than all of Shakespeare's plays combined." The literary scholar Gerald Graff, author of a magisterial account of the history of his profession, decided to count

> the texts assigned in Northwestern University's English department from the fall of 1986, when Alice Walker's novel was first assigned in a course, to the spring of 1990. Over this four-year period I located two courses in which *The Color Purple* was taught, while I found eight courses that required at least six plays by Shakespeare and eight that required at least two. Shakespeare's dominance became even more visibly one-sided when I totaled the number of students in these courses . . . for every reading of Walker there were approximately *eighty-three* readings of Shakespeare.

Graff cited national surveys of university literature syllabi to the same effect. In nineteenth-century American literature, the canon is still dominated by Hawthorne, Thoreau, Melville, and Emerson. In British literature, it is Austen, the Brontës, Dickens, Eliot, Hardy, and Thackeray. Of those works recently added to the American list, the one most frequently assigned was Harriet Beecher Stowe, and she "was listed by only 15 percent of the teachers surveyed."

Nor did D'Souza remind his readers that canons are not engraved in granite; nor that it took a bitter struggle before the above-mentioned "classics" replaced the Greeks and Latins a century ago; nor that one of those notorious white men of today's canon, good gay Walt Whitman, had to elbow aside John Greenleaf Whittier and James Russell Lowell a generation later. One could write a book as long as D'Souza's composed entirely of refutations and qualifications. Like an Afrocentrist who claims that Plato was black but still doesn't get around to reading him, D'Souza claims Plato for his side but shows himself innocent of the Socratic method. He worships at the shrine of history but is innocent of facts.

According to the right-wing correctors of left-wing political correctness, it was not bad enough that ill-conceived ideas and an intolerant atmosphere prevailed in certain departments of certain institutions of higher learning, or that there was a rash of censorious outbursts on many campuses. The claim had to be made that reason and civilization were being utterly overwhelmed by superannuated tenured radicals and their administrative puppets. It did not slow the exponents of cultural war when Jonathan Wiener, Louis Menand, Gerald Graff, Russell Jacoby, and others handily exposed and refuted many of the wilder excesses of the anti-PC corpus. Nothing seemed to shake the canonical standing of their most immoderate claims. The same horror stories circulated, unexamined and unrevised, from one right-wing pundit to another. Let one group of Stanford students chant "Hey, hey, ho, ho, Western Culture's got to go," and the echo reverberated for years.

One reason why the campaign against PC had legs—more legs than a caterpillar—is that identity politics and attendant censoriousness were real. Though many on the Left were reluctant to admit it in public, many true stories could be compiled to plug the holes left by D'Souza's sloppy research. Professor Leonard Jeffries of the City College of New York plugged a lot of holes all by himself. This know-nothing seemed to have been sent directly from Central Casting to kindle indignation. Here was the chairman of City College's Department of Black Studies holding his position—a position normally held at the pleasure of the administration—for twenty years in a row while teaching that whites are "ice people" and blacks "sun people," and specializing in anti-Semitic smirks. Here was a tenured professor who had never produced any relevant scholarship, but in 1989 was considered a significant enough figure to be appointed a consultant to an official task force by the New York State superintendent of education, where he delivered himself of the view that the dominance of "the European-American monocultural perspective" explained why "large numbers of children of non-European descent are not doing as well as expected."

It might be noted that, however egregious, Jeffries did not appeal to many students—his black studies program attracted fewer than ten majors on a campus of 12,000 undergraduates. But beyond Jeffries, in any event, there was no shortage of material to warrant censure of the censorious American university. Richard Bernstein of the *New York Times*, a far better reporter than D'Souza, compiled many serious cases in his 1994 book, *Dictatorship of Virtue*—cases that in their prosecutorial absurdity indeed deserved to become canonical: among others, the University of Pennsylvania bringing charges against a student charged with racism for yelling "water buffalo," a translation of a Hebrew swearword, at some noisy black students. Bernstein's rhetoric was extravagant: he took his title from the French Revolution, opened with an epigraph from Robespierre, and peppered his text with references to Stalinism and the Chinese Cultural Revolution. Still, he had a lot of goods, and by now, almost no one denies it. The question is what to make of them.

By 1994, independent-minded opponents of the trendily "correct" were acknowledging that the alarm had been excessively piercing. The prolific critic Robert Alter, himself an adversary of fashionable literary theory, wrote (in the same collection including Kimball and Kramer) that while illiberalism does "constitute a real threat to the variety and freedom and complex pleasures of intellectual life on the campuses, . . . my guess is that its scope and gravity have been exaggerated by most conservative reactions and in the popular media." Even the anti-PC National Association of Scholars was divided, with some convinced that the Left-PC-feminist-multiculturalist "monolith" (Kramer's word) had swept all reason and culture before it, others that the worst dogmatism associated with "political correctness" had been fought to a stand-off. It was as if the Cold War dispute between a rollback "forward strategy" and a long-view deterrence had been recapitulated, this time as farce.

In the meantime, long overdue, a range of neither/nor positions was emerging. The independent Left critic Morris Dickstein spoke of "a resurgence of liberal thought, rejecting both intimidation of the left and the hysteria of traditionalists," and ticked off, as exponents, John Searle, Frederick Crews, Irving Howe, C. Vann Woodward, Arthur Schlesinger, Jr., David Bromwich, Robert Hughes, John Higham, and this writer. Eventually, a higher order of debate, with clarifying potential, emerged in anthologies edited by Paul Berman, Patricia Aufderheide, and Michael Bérubé and Cary Nelson, and in articles by Barbara Epstein, Henry Louis Gates, Jr., and David A. Hollinger—no fault of theirs that many of their judicious writings appeared in small-circulation academic journals. In 1994 the range of neither/nors was extended by Russell Jacoby's *Dogmatic Wisdom,* which chastised the Right for a prosecutorial zeal that stopped short of rising in righteous indignation against the dramatic threat to higher education from economic impoverishment; and by Daphne Patai and Noretta Koertge, feminists who offered in *Professing Feminism* a devastating and knowledgeable critique of many women's studies programs.

But in wild disproportion to the actual strength of the wounded *bête noire,* much of the Right continued to emit a high pitch of horror and fervor. The fear of encirclement was apparently undiminished. Either/ors continued to sound as if the rebuttals (and frequent refutations) had never been uttered. How shall we understand this inconsolable fervor, and its success in setting the terms of the debate?

2. The Selectivity of Media Obsessions

The alarmism of Roger Kimball, Hilton Kramer, and Irving Kristol makes an easy target. Here are the 1990s' equivalents of the most lurid John Birch rhetoric, now that it will no longer do to draw a map showing red arrows slashing across the Iron Curtain into the Free World. But if ridicule or the brandishing of counterevidence affords the pleasures of aggressive indignation and wounded rectitude, it does not necessarily clarify. The question is not simply whether the panic was misguided but why it mounted so quickly throughout the media.

Any assessment of the genesis of the PC panic must start with two general observations. First, media panics are imperfect guides to the truth. Second, some things are true even if Dinesh D'Souza says them. The alarmists offered an interpretation for a widespread feeling, but did not invent the feeling. One explanation for the chorus of condemnation is that many would-be thought police *were* at work (though usually without the power to crack heads). But truth is neither necessary nor sufficient for a media crusade. This is only rarely because journalists are indifferent to truth. Sometimes truth is difficult to establish; in particular, when government propaganda goes to work. Certain obsessions begin with half- or quarter-truths and inflate them—the "missing children" campaign of the mid-1980s, which, in full hysteria down to its milk-carton portraits and President Reagan's claim that there were "well over a million children who disappear every year," neglected to note that, according to FBI statistics, of the 30,000 American children missing in mid-1985, the grand total abducted by strangers was exactly 67, while about 1,500 had been snatched by a parent in a custody dispute, and the remainder, the vast majority, were runaways in flight from domestic abuse. Some crusades start with almost no truth—for example, the "Africanized killer bees" periodically making their way northward over the Texas border to plunge America into a public health crisis. While maladies like chronic fatigue syndrome and Lyme disease balloon overnight into cover stories, other facts and dangers take years to rise to the threshold of media awareness—AIDS, for example, or breast cancer for many years, or, lately, prostate cancer.

Regardless of justifications, all media alarms share certain elements. Part of the explanation for the PC obsession is that there was, in conventional journalistic terms, "a good story." There were actual facts. There were delights of combat and exposé, with public values at stake. Journalists like conflict for the same reason dramatists and sports fans do. It catches the attention of their superiors, as it does that of their colleagues, that of their viewers and readers, and their own. In PC, journalists and editors, who don't ordinarily scrutinize topics for their deeper significance, found plenty of practical elements for a juicy continuing story: good guys and bad guys; an aura of menace; a promise of moral melodrama; an apparently ever-replenishable source of follow-up stories. Then too, once they have found their scandals, journalists like them simple. They do not like them comparative or overly mitigated. Comparisons end up in sidebars, if anywhere, but not in the headlines or the lead in the evening news. The news comes down with a clang of absolute factuality: THIS HAPPENED. Perspective comes trailing afterward, if at all. Anyway, one woman's perspective is another woman's extenuation. The easiest thing to do is to graft the latest round of facts, or claims, onto the previous round, and leave it at that.

Consider the controversy over race-based admissions at Berkeley, one of Dinesh D'Souza's horror stories. The charge was that affirmative action was excluding thousands of worthy white and Asian candidates. Scarcely any students, or faculty, for that matter, understood the administration's actual policy. For its part, the administration did a poor job explaining itself—as if they scarcely understood their own policy. Not surprisingly, journalists, too, were frequently content to remain ignorant. One of D'Souza's points was that many blacks and Latinos were being admitted to Berkeley with grade-point averages lower than those of whites and Asians—many of whom were being turned away with 4.0 averages. But hardly any protesters understood that there were so many California high school graduates with 4.0 grade-point averages (more than 5,800 out of the 21,300 who applied to Berkeley) that in 1989, even were there no affirmative action at all, 2,300 4.0s would have had to be turned away. (With affirmative action, the number actually turned away was about 2,800.) Hardly any understood that in a most Californian euphemism, high school students got bonus grade-point credit for doing well in college preparatory courses, so that a 4.0 average did not mean that a student had gotten straight As. Hardly any students or faculty, let alone journalists, knew that alumni "legacies" and athletic and special-skill admissions accounted for more exceptions to the "objective standards only" norm than affirmative action, so that in 1989, 24 percent of *white* students were admitted to Berkeley on criteria other than academic scores—still a much lower percentage than in the case of blacks and Hispanics, but not negligible either. Nor was it a staple of PC exposés that at Harvard, as late as 1988, preferences for children of alumni accounted for more admissions than all the African American, Mexican American, Native American, and Puerto Rican registrants combined. Alumni preferences were a tradition; affirmative action was news.

PC was a good story, but not all good stories cross the threshold of media attention to stand exposed in the floodlights and stay there. The world is brimming with potential subjects for media frenzy. The savings and loan banking scandal, replete with bad guys and consequences amounting to more than $150 billion, took years to get into the spotlight. (The details were many and hard to grasp. Since Republicans and Democrats shared the trough and the blame, the scandal lacked the drama of partisan confrontation.) Gay-bashing, at this writing, is not a crime that catches much attention in a nation that ostensibly quivers with the fear of crime. Many good subjects are eligible for a media furor, but few are chosen. So press obsessions can never be taken entirely at face value. An obsession cannot be altogether explained by the reality of its subject. Logically, it cannot be that reports of bad news simply mirror bad facts in the world, for the media have limited space, limited time, limited personnel, and at any given moment there are too many bad facts. One need not be a conspiracy buff to conclude that media institutions are selective. Even if the criterion for newsworthiness is actual or potential impact, there is a surfeit of possibilities, and the question is, Impact on whom? Media institutions have to select.

Theatrical, continuous conflict helps make the story. This is one reason why Stanford proved enthralling to the media in 1988, when the Western Civilization curriculum was revamped into a multicultural substitute, and not ten years earlier, when Western Civ was installed in the first place. All the better when a party to the conflict or a victim of the crime carries prestige—Stanford or the Ivy League universities are newsworthy, just as the notorious rape of the Central Park jogger, a white investment banker, in 1989 received hundreds of times more attention than all the contemporaneous, brutal rapes committed around New York City that year put together. On principle and on professional grounds, the press is prone to stand up against violations of freedom of speech—thus, campus speech codes made a compelling target for exposés. Furthermore, to break out, a story has to catch the fancy of editors, which is most likely to happen where national media have flung their news net—at Columbia or Stanford, not at San Diego State or Texas A&M. Of course, once the story is certified at a high journalistic level—a *New York Times* story being the most important certificate of significance—the momentum can grow. It helps when experts stand at the ready for consultation. (Recall

Roger Kimball, quoted in Richard Bernstein's original PC story in the *Times.*) Then subsequent incidents are ripe to be recognized as part of a pattern. An individual story makes most sense when it rhymes with an established story, when it comes with its own preaffixed label, and can be recognized as a chapter in an ongoing plot.

Of course, editors based in the Northeast will say that their audience cares about Columbia more than Texas A&M, and they are doubtless right. But what they do not say, what perhaps doesn't rise to conscious-ness, is that they feel the travails of Stanford and Harvard and Duke in a distinctive way. Disproportionately, they are alumni of these schools. They read their alma maters' magazines and keep in touch with gossip. Indeed, they may have a more intimate stake. It happens, for example, that *Newsweek*'s editor in chief, Maynard Parker, the man responsible for putting the 1990 "Thought Police" story on the magazine's cover, became a member of the board of directors of Stanford's Alumni Association the following year. Arguably, his attachment to the university was not deci-sive in Parker's thinking, which was little if any different from that of other editors not similarly placed, but was not irrelevant either, for such a link to university power bespeaks an established view of the world and a special disposition to worry about PC tendencies at elite universities. Other top *Newsweek* editors, though not all, agreed that "Thought Police" would make a smashing cover for newsstand sales, which, while only a small percentage of total circulation, impress advertisers, and mark how well the magazine is doing against the competition.

Beyond personal connections and the pleasures of reporting properly located combat, journalists leaped into the PC story because, like it or not, they are *engagé*—though not usually in the deliberate ideological way charged by many media critics. One need not be a radical relativist to note that, like all social groups, journalists have a social position to defend. Their institutions require that they make objectivity claims. The belief that a true picture of the world is possible is their occupational raison d'être. Therefore, whatever mixture of superior and inferior feel-ings they harbor toward universities, journalists have a stake in the legiti-macy of the sorts of activities that go on there. To the degree that the university loses face, or devalues the disinterested pursuit of knowledge, their own credentials are devalued. It was, after all, these institutions of higher learning that first certified them as adepts of information—as knowers. It is also both compelling and handy to defend the ideal of objectivity against its degradation by obscurantist professors who clot their writing with jargon and, with great flourishes, trumpet impenetrable translations of dubious French phrases. The journalists get to defend the ideal of transparent prose coupled with the ideal of objective standards. In the populist mood, all the educated classes are under suspicion together for "elitism." When they defend the ideal of objectivity—and yes, "Western Culture"—they defend some Platonic idea of themselves.

3. The Right Turn

But how, in particular, did the PC recoil begin? Media panics frequently start with, or get a significant boost from, the preoccupations of powerful groups who talk up certain social problems so vociferously, in the right journals, at the right resorts and the right dinner parties, as to land them on the journalistic agenda. In the case of the anti-PC panic, journalistic fascination, while sincere, also got a boost from the well-heeled right wing.

Respectable experts, as I have mentioned, help certify the legitimacy of a story. The issuance of a "report" from a think tank or a quotable figure with a book to his or her credit probably doesn't send a reporter running to write a story, but does help recommend it to an editor or a producer, and does move the story along. The prominent expert partisans who certified that PC was a menace—Allan Bloom, Roger Kimball, and Dinesh D'Souza in particular—were supported by the John M. Olin Foundation. It did not hurt their cause that many in the media were receptive to certain complaints from the Right.

This receptivity predictably belonged to the recoil against the movements of the 1960s. How could the palpable breakdown of authority in the 1960s, and the centrifugal identity motion that followed, fail to generate a countermovement, a conservative consolidation? With dialectical elegance, a new radicalism aroused a new conservatism. Only then could Political Correctness become a usable demonology in the eyes of politicians and the press. To begin with, the potential for a protracted crusade against the wrong ideas has always been latent in America. The locus classicus of right-wing laments about the subversive university was the 1951 book that put William F. Buckley, Jr., on the national map, *God and Man at Yale.* The lament was reinvigorated during the Nixon years in a popular reaction against militant student movements, a reaction that this time had large-scale academic support at a time when the university, replete with "radiclibs" and "nattering nabobs of negativism," seemed to have gone over to the enemy.

The political Right, reflecting on its loss of control in American culture, reasonably enough determined that the universities and the media, culture's two main institutional conduits, ought to be singled out for counteraction. The business class agreed. By the early 1970s, leaders of major corporations thought that, having lost control of the wellsprings of ideas, they needed to invest in reclamation. In their view, only ideological bias could explain the disrepute in which business was held. "Destructive," "misinformed," "slanted," "anti-establishment," determined to "tear . . . down our system": these are among the terms hurled at the media, intellectuals, and universities by prominent executives of multinational corporations during 1974–75. Neoconservatives supplied the theory, identifying the media and the universities as nests of a knowledge class that had no stake in business (or national) success and whose naysaying was subsidized outside the market.

By the late 1970s, the business-sponsored ideological rally was revving up for action. The temperature of the rhetoric mounted. In 1978, in the view of former Secretary of the Treasury (under Presidents Nixon and Ford) William E. Simon, "What is happening in this country is a fundamental assault on America's culture and its historic identity." But the newly energized conservatives were not armchair grumblers. These were practical men (and some women). Explaining why he had assumed the presidency of the John M. Olin Foundation in 1976, Simon declared that business was obliged to put its money where its interests were. He called for "nothing less than a massive and unprecedented mobilization of the moral, intellectual and financial resources which reside in those . . . who are concerned that our traditional free enterprise system, which offers the greatest scope for the exercise of our freedom, is in dire and perhaps ultimate peril." This "crusade" would mobilize "those who see a successful United States as the real 'last best hope of mankind.' " Simon concluded with three points:

> 1. Funds generated by business . . . must rush by mul-
> timillions to the aid of liberty . . . [and] funnel desperately
> needed funds to scholars, social scientists, writers and jour-
> nalists who understand the relationship between political and
> economic liberty . . . [and whose work would] dissent from a
> dominant socialist-statist-collectivist orthodoxy which prevails
> in much of the media, in most of our large universities, among
> many of our politicians and, tragically, among not a few of our
> top business executives. . . .
>
> 2. Business must cease the mindless subsidizing of col-
> leges and universities whose departments of economics, gov-
> ernment, politics and history are hostile to capitalism and
> whose faculties will not hire scholars whose views are other-
> wise. . . .
>
> 3. Finally, business money must flow away from the media
> which serve as megaphones for anticapitalist opinion and to
> media which are either pro-freedom or, if not necessarily "pro-
> business," at least professionally capable of a fair and accu-
> rate treatment of procapitalist ideas, values and arguments.

Thundering that "the only thing that can save the Republican Party . . . is a counterintelligentsia," Simon was no lone crusader flogging a crank cause. He was one of the more forthright and better-placed of the right-wing publicists who, through passion, organization, and not least, money, helped undermine the liberal-labor welfare state consensus. A paleoconservative free enterpriser, Simon and his cobelievers welded a common front with ex-leftist neoconservatives like Irving Kristol, Norman Podhoretz, and Midge Decter. In 1978, Simon and Kristol founded the Institute for Educational Affairs (in 1990 renamed the Madison Center for Educational Affairs), which proceeded to fund some sixty right-wing and sometimes scurrilous campus papers, one of them the *Dartmouth Review*, where Dinesh D'Souza cut his journalistic eyeteeth.

Struggle language like Simon's anticipated the rightward shift in the media—and nudged it on. Corporate funding from AT&T legitimized public television's *MacNeil/Lehrer NewsHour,* featuring circumscribed policy talk that rarely departed from the assumptions of Washington think-tanks. Right-wing foundations helped launch ideological auto-dafés like *The McLaughlin Group* onto the airwaves. Partly as a result of the prestige bought by canny investment, the public intellectual atmosphere changed. *Commentary* was now read widely in Washington, as was the Sun Myung Moon–sponsored *Washington Times* and its magazine supplement, *Insight.* The American Enterprise Institute, the Heritage Foundation, and more specialized right-wing think-tanks churned out op-ed pieces and briefing papers, which reporters felt obliged to pore over. George Will became ubiquitous in magazines, newspapers, and television. Ted Turner gave Patrick Buchanan a daily slot on CNN's *Crossfire.* When Ronald Reagan came to office, he was known to read—or at least consult—the right-wing *Human Events* and *Conservative Digest,* and if these were still considered slightly kooky tastes, they were so only by comparison with what instantly became the more respectable journals on the Right.

And then, of course, Reagan's election certified that the Right was not to be considered marginal. Their ship had come in. Reagan had the charm and ideological wherewithal to widen his political base beyond "movement conservatives," while his 51 percent of the vote looked like a landslide against Jimmy Carter's 41 percent, confirming a rightward ideological turn whose thoroughness was touted by the mainstream media. The urgency of the culture war against the barbarians progressed by fits and starts during the Reagan years. William Bennett banged bully pulpits in Washington at the National Endowment for the Humanities and the Department of Education. It was Bennett who, in 1988, converted the revamping of the freshman year humanities requirement at Stanford University into a national cause célèbre, declaring that "for a moment, a great university was brought low by the very forces which modern universities came into being to oppose—ignorance, irrationality and intimidation." It was during these late months of the Reagan administration that the National Association of Scholars was founded to fight left-wing academics, and a turgid, quirky, demanding, obscure, and frequently obscurantist book by a political theorist named Allan Bloom soared onto the best-seller list with its blanket assault on student activism, relativism, German philosophy, and rock 'n' roll.

Where Bloom was ornery and idiosyncratic, lesser conservative intellects set out to break down his assault into a set of distinct issues in higher education, and then to clump those issues into an indivisible amalgam called Political Correctness. This campaign came during the damp, declining presidency of George Bush, when the right wing, distrustful of Bush, feeling that (whatever his protestations) he was not quite *their* man, were in need of a focus of evil to concentrate their minds and their resources. The change in political climate from Reagan's years to Bush's helps account for the timing of the PC panic.

Bush began his successor regime in an ideological disarray brought about by a collapse of enemies. He no longer had the Cold War as a magnetic force to line up supporters into a solid front. Within his first year in office, the Right's intellectual map dissolved. "Movement conservatives" found the situation anticlimactic at best. What were conservatives going to do without identifiable barbarians? They looked homeward, and found new barbarians among the superannuated old barbarians, for it was not lost on them that what they labeled the PC forces had roots in the 1960s Left—the very amalgam of minorities that had triggered the "silent majority" reaction in the first place, helping resurrect the Republicans and converting them into a majority party under Richard Nixon. The crusade to correct PC promised to hold together the disparate sectors of the Right. Even the victorious long march of the Right through the institutions of politics had failed to roll back the feminist, gay, and multicultural movements that had indeed acquired niches in the institutions of image and word. Conservatives accurately observed that, having taken the White House, they still had not taken back Harvard, Hollywood, the Modern Language Association, or the National Endowment for the Arts. Just after the Gulf War, George Will could write with a straight face that as Bennett's successor at the National Endowment for the Humanities, Lynne Cheney, "secretary of domestic defense," faced enemies who were more dangerous in the long run than the adversaries her husband, Secretary of Defense Dick Cheney, confronted abroad.

The media panic was encouraged by another background factor—the weakening of the universities. Universities made journalistic targets partly because they were already losing public respect. Declining in wealth, universities also declined in prestige. There were scandals— misappropriations of government funds and episodes of sexual harass- ment—and although there might have been just as many or more aca- demic scandals left unexposed during the decades preceding 1990, journalists were now primed for the hunt.

The sense that the university was vulnerable was driven by the domi- nant ideology of the Reagan years and accelerated during the waning of the Cold War. For decades after the Soviet Union launched Sputnik, the world's first satellite, in 1957, and the Eisenhower administration sounded the educational alarm and began pouring government money into efforts to ensure that Johnny read and multiplied with little Ivan's facility, scholarship had been justified as a contribution to national defense. Big science education would mean a bigger bang. Fellowships that the federal government would never have dreamed of justifying in the name of knowl- edge were now justified by their contribution to The National Defense— hence the enactment in 1958 of the National Defense Education Act, one of the major sources of stipends for a generation of graduate students. But by the time of Reagan's presidency, the shine was off federal spending. Reagan's cuts in university funding, in fact, predated the end of the Cold War. Between 1981 and 1986, federal funding for higher education plunged by 14 percent in real dollars. Moreover, during the Reagan and Bush years, the federal government shifted the burden for public pro- grams to the states, absorbing funds from their own education budgets. State budget cuts, worsened by recession, were disproportionately leveled at higher education. In Illinois, for example, university spending fell from 23.5 percent of state funds in 1968 to 18.3 percent in 1990; in Colorado, from 23.5 percent in 1982 to 19.2 percent in 1992. Between 1980 and 1989, spending for higher education at all levels of government plunged by 24.3 percent in constant dollars.

At the same time, an aging population of taxpayers was losing sympa- thy for public schools. The elderly were not only growing as a percentage of the population, they made up an even larger proportion of the voters and a higher proportion still of those who vote in off-year elections on university bond issues in states like California, which submit such votes to the public. The elderly were increasingly willing to dispense with public funds for schools that they thought inessential or worse. Let the young fend for themselves!

Inside the academy, scarcity inflamed faculty turf fights and fueled the intensity of PC and anti-PC crusades. Student fees increased dramatically. So did student debt. In the early 1990s, about half of enrolled university students held jobs while attending classes. Students wondered whether, after graduation, they would be able to live in a house half the size of the one they grew up in. The dominant tone was anxiety. Identity politics was one way to crystallize this anxiety and shape it into a worldview. For many a white male (and not only him), the more attractive receptacle was the conservative counterforce. Conservatives apparently cared for his freedom, while liberals, in the name of diversity, counseled discretion that he could easily mistake for self-censorship. He grew less likely to care about racist, sexist, or homophobic harassment, and cared more about being the victim of stereotyping himself. If he had started out with a tolerant disposition, he was dismayed to find that integration had become the goal that dared not speak its outdated name (except, curiously, in parts of the Deep South). He encountered cliquishness—though it would not have occurred to him that a living unit where students spoke Italian was cliquish. He was caught between his individualism, which wanted to be color-blind, and his social liberalism, which acknowledged a history of racial oppression. If he was not conflicted, he got the idea that everyone else got to speak bitterness but himself. If he was aggressive or self-pitying enough, he would complain anyway. He was ready to have conservatives name his malaise: victim of PC.

Feeling chilled in the 1990s, he was not interested in being reminded that he was warm compared to, say, his parents. If he came from the working or middle classes, he resented the imputation that his life was a breeze and that he was not deserving. If he had friends of color in high school, he resented their receiving fellowships to which he was not entitled. If women, or blacks, or gays had their afflictions, well, then, in a world of interest groups, he felt that he had his, too. If the world was divided up by identity cards, he, too, would learn to define his discomfort as a stigma, identify with it, wear it with pride. His card would say that he believed in color blindness and individual rights, that he was free from responsibility for the sins of his (or anyone else's) ancestors.

4. Another Dubious Battle

Late in 1994, three years after Oakland's school board voted against his textbooks, UCLA's Gary Nash was back in the news along with Charlotte Crabtree, who had helped write the California history–social science framework. Nash and Crabtree had supervised the development and publication of a set of national history "standards"—a compilation of topics, concepts, ideas, arguments, and facts that every American student ought to learn. Now the charge was that the standards "make it sound as if everything in America is wrong and grim," were "politically correct to a fare-thee-well," "really out of balance," the "politicized" products of an "academic establishment" that tended "to save [its] unqualified admiration for people, places and events that are politically correct."

The critic leading the charge was Lynne Cheney, formerly President Bush's chairman (her preferred locution) of the National Endowment for the Humanities, now feeling "flimflammed," as she said, because she had helped launch the project in the first place. In 1992, her National Endowment for the Humanities had given Nash and Crabtree's National Center for History in the Schools at UCLA a grant—supplemented by the Department of Education—to develop national standards for the first time in American history. In contrast with a country like France, which holds students accountable for a standard curriculum—it used to be said that at any given moment you could tell exactly what subject students were studying anywhere in the country—the United States had never promoted a national body of knowledge. To the contrary: states' rights made such a notion anathema. But with American students doing poorly in cross-national competition, Cheney and other Republicans, as well as Democrats, had come to think that common historical knowledge was too important to leave to the states and localities. At the least, there should be available a set of common standards on the basis of which new textbooks could be commissioned and curricula worked up at the local level.

The standards would be optional, not mandatory, but at the same time, with their national imprimatur, they would be widely regarded as exemplary.

An elaborate structure was set up to ensure that the writers of the standards would consult many interested parties. Teachers and state curriculum officials would be heard from, as well as academic historians. Since Nash and Crabtree were known to be sympathetic to multiculturalism, Cheney insisted that historians of a less multiculturalist bent be added to the council of thirty-one scholars and teachers that would have the responsibility of approving the standards that would emerge through the consultative process. The council now included, among historians of the United States, Emory's Elizabeth Fox-Genovese, a member of the National Association of Scholars and a frequent critic of PC, and Columbia's Kenneth Jackson, who, with Arthur M. Schlesinger, Jr., had dissented from the Afrocentrist Leonard Jeffries's views during the New York State history revision a few years earlier. The council also included several distinguished practitioners of world history who were far from trend-setting New Left alumni, among them Bernard Lewis of Princeton, a trenchant critic of Edward Said's critique of "Orientalism," Akira Iriye of Harvard, and William McNeill, emeritus of the University of Chicago. Cheney also insisted on adding two nonhistorians: Gilbert Sewall, a professional critic of multiculturalist textbooks, and David Battini, a conservative teacher from Cairo, New York.

Two years later, the standards were ready, in the form of three volumes —one covering all history for kindergarten through the fourth grade, and one each for U.S. history and world history through the eighth grade. But six days before the books' official release, and two weeks before the midterm elections, Cheney let loose with a *Wall Street Journal* op-ed tirade crying foul. Her own earlier judgment was at stake. She had been impressed, she wrote, with earlier work from Nash and Crabtree's center, which emphasized "individual greatness," "convey[ed] the notion that wealth has sometimes had positive cultural consequences in this country," and was "honest about the failings of the U.S., but . . . also regularly manage[d] a tone of affirmation." Not so the new standards, which, Cheney wrote, gave George Washington "only a fleeting appearance and . . . never described [him] as our first president"; considered "the foundings of the Sierra Club and the National Organization for Women . . . noteworthy, but [not] the first gathering of the U.S. Congress"; never mentioned the Constitution; mentioned McCarthy or McCarthyism nineteen times and the Ku Klux Klan seventeen times; mentioned Harriet Tubman of the underground railroad six times but "two white males who were contemporaries of Tubman, Ulysses S. Grant and Robert E. Lee," one and zero times, respectively; and Paul Revere, Alexander Graham Bell, J. P. Morgan, Thomas Edison, Albert Einstein, Jonas Salk, and the Wright brothers not at all. "Students are encouraged to consider Aztec 'architecture, skills, labor systems, and agriculture,'" Cheney wrote. "But not the practice of human sacrifice." "They would sacrifice 10,000 people at a time," Cheney told a reporter. "If it had happened in the United States, I guarantee it would have been included in the standards." Cheney quoted two unnamed members of the National Council for History Standards, charging that "the 1992 presidential election [had] unleashed the forces of political correctness" and that in its wake the American Historical Association "had become particularly aggressive in its opposition to 'privileging' the West" and "threatened to boycott the proceedings if Western civilization was given any emphasis."

If Cheney felt "flimflammed," Nash once again felt blindsided. He thought two years of consultations had produced a "consensus." There had been no tremendous controversy about the U.S. history standards, although with respect to world history, there had indeed been what Nash called "a significant controversy on how much to stress Western civilization as against world civilization." "The process was as reasonable as one might expect something like this to be in our fractious time," one historian member of the council, Morton Keller of Brandeis, who describes himself as "a moderate (that is to say, a liberal who was only mildly mugged by radicalism)," wrote to me later. "I was deeply impressed with the good will exhibited by scores of organizations and their representatives toward the project at every stage of the standards' writing, and by the seriousness and thoroughness with which the actual writing (including the review of various drafts) was undertaken," wrote another, Akira Iriye of Harvard. "Some were more multiculturalist than others (I, for one, argued for a more forthrightly Western orientation). . . . It is of necessity a compromise document as far as ideological orientation is concerned, but in achieving a compromise, we never sacrificed, distorted, or misrepresented historical data." In the end, only Sewall and Battini opposed the standards.

The rest of the onslaught was not long in coming. "A classic of political correctness," declaimed Charles Krauthammer in his syndicated column. "Where is Plymouth Rock . . . ?" wrote LynNell Hancock in *Newsweek*. "What happened to the Niña, the Pinta and the Santa Maria? John Smith and Miles Standish, too?" The standards were products of "a secret group" and should be "flushed down the toilet," said Rush Limbaugh. In *U.S. News & World Report*, John Leo, a syndicated columnist specializing in culture wars who likes to style himself "Two Steps Ahead of the Thought Police," found "the usual multicultural excesses" among these "sour and negative" standards "written from the countercultural perspective by oppression-minded people who trashed the dean's office in the 1960s (or wished they had)," with "no uprising or rebellion . . . unmentioned" in a book whose "story line" was "the gradual rise of more and more rebellions against the selfish and hypocritical ruling white elites."

John Leo began by mocking the notion that children should "examine the lives of individuals who were in the forefront of the struggle for independence, such as Sam Adams, Thomas Paine, Mercy Otis Warren and Ebenezer McIntosh." Warren, a playwright, was the obligatory token woman, but four historians he phoned had never heard of McIntosh. The fifth, however, told him that "McIntosh was a brawling street lout of the 1760s who whipped up anti-British mobs and sacked the homes of various colonial officials." When I told Nash I hadn't heard of McIntosh either, he enlightened me: a leader of the Boston Tea Party, which surely has a more heroic ring in the most traditional of textbooks than "brawling street lout." In the *Wall Street Journal*, Albert Shanker, president of the American Federation of Teachers, was quoted as calling the world history standards "a travesty, a caricature of what these things should be—sort of a cheap-shot, leftist point-of-view of history. . . . Everything that is European or American, or that has to do with white people is evil and oppressive, while Genghis Khan is a nice sweet guy, just bringing his culture to other places." In fact, as Nash wrote the *Journal*, the book asked students to "assess the career of Chinggis Khan as a conqueror and military innovator in the context of Mongol society," to "describe the destructive Mongol conquests of 1206–1279 and assess their effects on peoples of China, Southeast Asia, Russia, and Southwest Asia," and to "debate the concept of the 'Pax Mongolica,' " asking, *"Is it worth the cost of terror to have an enforced peace?"* Nash's letter was never published.

As usual, accusations circled the world in a flash while refutations lumbered along behind. In a press release, interviews, and radio and television appearances, Nash and others scored points against Cheney's attacks. For United States history, the book proposed thirty-one areas for students to master, and in each case gave examples of facts that students should learn. Five of the thirty-one did indeed address the creation, compromises, provisions, and ratification of the Constitution. Three did indeed deal with major issues of the first Congress. White males were still the vast majority of individuals named in the standards (Washington was mentioned four times, once in a caption referring to his inauguration), but few names were mentioned among the standards proper, for the standards were conceptual—they were guidelines for teachers, not a history text. Most concerned causality and interpretation, not facts, while it was precisely the facts, names, and dates that the critics wanted to see. While Robert E. Lee was not, in fact, named, the U.S. history book said that students should be expected to "evaluate how political, military and diplomatic leadership affected the outcome of the Civil War," and, wrote Nash, "teachers and textbook writers certainly know what that standard means." Indeed, most of the names that Cheney wanted to see appeared in examples scattered throughout the U.S. history book. Although Alexander Graham Bell was not mentioned, Robert Fulton, Eli Whitney, Samuel Morse, John Deere, and Cyrus McCormick were. Bell, Edison, Einstein, and Salk duly put in appearances in the K through 4 and world history books. In any event, as Nash underscored when I spoke to him, the point of the standards was not to itemize inventors but to propose questions about the social effects of their inventions. About the Aztecs, Nash's view was that "it's absurd to say that [children] ought to know about African tribal warfare and Aztec human sacrifice (unless we focused as well on capital punishment for minor theft in England, legalized wife-beating, medieval torture, etc.)," all neglected as well. "Cheney argues that Aztec culture was organized around human sacrifice. That's not my reading of anthropological accounts."

Project codirector Charlotte Crabtree maintained, somewhat defensively, resorting to conventional textbook boilerplate, that "the standards strongly affirm the strengths of the nation's peoples—of *all* its peoples, in all their diversity; of the political and economic systems they have created; and of the progress that has been made toward bringing all our citizens the benefits of the nation's economic opportunities, civil liberties, and constitutional protections." The books' discussions of the Ku Klux Klan (thirteen of the references appeared in one two-page section) and McCarthyism (all nineteen references appeared in another two-page section) were meant to be civics lessons, she argued, "alert[ing] students to . . . assaults . . . and demonstrat[ing] . . . the strength of the democratic system to protect itself, provided concerned and vigilant citizens use the power of its institutions—free press, due process, and representative government—to turn back the assaults against them. These triumphs over the grim episodes in our history are powerful case studies, ennobling and inspiring to students, and an essential part of a sound education for active citizenship."

Here, the UCLA group was reaching. In truth, although Cheney surrounded her argument with a bodyguard of errors, she had a real argument. The topics and questions did not carry the triumphalist tone long associated with history textbooks. They directed attention to social conflict more than to social consensus. They invited arguments, not celebration—asking students to make the cases for and against slavery, for example, or to explore Mexican as well as American views of the Alamo. The standards did place African Americans and Native Americans at the center of American history, and John Leo was right that, in the process, white ethnics more or less disappeared. The standards were skeptical about the achievements of capitalism and skeptical of its myths. Although the section on industrialization included a quote from Andrew Carnegie's *Wealth,* students were indeed invited to debate whether business leaders were "captains of industry" or "robber barons," and (as Lynne Cheney pointed out) to conduct a mock trial of John D. Rockefeller for "unethical and amoral business practices," but were not invited to debate whether "labor leaders" were "bosses," or to conduct a mock trial of Jimmy Hoffa for unethical conduct. Rather, they were to be asked "how many of the great business leaders of the late 19th century fit the Horatio Alger model" and invited to "contrast the romantic depiction of life in the West with the reality."

Yet the standards were not a catechism, though Cheney sometimes addressed them as if that was what they were. *(Newsweek* at one point called them a "text," though most articles did accurately refer to "standards" and "documents.")* They were recommendations for textbooks, suggestions to curriculum writers and teachers. Moreover, the questions the standards raised and the emphases they chose were, in fact, the questions and emphases favored by the mainstream of the history profession over the past quarter of a century. "While the standards do reflect some of the objectionable conventional historiographical wisdom of our time," in the view of the self-proclaimed moderate historian Morton Keller, they also included "so much of what is positive about American historiography in recent decades—a new social and cultural history that for all its radical politicization has greatly expanded our sense of the American past."

Gary Nash's widely quoted claim that the standards amounted to "nothing short of a new American revolution in history education" was really making two points, neglected by almost all the critics. First, traditionally, American history was mainly the history of power, and power was white, male, and elite. (What else would it have been?) But the new standards carried a sense that history was also the struggle *against* power. They emphasized social history and social movements—though not indiscriminately, for they made a much larger place for feminists than for evangelical Protestants. Cheney was wrong to say, "This book is just the sad and the bad," but the standards did carry a sense that history was significantly, if not essentially, the struggle *against* the sad and the bad. Second, the standards aimed to teach students not simply *what* to know but *how* to think about history. Indeed, they took a position on how to attempt that awesome task. "The study of history," the U.S. history standards volume said, "involves much more than the passive absorption of facts, dates, names, and places. Real historical understanding requires students to think through cause-and-effect relationships, to reach sound historical interpretations, and to conduct historical inquiries and research leading to the knowledge on which informed decisions in contemporary life can be based." Toward this end, the book proposed to help students become competent in assessing the experiences of "those who were there," "to consider multiple perspectives . . . and multiple causes; to challenge arguments of historical inevitability; to compare and evaluate competing historical explanations . . . ; to judge [the] credibility and authority [of documents] . . . ; to analyze the various interests and points of view of people caught up in these situations." Using flow-charts and the usual high-minded pedagogical jargon, the standards proposed, for example, that "to demonstrate their understanding of the causes of the Revolution," students should be held responsible for three topics: The Causes of the American Revolution, The Ideas and Interests Involved in Forging the Revolutionary Movement, The Reasons for the American Victory. Not exactly a purge of white males, but neither was it names-dates-and-places history, or an exaltation of Founding Fathers.

The new standards were not an honor roll of heroes—or rather, they implied an honor roll so expanded as to burst out of the precincts of any pantheon. They were indeed, as charged, relatively light on traditional heroes and strong on abolitionists, feminists, unionists, and Native American chiefs. Mainly, they were not trying to inspire greatness but to question how much the greatness of individuals matters—something historians have been doing for more than a century. They wanted students to be critics and historians, not worshippers in the pantheon. They were, in short, trying to teach a (lower-case) democratic history—and to develop it, moreover, by a democratic process. This is where Lynne Cheney's objections, and those of the columnists in her wake, were coherent. The generalizing of reverence to raucous elements and ordinary people was not the reverence conservatives have in mind. But not just conservatives would be offended by the new standards. The offense was against a traditional conception of how to educate the young in (lower-case) republican virtue. Lynne Cheney wanted a republican history—schooling in the virtues of traditional republican leadership. The problem was that American history was inexplicable if it were nothing but a tour of the pantheon. Where was the emphasis to lie: reverence or explanation?

Democrats (also lower-case) are generalizers. If the Declaration of

Independence held that "all men are created equal," then the Seneca Falls Declaration of Sentiments of 1848 held that "all men and women are created equal." But democrats, too, carry a contradiction—the same contradiction, or at least tension, carried by all postmodernizations of history. The tendency of multiple identities and perspectives is to multiply boundlessly. The result is vertigo. Textbooks fall apart. Traditionalists want to shore up the former center. Radical perspectivists resent any center at all. From the logic of their point of view, it is never possible to be polycentric enough. To try to create a commons athwart these currents is a perilous project indeed. A progressive democratic multiculturalist like Gary Nash was bound to be whipsawed—attacked by California's extreme perspectivists and Washington's traditionalists alike.

I have taught American university students for a quarter of a century, most of them from among the top one-eighth of California high school graduates, and I have run into a good number who do not know the difference between an assertion and an argument; who purport never to have heard that there is a difference; who think that an opinion is a fact, perhaps expressed a bit more vehemently; who do not know how to make a case for or against a historical, philosophical, or sociological proposition. I once asked a class of upper-division Berkeley students, not for credit (or discredit), in what year World War I ended. The answers ranged from 1898 to 1939. I would be thrilled to meet students who could achieve what the National Standards propose be taught in grades 7 and 8, let alone 9 through 12. In "History Hijacked," Charles Krauthammer demanded: "How can [students] discuss anything without first having mastered dates, facts, places and events? History, like journalism, has to start with who did what when." Fair enough, but if Krauthammer had begun with who wrote what on what page, before filing his column, he would have found on page 21 of the U.S. history standards book that students of *grades 5 and 6* ought to be able to "calculate calendar time, determining the onset, duration, and ending dates of historical events or developments."

Fortunately, the vast majority of the overseeing council of thirty-one, including several historians who had been less than thrilled by all the standards, successfully resisted the logic of polarization. Morton Keller wrote:

I don't think Lynne Cheney is dead wrong in her criticism. I do think that she has dwelt on some of the standards' questionable features, and slighted some of their more admirable ones. . . . I agree that the standards should give students a greater appreciation of how remarkable some of the achievements of the nation's history have been. But I worry less than she does about this because the celebration of those achievements is deeply embedded in our culture, and I do not think that they are in danger of being overwhelmed by these standards.

Princeton's Theodore K. Rabb, the only European history specialist on the standards council, wrote in the *Washington Post* that while he had objected to "reducing the West to about 40 percent" of the world history standards—"in other countries," he pointed out, "such diminution of the central influences in a nation's heritage would be unthinkable"—the standards were defensible as "sets of recommendations from which [teachers could] select the topics that arouse their own and their students' interests," and that they amounted to "a serious effort to remedy the shortcomings of history education." Harvard's Akira Iriye, who had also wanted "a more forthrightly Western orientation," said more bluntly: "Those who condemn the [standards] project simply don't know what they are talking about or don't care to find out what is really in the text."

In this category were numbered the majority of the U.S. Senate, which, in January 1995, in the wake of the Republicans' midterm sweep, stampeded into a vote of 99 to 1 to condemn the new standards. The one holdout wanted an outright prohibition against expending a penny of government money to distribute the books. Liberals, voting to condemn, thought they were avoiding the worst. Thus during the glorious hundred days of the Republican Congress's "Contract with America," when the tone of the nation's discourse was being sounded by Rush Limbaugh, did politicians whose grasp of American history is feeble by any standards, new *or* old, stand up for piety. Thus do the culture wars rage on in a nation with a soured soul. Thus do dubious battles resist truces, let alone peace.

Here is the unacknowledged truth of the nation's identity crisis. The publicists and scholars who obsess about political correctness, and the politicians who seize the opportunities they open up, are frozen into their own correctness. They are the faction against factions. They feel victimized by those they accuse of cultivating victimization. Deploring hypersensitivity, they are hypersensitive to every slight directed at white men. Humorlessly, they decry the humorlessness of feminists and minorities. Those who charge distortion, distort. Advocates of the *unum* that holds together the *pluribus* are not themselves disinterested. True enough, not all Republicans believe that Patrick Buchanan was cultivating common ground when he told the 1992 convention: "There is a religious war going on in this country, a cultural war as critical to the kind of nation we shall be as the Cold War itself, for this is a war for the soul of America." But in the thick of the culture war, the movement that purports to wish to shore up the American center is itself a centrifugal force.

7

Where We're Coming From

1. Blinded Identities

How men and women think is not simply a function of what they have seen or felt in their own lives. Nor is their form of thought a genetic shadow cast by their parents or grandparents. People think within the intellectual and cultural currents that surround them—currents with histories, even if the sources cannot be seen from downstream. Even dissenters are soaked in the currents that they believe themselves to be swimming against. To paraphrase Marx, men and women think, but not in a language or concepts or even emotions utterly of their own making. To paraphrase Marshall Berman paraphrasing Trotsky, you may not be interested in philosophy, but philosophy is interested in you.

It is no small contribution to the triumph of identity politics that a form of intellectual parochialism has triumphed, a style of thinking that its detractors call relativism and its proponents, more clumsily, call perspectivism or standpoint theory. For all the specialization of culture today, the premise of much thinking in universities and popular lore alike is that how you see is a function of who you are—that is, where you stand

or, in clunkier language, your "subject position," the two nouns constituting an unacknowledged gesture toward an objective grid that prescribes
where you stand whether or not you know it.

Everywhere, the automatic first question is, "Where are you coming
from?" leading frequently to the conversation-stopping "We know where
you're coming from." Although alarmists of the cultural Right, claiming to
speak for a single morality, trace this form of thinking variously to English empiricism, American anthropology, German Marxism, or French
deconstruction, the academy has no monopoly on the decline of the claim
to truth. Perspectivists crop up everywhere, from op-ed pages to the
Grand Ole Oprah of daytime talk shows in which Klansmen and Afrocentrists, anorexics and abusers, rapists and rape victims all get their hearings. In a culture saturated by therapeutic talk, where even the president
"feels your pain," a sign of "caring" is the assurance: "I know where
you're coming from." There are said to be no privileged positions from
which to know anything. Our discussion, or "discourse," is fatally limited
to our language, our "interpretive community," our vantage point—by
which is usually meant our race, ethnicity, gender. There is no fixed,
stable meaning for the very terms with which, imperfectly, we strive to
know. There is, instead, a veritable orgy of "discourses" and "knowl-
edges," each of which—except perhaps that of the speaker—is limited by
its "silences." What there isn't is truth. There are only stories.

Of course, so pure a relativism is brittle. After all, human beings cry
out to know what is *true*, not just "true for them," and *right*, not just "right
for them." They may take a walk on the wild side to sample the daily
freak-show in the *National Enquirer* or on *A Current Affair*, but they
surely wish and expect, once the remote control has transported them to
the next sideshow, to confirm the rightness and stability of their moral
system, not to challenge it. In practice, the partisans of fundamental
group difference do not experience all stories as equivalent and equally
arbitrary. They rank their own stories higher than those of others. Often
what this means is that the story that, according to them, deserves to be
"privileged" is either the one told from the victims' point of view or the
one that casts the underdog group in the most flattering moral light. The
critics of the Houghton Mifflin textbooks spoke of truth, claiming that
they had it (or, with a summer of research, could get it) and that Gary

Nash didn't. To the challengers' ears, Father Junípero Serra's view that the California missions saved souls was not worth hearing; only the view of the "mission Indians" was. To the challengers' eyes, the Iroquois Confederation *was* the model for the federal system of government enshrined in the Constitution—although the evidence that the Iroquois system decisively influenced the writers of the Constitution is mixed.

Truth remains the Holy Grail. Beneath the smoky "instability" of postmodernism, virtually everyone claims to be telling it like it is. Everyone strives to make sense of the world and not just of his or her personal state of mind or tribe. The most passionate critic of "male" science believes that she should step out of the way of an oncoming bus, whether or not she believes in the Cartesian mind-body split. The most passionately separatist member of the Nation of Islam cites authorities and documents, presents a caricature of evidence to blame the Jews—not the Christians, not the Muslims, but the Jews—for slavery. He claims that it is true, not just "a story," that significant numbers of Jews profited from the slave trade.

But the perspectivist attack is not to be dismissed as an insult with a pedigree, a self-serving cover for the blind assertion of self-interest. However eager it is to be "transgressive" and "subversive," however much it claims to be a departure from false Enlightenment promises of a universal knowledge accessible to and true for all humanity, standpoint theory is a creature of the Enlightenment. Those who deplore false universals still address arguments to a wide variety of human beings whom they presume have the power to reason. They propound what they claim are true, or truish, universals—not least of which is the insistence, across the board, that *all* knowledge, not just that of their group, is local, limited to the territory where their standpoint prevails. Those who defend the proposition that different groups have fundamentally different views of the world and cannot understand one another are unlikely to protest that the enterprise is futile when a publisher offers to translate their books into other languages.

At conferences in recent years, when I have argued against the excesses of identity politics, I have heard something like this:

"What he says is easy to say, therefore easy to discount. It follows directly from his social position. In fact, it is not 'he,' an author, who speaks, it is his 'subject position.' It is his objective social interest who 'speaks him.' Face it: His is the *cri de coeur* of a white male, heterosexual to boot, and no longer young. It expresses nothing other than the lament of his caste, which needless to say feels threatened. With reason—it has lost some of its power and resents it. Moreover, this particular white male heterosexual experiences a particular loss. He mourns the loss of a Left that can no longer be—that would have given him an honorable, even central place to stand. Once, he and his generational gendermates could with confidence have presented themselves as the Left, feeling themselves justified in their life-choices, for they did well by doing good. They felt secure in a lineage, for were they not the good sons who would in the course of events inherit the family business, that business being, in this case, a political tendency? Imagine their chagrin and disturbance to find that they had been swept aside, that the mantle of liberation had itself been liberated by young upstarts, exposing erstwhile radicals as nothing but nostalgic *conservateurs!* To be sure, like all interested parties, the author casts his views in the shape of disinterested observations. He purports to reason his way to his conclusions. Well, this is ever the way in which the powerful claim a mantle of justification—choosing which arguments to accentuate and which to neglect. In fact, his reasons are *post hoc.* His conclusions came first. His arguments amount to nothing more than rhetorical gestures."

These are not trivial objections. They make a point eminently worth making: all thought begins with persons, and all persons are situated—in times, places, societies, cultures. That is to say, all thought begins within boundaries. The subject and tenor of thought are frequently (though not always and not totally) predictable from the origins of thinkers. Blacks are more likely than whites to doubt the promise of America; women more likely than men to care about children and fear rape; Jews more likely than Buddhists to study the Holocaust. Human beings neither live in a state of nature nor give birth to themselves, but encounter the world through categories passed on via nations, classes, castes, generations, eras, genders, occupations, races, and so on.* We are interested parties—

---

* I deliberately avoid the academic boilerplate terms "constitute" and "construct." These drastically overused jargon items began as useful correctives to the individualist assumption that individuals are

persons with angles of vision, persons to whom certain questions, points, and facts occur nonrandomly because of our life experiences, psychic makeups, and solidarities. It is in the nature of the human situation that our interests are inevitably accompanied by blind spots, by—to use the jargon—"silences," "erasures," "exclusions," and "repressions." Knowing this, we make assumptions about the validity of what is said from our knowledge of who is speaking. We consider the itemizing of "context" a necessary part of the full understanding of human beings.

But just how deeply and unalterably are we mired in our limited selves and meager understandings? And how are we to know in advance just how deeply we are mired? Historians of life and literature worry the question to death these days, and biographers are frequently locked in a death-grip with their subjects, and are preoccupied with that fact. Knowing how the world looked to the dead would seem to be even more difficult than knowing how the world looks to a living member of another group—though why it should automatically be easier for a Navajo living

---

sole producers of their destinies, but quickly curdled into cliché—misleading cliché at that. Through automatic recourse, these terms and their equivalents lend themselves to routine overstatement. Take these observations of the influential historian Joan W. Scott: "[D]ifference and the salience of different identities are produced by discrimination." And: "[D]ifferences are created in power relationships. . . . Difference has to do with something that's vital to the sense of self of an individual or a group, and it constitutes a power relationship with a set of interests and problems that are not easily resolved or given over by the notion of universalism." Leave aside the questions of what produces discrimination, what is a group's "sense of self" and where it comes from. If the first sentence in Scott's second quotation means that differences are reducible to power relationships, it is demonstrably false. (Russians perceive that Africans are "different," but not because they necessarily have any power over the Africans, or because the Africans necessarily have any power over them.) If the first clause of the last sentence means that difference automatically creates a power relationship, it is demonstrably false. (The Kurds and the Tutsi are different, but they have very little if any relationship at all.) If it means that difference creates nothing but a power relationship, it is also demonstrably false. (If I like the raps of Sister Souljah, it is not because she has the power to compel me to buy her compact disc.) If it means that there are no power relationships without difference, it is tautological. (I cannot exercise power over myself—except insofar as one part of myself is "different" from another part of myself.) The unexamined use of these terms presumes that life experience amounts to nothing but the language and institutions of the milieu. Likewise, to say that identities (for example, woman or homosexual) are "constructed" in history catches the truth that labels shift and categories come and go but is frequently stretched so far as to presume that they are constructed *out of thin air*. We may construct a house, but it helps if we bring bricks, lumber, labor, plans, and so on to the site. Habits are not changed at will. Dennis Wrong has pointed out the overuse of "constructed," and attributed it, in my view correctly, to the resounding success of sociology in popularizing concepts like those of Peter Berger and Thomas Luckmann's *Social Construction of Reality*.

at the end of the twentieth century, say, than it would be for a sensitive white man to recover the experience of a Seminole living at the end of the eighteenth century is not altogether clear; nor is it clear how anyone could know. Even in the present, the difficulties of reaching into the lives of sociological or anthropological subjects are daunting. Yet a moment's reflection also suggests the limits of epistemological doubt, especially when it is so firmly embraced as to become doctrine. Difficulty is in the human condition, but what of that? The question is not whether we start with perspectives—of course we do—but where we go with (and from) them.

So many difficult matters, so crudely brushed over by the perspectivist *ad hominem!* Perspective may lead to falsity or to truth, may be conducive to some truths and not to others. Perspective may be conducive to accurate observations or distorted inferences, may lead to promising notions or idiotic ideas—but to evaluate the observations, inferences, or ideas, we need to do more than inquire into their origins. Whoever brings forth an argument, discussions, arguments, analyses, and reasoning need to take place.

This is easiest to see in the realm of science, where truth-seeking, in principle, overrides all other considerations. The science that cheaters do is no less bad if their motives are good or, for that matter, if they are kind in their private lives. To know whether the science is good or bad requires a perspective different from all other perspectives: a commitment to truth-seeking above all else. Of course, it can be argued that the problem is simple in the case of hard science; among scientific practitioners, there is a strong consensus—even if honored in the breach—as to what constitutes legitimate scientific work and what incompetence or fraud. Still, even when we turn to ideas about society, not nature, there is no reasonable way to maintain that the worth of an idea is exhausted by the identities of its exponents. All ideas about cause and effect, and all moral judgments, include factual claims that have to be assessed apart from their source. The question of whether Junípero Serra enslaved the Mission Indians is rationally debatable by Mexicans, California Indians, or Ethiopians. The claim that Auschwitz was not a death camp for deliberate genocide is false even if the person making the claim happens to be Jewish. Not even the most relativist of cultural anthropologists or the most multiculturalist of literary critics could rationally maintain that social position determines value in a one-to-one fashion.

Anyway, just how firm is "women's" or "the Latino" or "the African-American" or "the Jewish" perspective? Not only are there class, regional, age, political, and plain individual differences among the different, but people of every description change their perspectives. Indeed, to ride and guide and temper and live these changes is one of the great adventures of modernity. The onslaught of economic, organizational, and technological change inexorably erodes the very ground on which one's parents walked. Surely no culture has undermined the stabilities of tradition more consistently than America's. Perhaps the firmest American tradition is the undermining of tradition—regardless of color. Long before the throwaway styles of the mall world, American culture was a culture of self-invention—even if the conquerors believed that to create themselves they had to destroy those who stood in their way. Americans have recreated themselves often enough—from Crèvecoeur to Alcoholics Anonymous and "born again" Christianity—to puncture any belief in unyielding "identity."

To cultivate perspectives and shake them up is one thing schools are for, and sometimes they succeed. Fresh experience undermines and reworks what young people take for granted. Under pressure from events and books, movies and speeches, conversations and courses, many rethink themselves and their relations to the world. They mature, regress, move sideways. They open themselves to thoughts that they hadn't thought before—including thoughts about "who they are." Religious and political renewals also challenge the rigidities of identity politics. Indeed, the possibility of a radical change in perspective is the very premise of that central element in religions and political systems, the narrative of conversion. Abraham, Paul, Mohammad, Augustine, the Buddha—for each, there is the moment of truth when scales fall from the hero's eyes and he rethinks, reinterprets, shucks the old skin, and takes on a new identity. So, too, for heroes of identity politics like Malcolm X. It is precisely the brand-new identity that followers are inspired to take on, and precisely this identity that the exponents of identity politics want to cultivate. If identity were a fixture of human life, why bother fighting so hard over what is to be in the textbook or who is to control the reading list in women's studies? If some people at some times change their perspectives, who is to say in advance who will and who won't, and when or why?

Moreover, interested parties have compound, multiple identities and, accordingly, interests. This, too, is part of what it means to be modern: to be complicated. Identities overlap within the scope of a single human life. We—Americans in particular—are populated by more than a single category. Leon Wieseltier has said it well: "The American achievement is not the multicultural society, it is the multicultural individual. And the multicultural individual is what the tribalists and the traditionalists (they are not always the same people) fear. Identity is a promise of singleness, but this is a false promise. Many things are possible in America, but the singleness of identity is not one of them." Perspectives grow in the crosshatched zones where memberships intersect. The purity of "subject positions" exists only in the geometry of theorists. We are not only but also.

Then is the freedom to choose from among one's identities, to develop new ones, to combine and recombine them as one likes, a privilege of straight whites whose identities are not punishable by bigots? To varying degrees, yes, but the fact that skin color and sexual orientation are privileges does not make the freedom to be oneself, or oneselves, less valuable. To the contrary. Many people suffer because their identities are despised, but that is an argument for increasing their chances for satisfaction, not an argument for restricting identity to the current array. If some people have less freedom to choose identities—which is certainly the case—that is a good argument for fighting discrimination and supporting their right to more freedom.

At any given time, in any given situation, one or another of my identities may come to the fore and the others recede. Even within a given group, there is no one-to-one relation between membership and perspective. Subidentities, too, blur and shift. By none of my identities am I "determined" in the sense of "compelled." I am shaped, no doubt. Disposed, perhaps. Limited, definitely. Completed, no. I disagree with other Jews, middle-aged folks, and old New Leftists about, for example, what should be done in Bosnia or Israel. If my membership *is* my perspective, how can such disagreements be possible? If I change my views on the

Palestinians, or how to respond to Louis Farrakhan, have I crossed a line and ceased to be a Jew? (Some of the essentialist Jews in the organizations that regard themselves as "the Jewish community" might say so.) Identity, love it or leave it—this is the pseudo-logic of loyalty oaths, bullying at worst, absurd at best.

Just what is a "group" anyway? Exactly who authenticates an authentic identity? Who is entitled to issue membership cards? Boundaries shift in time and space. Resemblance is relative to the culture and the purpose of classification. To a passerby or a census-taker, I am white. To an anti-Semite, I am simply a Jew. To a German Jew, I may be one of the *Ostjuden;* to Sephardim, an Ashkenazi Jew; to an Israeli Jew, American; to a religious Jew, secular; to a right-wing Zionist, an apostate, or no Jew at all. Advocates of identity politics will insist that the issue is not simply the elusiveness of categories or the American tradition of self-naming, but oppression and persecution. Hasn't history already done its detestable and irreversible work, stamping inferiority on dark-skinned peoples, enslaving them in the name of that classification? Without doubt, the group identities that have lasted longest and cut deepest are the ones that persecution has engraved. Once engraved, they stay engraved—that has been the reality. Thus has it been for centuries in the West, where white supremacy is the main lie that has rationalized detestation, enslavement, and slaughter, not to mention the ingenious variety of discriminations to which human beings are prone. Often the persecuted revolt by converting the mark of their subordination into a badge of pride.

But what follows from these categories once they are imposed? Identity is no guide to accuracy, to good judgment or political strategy. Race (or gender, or sexual preference, or disability) is far from an adequate, let alone complete, guide to the world, since all identity is a blindness as well as a way of seeing. A map colored strictly by gender (or race, or religion) does not account for the complexity of the world, does not allow anyone to navigate a society that is, by any definition, multiple, replete with perspectives.

Today's popular line of argument to the effect that people can only comprehend people like themselves does not convince. In fact, across boundaries, at least in complicated societies, people are always translating differences into mutually intelligible terms and reasoning about the good. Whatever relativists may say about the impossibility of John Doe grasping what Jane Roe means, John can translate from Jane's speech into terms that John understands, while Jane does the equivalent for John. If there is not to be irresolvable conflict, then people have to agree to limit the severity of their differences—even while pounding the table and claiming the uniqueness of their communities. They have to share a framework in which differences exist amid what does not differ—the common element, the shared ways of seeing and rules of the road that decree that, for example, whatever one's social origin, it is reasonable, in the United States, to drive on the right side of the highway. If the value of thought were determined in a one-to-one fashion by the identity group, then there would be no way to adjudicate disputes but to cede—or secede. Not only would differences within the group be impossible, so would change.

In a more or less democratic society, it is an observable fact and a general good that people of all identities and perspectives go to the trouble of trying to persuade others to side with them. That is what happened in the California textbook dispute. The groups who opposed the Houghton Mifflin series did not restrict their advocacy to people who resembled them on the premise that resemblance automatically causes perspective. They could not afford to. They had to raise their voices over their ghetto walls. The most fervent advocate of identity politics makes appeals intended to reach beyond the boundaries of the foreordained identity group; makes a pass, at least, at a more generally accessible truth; appeals to a common reason; holds certain truths to be self-evident. Even to speak to the group, the advocate of identity politics routinely has recourse to evidence, deductive logic, claims of rights—assumptions and techniques drawn from the despised apparatus of the ("white male") Enlightenment he purports to negate. He may believe that there is no legitimate way to argue his way over the walls of self-interest—that only might, in the end, makes right—but it ill behooves him to say so.

Partisans of cultural politics think they are resisting the uniformity, the dizzying anonymity, of American life. They refuse to be unmoored, adrift in the swirls and malls of contemporary existence, overpowered by the unbearable lightness of advertising, television, movies, video games. Sooner than remain rootless and disembodied, gnawed at by endless propaganda, they will remain loyal to traditions and ancestors, will find a place to stand in the company of the community, the group, the tribe. If identity is both the starting point and the end point of all intellectual dispute, they need not tarry anywhere in that difficult, rugged, sometimes impassable territory where arguments are made, points weighed, counters considered, contradictions faced, and where honest disputants have to consider the possibility of learning something that might change their minds.

2. The Shadowed Enlightenment

The Enlightenment has had a bad century. Any graduate student with an ear to the ground can tick off a list of the philosophical pallbearers— Nietzsche, Weber, Horkheimer and Adorno, Heidegger, Foucault, Derrida, Lyotard—in different permutations and combinations depending on the department in which he or she is enrolled. The Enlightenment has come in for a pounding not only in the theory seminars of the academy but at the mall and the health food store, in the astrology columns and on the afternoon talk shows. Plenty of Americans may not be interested in philosophy, but philosophy is interested in them.

The lineage of perspectivism begins with reactionaries, nationalists, and romantics, the likes of Burke, de Maistre, and Herder mocking the pretensions of the Enlightenment. The critical spirit praised by Enlightenment *philosophes* could be—and was—turned against them. In fits and starts, and then with a rush at the end of the nineteenth century, the claims of reason were weakened, morality relativized, language peeled away from the heart of things. The philosophical unfounding father of the trend was Nietzsche, the patron saint of today's irrationalists, insisting that reason and so-called civilized morality have a less than enlightened history—that they are the products of enslavement and repression. The sociologist Max Weber, himself a partisan of objective knowledge that was not reducible to the world view of the knower, tracked the inexorable triumph of a broken version of reason, instrumental reason, or "rational-ization," with which bureaucracies promoted efficient means and not moral ends, forging bars for an "iron cage" that locked up modern humanity. Anthropologists demonstrated that cultures existed, in the plural, that they had their logic, that they "worked." The American pragmatists Charles Peirce, William James, and others, opened still other doubts about the scope and generalizability of reason. From a different direction, so did the Viennese philosopher Ludwig Wittgenstein in his exploration of the fluidity of language. ("We never arrive at fundamental propositions in the course of our investigation," said Wittgenstein in 1930. "We don't get to the bottom of things, but reach a point where we can go no further, where we cannot ask further questions.") The German Martin Heidegger, on his way to embracing Hitler, pronounced the technological form of reason a form of estrangement from Being. From a Marxist angle, during World War II Max Horkheimer and T. W. Adorno declared the Enlightenment "self-destructive," "totalitarian," "patriarchal"—hell-bent on undermining the promise of its own achievements. Science itself, in the view of these disabused émigrés from Nazi terror, enshrined abstract reason, which "liquidated" the very individuality the Enlightenment claimed to be liberating. "Even the deductive form of science," they wrote, "reflects hierarchy and coercion."

Half a century ago, then, a philosophical setting was already in place for perspectivism. The academy was already primed for the revolt against universalist faith. Those who thought they were building the edifice of knowledge on firm foundations were told that they were actually constructing a dungeon. Then the street came into the seminar room. Present-day quandaries concerning multiculturalism and identity arrived in the library, the museum, the school board meeting not only through the force of argument, or the contradictions inherent in the Enlightenment, but through blacks in Watts, feminists in Atlantic City, and gays at Stonewall. The black, feminist, and gay movements demanded to be present wherever goods were allocated, textbooks written, teachers hired, plays performed. They formulated demands in the Enlightenment language of universal rights and, once they got inside, changed the look, the literal coloration, of intellectual life. They brought new blood to perspectivism because they brought perspectives. They jolted institutions with identity politics because they brought unacknowledged, unfamiliar identities with them—and brought them into universities so populous that it was easy to mistake them for the world.

The premise of mass higher education, moreover, was that knowledge mattered deeply. And yet, it came to be argued, the society that resulted was destructive, the order disorderly, the knowledge poisonous! Deep reason seemed futile. Deformed and deforming instrumental reason was evidently in charge, personified by the likes of Robert S. McNamara and Henry Kissinger. Confronted with the Establishment's claim that America was the incarnation of goodness hand-in-hand with reason, the revolted doubted both. Loathing what "the best and the brightest" of purportedly enlightened America were doing in Vietnam, they looked for a way of recasting the good and the bright, rethinking not only America but thought itself.

The 1960s were more than action, they were thought—and the thought whose time had evidently come, the most heady thought, was deep doubt about the foundations of knowledge itself. Even before French anti-foundationalists like Michel Foucault and Jacques Derrida were imported onto these shores, there was a homegrown revolt brewing against the received idea of knowledge at its most unassailable: science itself. If objective knowledge was possible, surely the proof was in science! But Thomas Kuhn's *The Structure of Scientific Revolutions,* a short book that could be read by the resolutely nonexpert, made a powerful case for the idea that science was not a simple matter of producing pictures of the world "out there," outside history, each more accurate than the last, but rather was a human creation that took place *in* history, a succession of discontinuous, flexible, temporary, changeable ensembles of theories, methods, and instruments. This most influential twentieth-century American work in the history of ideas was first published for specialists to little fanfare in 1962, but its reputation grew until the word it introduced, "paradigm," became the stuff of *New Yorker* cartoons.

Oversimplified versions of Kuhn's idea swept the social sciences and humanities in the 1970s. Reworking materials that had seemed the very bedrock of received wisdom about the onward march of knowledge, Kuhn calmly undermined universalist reason at its apparent strong point. New facts, all by themselves, Kuhn argued, did not change scientific theory. It was, rather, new theories that led scientists to look for new facts in new places, to understand even the old facts differently, and thus to produce "revolutions" in knowledge. Kuhn's idea of scientific revolutions caught fire among people who would otherwise not have been much interested in the history or philosophy of science. This was dizzying, mind-bending. If science was not a direct report from the world "out there," then it was freed to become a creature of, well, perspectives. Forget objective knowledge: it was perspectives, theories, "discourses," all the way down. If this were so for ideas about nature, would it not be all the more assuredly true for ideas about society? Never mind Kuhn's protestations that he had never meant that all knowledge was always a trumped-up rationalization wheeled out by interested parties.

Intellectual doubt joined political despair. Just as Enlightenment faith in universal reason was collapsing, this very faith was taking a bad rap for social catastrophe. The mood and the argument sounded like this: Look at the twentieth century! Need anything more be said than those dreadful words, *twentieth century?* Civilization, ever more rational in its means, has become ever more conquistadorial in its conduct, more deadly in its consequences. A whole civilization can chant along with Ahab: "All my means are sane, but my end is mad." Can it be an accident that the century of inoculations, sanitation, and mass production is also the century of extermination camps, Gulags, and the bombing of whole cities? Does the connection not speak for itself? As the Polish-Jewish-English sociologist Zygmunt Bauman has argued, it was precisely the triumph of industrialized reason—smoothly running trains, elaborate record-keeping, mass-produced lethal chemicals—that made organized, barbaric mass murder possible. Auschwitz has to be counted not as a gaping hole in the Enlightenment, but as part of its built-in potential. And if mechanized genocide is still extraordinary, the mechanized devastation of the environment is routine. The same science that created the steam engine and the automobile presides over the pulverization of nature—pollution, desertification, ozone depletion, global warming—all on a grand scale. Once humanity has learned to measure the rain forest in board feet, we are on our way to destroying it. The apparatus of mass production, owing no obligation to nature, or to weaker societies, undermines both. Is it not self-evident, then, that the Enlightenment is the theme song of imperial conquest, destruction and self-destruction?*

No, it is not. Indeed, the immense gravitational field of the Enlightenment is not so casually escaped, even by its critics. Those postmodernists who propose to discard the Enlightenment as an excrescence of male, imperialist, racist, Western ideology are blind to their own situation. For all their insistence that ideas belong to particular historical moments, they take for granted the historical ground they walk on. They fail, or refuse, to recognize that their preoccupation with multiculturalism, identities, perspectives, incommensurable world views, and so forth would be unimaginable were it not for the widespread acceptance of Enlightenment principles: the worth of all individuals, their right to dignity, and to a social order that satisfies it.† The debate about the knowability of reality would not be taking place on such a large scale were there not a public education system that admits tens of millions of people to the possibility of a conversation about such topics. For that matter, those who worry that the industrial system directed by imperial male egos is destroying the world through global warming gleefully brandish the measurements gathered by scientists who surely believe that what they are measuring is actually "out there" and not simply a "construction" of imperial egos.

Even the ideals of perspectivism and its political equivalent, self-determination, are the still uncompleted, indeed uncompletable unfolding of one of the Enlightenment's major potentials. That ideas carry the

---

* The most common form of this argument today is so-called standpoint feminism, the idea that so-called objectivity and so-called emancipation are nothing but the trappings of the imperial masculine ego at work, consuming, obliterating, or paving over everything in its path. In this view, patriarchy's rage to rule is the inevitable consequence of the Cartesian illusion that the mind is separate from the body and hovers in free space, like God's eye, treating the world as an object. At the root of male supremacy and ecological disaster alike lies the false assumption that the world has no life of its own but exists for the pleasure and conquest of the (white, Western, heterosexist) male ego.

† The most cogent defense to date of the politics of difference, that of the Canadian philosopher Charles Taylor, traces it to Rousseau's emphasis on personal authenticity and Herder's insistence that "each person has his own measure." Then, "the politics of difference grows organically out of the politics of universal dignity." But the principle of universal human rights also imposes a caution: one tribe's dignity must not infringe on that of another tribe. That is, universalist principle restricts the prerogatives of a culture, however much it prides itself on its right to recognition. On this most universalist ground, the Confederacy did not have the right to secede from the Union in 1861 and take the slaves along, and Croatians were bound to make room for the rights of Serbs when they seceded from the former Yugoslavia in 1992.

marks of experience, that individuals have the right to be individual—these are offshoots of the value placed by Enlightenment thinkers on the critical life. The Enlightenment did not propose to reduce thought to a diagram, it was—it continues to be—a force-field of ideas encouraging people to discover the world, and themselves in it. A humane respect for difference, an understanding that *one aspect* of the human condition is to live in a distinct milieu, an acknowledgment of the limits of what anyone can know—these remain the basis for common human rights. The Enlightenment's enduring ideal of universal rights, once extended logically, guarantees the right to be different—although it is also a reminder that human beings have good reason *not* to differ about one elementary right: the right to be who one wishes to be.

The Enlightenment is not to be discarded because Voltaire was anti-Semitic or Hume, Kant, Hegel, and Jefferson racist, but rather further enlightened—for it equips us with the tools with which to refute the anti-Semitism of a Voltaire and the racism of the others. (Jefferson in particular promoted a useful First Amendment.) In none of these cases was bigotry at the core of the man's intellectual system; it reflected the routine white prejudice of the time. The Enlightenment is self-correcting. The corrective to darkness is more light. Far from ramming a partial ideal of reason down the throats of the unenlightened, the Enlightenment at its best proposes conversation among individuals and groups as an important source of insight into our common condition. It is from the much-maligned Enlightenment that the idea emerges that we must all, in the philosopher Richard Rorty's words, "lend an ear to the specialists in particularity." But lending an ear does not mean turning one's face from the Enlightenment. The fact that Jefferson owned slaves and cavalierly presided over the refusal to enfranchise women does not justify any particular view that happened to be held by a slave or a woman.

No, the Enlightenment is not so easily shrugged off. Even Horkheimer and Adorno did not believe that the Enlightenment ought to be junked, but rather that it needed to be bolstered against its worst propensities. In the time of the war against fascism, they did not want "consideration of the destructive aspect of progress . . . left to its enemies." Today's identity theorists are properly skeptical toward imposed, imperial, arbitrary, unwarranted universalizations. They pursue what one feminist theorist,

Lata Mani, calls the "revolt of the particular against that masquerading as the general." But where did they get their skepticism? How do they justify their revolt? Why does it seem legitimate to them? Not on Confucian or Islamic or Aztec grounds. Not as an inevitable consequence of the human condition. The revolt rests precisely on the Enlightenment's taste for human equality *and* diversity, its ideal of self-determination, its objection to arbitrary power. The business of the Enlightenment was, indeed, to enlarge the scope of the differences that deserved respect— and challenge. Where there was respect for others, there was bound to be self-questioning and all the transformations spawned by self-questioning. The Enlightenment erected great structures of thought but also manufactured the acid to dissolve them. It was self-reinforcing and self-devouring. It was a philosophy for leaving home, not least one's ideological home, wherever that was. To hate absolutism was also to hate the absolutist claims of one's nation, tribe, family. For precisely that reason, the Enlightenment is not to be disposed of with a wave of the moment's identity cards.

If the Enlightenment is intrinsically incomplete—indeed, intrinsically incapable of being completed—what then? Does it follow, as Richard Rorty writes, that "the vocabulary of Enlightenment rationalism, although it was essential to the beginnings of liberal democracy, has become an impediment to the preservation and progress of democratic societies"? Should the whole project of trying to know and attain the general good be junked? One might just as well discard the right to the pursuit of happiness because people remain unhappy. Why does the vocabulary of "differences," "identities," and "stories" stand a better chance of helping preserve democracy or the mutual respect that is its underpinning? Rorty, the most articulate exponent of present-day skeptical pragmatism, has claimed that, in the real world, people act in the name of their particular tribes; that when they have acted altruistically, for example to rescue Jews in Nazi-occupied Europe, they have "usually" given parochial reasons for doing so—that the Jew was "a fellow Milanese, or a fellow Jutlander, or a fellow member of the same union or profession, or a fellow bocce player, or a fellow parent of small children." But the political theorist Norman Geras examined some eighty accounts of Gentiles who saved Jews during the Holocaust. Only one failed to mention universal moral obligations. Even those who saved their friends cited universalist motives as well. The rescuers spoke of defending "human dignity," of helping "a persecuted human being," of helping "because a human being ought to help another," of "our human duty to open our home . . . and our hearts to anyone who suffers."

The question is how to cultivate the spirit of solidarity across the lines of difference—solidarity with "anyone who suffers." For surely that spirit cannot be expected to generate spontaneously inside fortified groups, each preoccupied with refining its differences from other groups. And yet that is precisely where the emphasis has been placed. "There is no transcendence of cultural, religious, and national particularity," writes the political theorist Michael Walzer, another lucid proponent of what may be called a soft version of multicultural politics. "There is no 'higher' social formation than the local group, no historically necessary universalism beyond the newly articulated universe of difference." The most that distinct identity groups may expect, Walzer argues, is to baste together commonalities for a time, using arguments that are "secular, pragmatic, inconclusive," differing "even in the schemes we devise for incorporating difference." To think otherwise is a rationalist or metaphysical illusion— or worse, a violation of democracy, for as long as large groups insist on organized respect for their distinct identities, "there is today no democratic way of opposing the politics of difference." In a culture of centrifugal motion, Walzer maintains that "our only stable and common commitment" is to "principles of government," and hopes that "stronger organizations, capable of collecting resources and delivering real benefits to their members, will move these groups, gradually, toward a democratically inclusive politics," where "religious and ethnic activists begin by defending the interests of their own community and end up in political coalitions, fighting for a place on 'balanced' tickets, and talking (at least) about the common good."

I share the goal, but the hope needs a great deal of help. To develop a political majority requires more than occasional coalitions knitted together by overlapping interests. It requires also, and urgently, a *culture* of commonality. If groups spend Monday through Saturday turned inward, separately cultivating their differences, consolidating their internal unities, practicing cordiality to the exclusivists in their midst, it will not do for them to gather together on Sunday morning to speak of commonalities. To be active citizens of the whole, they must also spend time Monday through Saturday fraternizing across the lines, cultivating cultural hybrids, criticizing the narrowness of the tribe, working up ideas that people "unlike" themselves might share. One may respect the democratic rights of distinct groups to organize as they choose and still argue vigorously against the aggrandizement of difference.

The Enlightenment accepts the paradox that we are, in Rorty's words, at once "connoisseurs of diversity and Enlightenment rationalists," and refuses to dissolve the paradox on the cheap, either by annihilating the partisans of the wrong positions or by giving up the aspiration to better thinking and clearer sight. The Enlightenment says human beings are born and die, and in between, they seek to live. As for the rest, human nature is what human beings make of themselves. The Enlightenment obliges all of us to recognize that everyone sees the world through a prism—and that a prism is also a prison, a perspective is also a limit.

The bearers of all identity cards need to know more than where they're coming from; they need to know where to go, and where others are coming from and want to go. Toward this end, it helps all of us to listen, to know that we, all of us, are capable of reason, respect, insight, but also of unreason, cruelty, error. It does not help to sneer at universal rights and capacities as if all general statements about the human condition amounted to nothing other than glossy masks over the skull called power.

The enlightened democrat believes in an open universalism, not the hand-me-down sort. The enlightened democrat believes in pursuing the common good, not taking it on faith. The enlightened democrat has a different faith: that particular thoughts and experiences can be accessible to those whose thoughts and experiences are different. The work of the democrat is to find points of contact, to sympathize, to explain, to reciprocate and to appeal to reciprocity. The democrat believes that translation is feasible—perhaps only "up to a point," but when all is said and done, up to that point, which cannot be known in advance.

In other words, the Enlightenment is best understood as an aspiration, an invitation, a commitment to a process that seriously aims to bring about understandings that do not yet exist. It is not a Hall of Fame or a pantheon or an archive of preserved knowledge about how human beings ought to live. It is available only in a loose-leaf edition. The point is not to celebrate the achievements of some accomplished Enlightenment, as if its Declaration of Independence and *Encyclopédie,* its Federalist papers and Constitutional debates established once and for all the master list of what there was to be enlightened about and who was worth hearing on the subject. We don't need resurrection, we need sensible conversation. The golden years of the Enlightenment do not lie in some distant past, when Indians were slaughtered and Africans enslaved in the name of the higher virtues of Western civilization. If we are lucky, the golden years remain to be lived.

IV.

The Poignancy of Multiculturalism

Drive your cart and your plow
over the bones of the dead.

—WILLIAM BLAKE, *The Marriage of
Heaven and Hell*

8

The Fate of the Commons

Identity politics confronts a world in flux and commands it to stop. Because the flux is not going to stop, neither will identity politics. Many varieties will rise, flourish, fall, give way to others, some more strident, others (one can hope) more temperate. Today, some cultural fundamentalists defend the formulas of "multiculturalism" as solutions to the riddles of national identity in a world where the powers of any nation or state are steadily being eroded. Other fundamentalists, probably more numerous, claim that multiculturalism, racial preferences, and the like are instruments of an elite of usurpers from Harvard and Hollywood who are uncivilizing a formerly robust nation. The apparent opposites are twins. What frightens both is the flimsiness of a culture where everything is in motion and authority has perpetually to prove itself, where marginality is no longer always so marginal and the fragments of identity are on sale everywhere from the university to the mall. In the minds of all fundamentalists, porousness makes for corrosiveness. A porous society is an impure society. The impulse is to purge impurities, to wall off the stranger.

Today, these currents are at work almost everywhere to one degree or another. The stability of communities is undermined by the expatriation of capital, the migration of peoples, and the bombardment of images. Never before have hope, greed, and fear had so many channels through which to rush so fast. Jet planes transport immigrants overnight from Seoul to Los Angeles, while back in Seoul, engineers clone computers from Silicon Valley, taking the jobs of workers in San José, and the computers they build in Kuala Lumpur move capital instantly from Los Angeles to Tokyo. By contrast, the Korean engineer's brother in Los Angeles has no reason to phone the black man in Compton, a direct-dial telephone call away. In the not so United States, ethnic enclaves coexist in blissful or not so blissful ignorance. They are most aware of each other at points of friction. The collisions are widely reported, filmed, videotaped. They become lore. Over time, they congeal into history.

The collisions and suspicions feel all the more intense within a dynamic of economic decline. Under pressure from globalization, the nation-state loses its will and capacity to remedy what the conservative economist Joseph Schumpeter called the "creative destruction" that the unbridled market brings. Such controls as Western societies succeeded in imposing on capital's license during a century of reform have weakened. Growth is wildly uneven, inequality is immense, anxiety is endemic. The state, as a result, is continually urged to do more but deprived of the means to do so. When Americans think of the *res publica,* the public sector, they tend to think of unsafe streets and bad schools. It is mostly the private sector that they associate with efficiency—Federal Express, not the hapless U.S. Postal Service. Public schools graduate semiliterates while parents with no particular affection for Catholicism send their children to parochial schools. Public buses are infrequent and overloaded while limousines glide by. Observing the state's incapacity, resentful of those worse off than themselves, people blame the government, refuse to vote, hate taxes, doubt democratic institutions. Political parties are hollow shells for the convenience of contributors. People withdraw from public life altogether.

In these circumstances, decline mocks the notion of a common human condition of shared rights and mutual obligations. For an entire generation now, the majority of Americans have been losing ground. In income and wealth, they have been losing not only relative to the very rich, but in absolute terms as well. The shrinkage of real per capita income that began in the early 1970s has now continued for more than two decades. Average real wages fell by 18.8 percent between 1973 and 1994. While the wealthiest one-fifth of the population improved its economic position during the 1980s, the rest of the middle class—to which the majority of Americans feel they belong—plunged into insecurity. The upper reaches of unionized manufacturing jobs were riddled by plant closures, demands for givebacks, and—in that contemporary euphemism—corporate "downsizing." Total household income also declined, especially in families headed by women. The percentage of *full-time* workers who earn what the Commerce Department defines as less than a living wage ($13,091 in 1992) rose from 12 percent in 1979 to 16 percent in 1992. Since 1973, the number of American children living in poverty has increased by half, to 22 percent of the total.

The gulf in opportunities widened accordingly. If higher education is the embodiment of the American dream, the price of access is soaring. For all the hue and cry about imperiled canons, unfair affirmative action, and the horrors of political correctness, the question left in the shadows is: Who can afford the price of admission? The popular imagination has not been seized by the growing polarization between those who benefit from higher education and those who do not. In 1979, the student from the top quarter of American families had *four* times the chance of earning a B.A. degree by the age of 24 as a student in the bottom quarter. In 1994, a student from the top quarter had *nineteen* times the chance. This is class division with a vengeance, but it is the subject of no national debates, no newsmagazine covers, no congressional resolutions, no political campaigns.

Growing inequality erodes social solidarity. Yet the majority who have lost ground, and whose children stand to lose still more in the future, do not imagine themselves a majority. They have little collective imagination, no shared institutions, no political party, no common church, no unified school system, no one big union. Affirmative action for racial minorities has to some degree retinted the class gulf without changing its depth. No significant political counterforce insists on reducing the staggering inequality that has come to be accepted as normal in a country where the average chief executive officer in a large corporation collects 149 times the pay of the average factory worker. By and large, those who deplore the lack of a common history and curriculum do not object to these staggering disproportions. They are willing to live comfortably in a society where the rich and poor are equally free to read their Shakespeare in the gutter.

The impersonal mobility of capital, the pell-mell pace of technological change, and probusiness state policy all have combined to undermine what might otherwise have been a significant instrument of cross-racial, cross-ethnic, cross-gender, cross-regional solidarity: the union. In the United States, where forty years ago almost one in four American workers belonged to unions, fewer than one in six does today. Management-union relations have regressed to their condition of the 1920s. Among the majority who work, the experience of class solidarity is at its lowest ebb in three-quarters of a century. Even many workers see unions as nothing more than bureaucracies that pursue "special interests." But far more than a spontaneous onrush of individualism is at work. Unions are also undermined by the *other* special interests. "Strong organizations and group affinities based on sex, sexual preference, racial and ethnic ties, religion, physical handicap, and the like . . . have severely compromised the status of trade unions," the economist Michael J. Piore writes. "Federal labor policy . . . has substituted legislative remedies to the particular grievances of . . . groups (the handicapped, the aged, the racial minorities) for collective bargaining, and in the process has encouraged people to define their grievances and to organize in this way." No idle bystanders to social trends, many companies encourage the growth of particularist organizations in the workplace—one example is the anti-union Digital Equipment Corporation, which cultivates groups of women, blacks, and gays, to the point of buying a corporate page in the program of the Boston Gay Rights parade.

The paradox is that as investment, communication, organization, migration, and trade become more intensely global, the reality that people experience, the one that comforts them and fills them with feelings of membership, becomes even more stubbornly local—all the more so because competing claims of commonality feel hopelessly abstract and remote. The upheavals that once undermined traditional attachments end up generating pressure to reinvent—the oxymoron is deliberate—new traditional attachments. The globalizing current kicks up a backwash. People feel some deep, only half-understood desire simply to belong to some zone, any zone protected from the dominant power, and some way to differentiate themselves from the mass into which they fear they will disappear. The solidarity they trust is the one closest at hand: the one defined by people who look or speak like themselves. Here is the promise—however elusive it may prove—of roots, security, and, not least, prospects for advancement. Here is a dignified place in life.

But today, the identity obsession is not just practiced by history's most beleaguered people. American culture in the late twentieth century is a very stewpot of separate identities. Not only blacks and feminists and gays declare that their dignity rests on their distinctness, but so in various ways do white Southern Baptists, Florida Jews, Oregon skinheads, Louisiana Cajuns, Brooklyn Lubavitchers, California Sikhs, Wyoming ranchers, the residents of gated communities in Orange County, and "militias" at war with the U.S. government. The difference is that the people who like their America white and well-armed purport to speak in the name of "normal Americans." They are proud to proclaim that they have "traditional values" on their side. *Their* particularity is frequently camouflaged, at least for now, as universality.

It is the identity obsessions, all of them, each fueling the others, that give the question of multiculturalism its charge and its venom. If multiculturalism were nothing more than an acknowledgment of certain facts about the different ways in which people live, whom they like, what languages they speak, there would still be practical controversies, but they need not have bunched up and ignited a culture war or an identity panic. Why shouldn't a population have bilingual schools, to ease their way through the difficult transition to English? It does no harm to the larger community to hire bilingual police or ambulance drivers to save the lives of Vietnamese or Dominican immigrants. It cannot but encourage the learning of American history as something more than a pageant if that history is more than a chronicle of selected great men. It cannot hurt parochial Americans' capacity to live more fully in the world to know that Western civilization, for all its achievements, is hardly alone.

There is no necessary contradiction between a recognition of difference and the affirmation of common rights. To the contrary: it is in the universalist grain to protect women from genital mutilation; to defend gay men and women against being assaulted because of whom they love; to oppose racial discrimination in hiring, housing, lending, even in the meting out of the death penalty. A commitment to commonality should forthrightly entail an opposition to class bias in school expenditures and university admissions. None of these commitments requires severe identity politics. To the contrary: they are far more easily dismissed if couched as the demands of groups enraptured by how different they are from the general run of humanity.

Uneasy with the actual variety of American lives, many Americans signal their "normality" by shuddering at the very thought of multiculturalism. In fact, it is sometimes hard to tell who uses the term more insistently, those who embrace the phenomenon, whatever exactly they mean by it, or those who find it deplorable. The word is baggy, a mélange of fact and value, current precisely because it is vague enough to serve so many interests. Partisans may use the term to defend the recognition of difference, or to resist policies and ideas imposed by conquerors, or to defend cosmopolitanism—the interest and pleasure that each may take in the profusion of humanity. The purists of identity politics use it to defend endless fission, a heap of monocultures. On the other side, multiculturalism and its demonic twin, "political correctness," serve conservatives as names for a potpourri of things they detest—including an irritating insistence on the rights of minorities.

Yet in many ways, the jargon of multiculturalism, whether as angel or bogeyman, evades the central wound in American history. America's national history is short, as histories go, but it is thick with slaughter and misery, and none of the consequences are more biting, more disturbing, than today's conflicts between whites and blacks. The crime of slavery has shaped America's destiny so thoroughly that it might almost be said that the answer to "Who Are We?" is: We are a people who tried to live "half slave and half free." For all the complexities of today's identity quarrels, race is the origin or at least the template for most of them, and the concept of "race," the way most people use it, usually means the most profound either/or: black or white.

The core of our current predicament is that for centuries, in a culture that affirmed the rights of the individual, American blacks were subject to slavery—"social death," as the sociologist Orlando Patterson has called it—and that slavery was followed by more than 125 years of frequently violent discrimination. The forms of that discrimination have changed, and in many cases diminished, thanks to a civil rights movement that won the support of a majority. But history is stamped on the skin, a remark or a flash of anger away. The present is always rekindling the flammable past. In the thinking of many blacks—but not only blacks—the difference between slavery and immigration is fundamental, and the consequences for present-day generations equally fundamental. To be white, when all is said and done, is to have the privilege of being *not black*. Compared to this difference—"as different as black and white"—other differences, well, pale. Blacks made more than "contributions" to American history. There is a strong case to be made that slavery is central to the whole history of American prosperity. After such knowledge, what redemption? Why should the descendants of slaves have to make compromises, pitch in, help form majorities?

But the brutal fact is that the descendants of the Africans seized and shipped to America have no practical choice but to remain here— here where their ancestors were chained, sold, and lynched, where they too, regardless of achievement, are often despised, belittled, or feared, and where they have still, against all odds, struggled to make such homes as it is possible for the descendants of such a history to make. The past was murderous, but the survivors live in the present. Democracy is precisely that system in which people have the chance to overcome the past, to "drive their carts and their plows over the bones of the dead," in William Blake's words, with the least violence to the living or to those yet to live. The calculus of a people's suffering is a poor basis for organizing a society in real time. This is a political truth as well as a comment on the practical difficulty of calculating, no less securing, reparations. Minorities at war with majorities generally lose. Their prospects for protection and advancement rest on common interests and moral appeals to majorities, not on evanescent "rainbows," self-segregating "unities," phantom "people of color." Misrecognition of the actual situation is unforgiving.

What, then, are the risks of the go-it-alone mood that identity politics encourages? The hardening of difference today, the periodic showdowns, the cutthroat competition, evoke the nightmarish images that fill the daily news. Tribalism rampant has led to steady carnage in Bosnia and the civil war firestorms burning throughout the borderlands of the former Soviet Union. We properly fear what might be waiting in the wings from racial and ethnic conflict. If "ethnic cleansing" could arise in a Europe that was supposed to have learned to say *Never again* to mass slaughter, after the war after the war to end all wars, then metaphorically at least, Bosnia stands as some desperate dead end point of no return. "Balkanization" is a metaphor with a built-in unhappy ending. It is also a reminder of the futility of using history as a basis for endless recrimination. There, Ortho- dox Serbs are still trying to punish Catholic Croats and Muslim Bosnians for the losses of centuries past. This revival of the wars of religion is a grave defeat for the cosmopolitan credo that when different people coex- ist, mix, intermarry, their familiarity with one another makes life more rewarding for all.

But appalling as it is, Bosnia is not the nightmare America has to fear—not in the foreseeable future. A scenario of the war of all tribes against all other tribes is not in the cards here. Despite the inflamed metaphors of the day, America is not "coming apart at the seams." Amer- ican civic life has been spared the worst by democratic institutions that have lasted—institutions that were, to say the least, thin in Tito's Yugo- slavia and nonexistent in the Soviet Union. It is Canada, and perhaps Mexico, but not the United States, that flirts with dissolution.

But the more likely prospect facing the United States is nothing to crow over, either. It is more of the same soft apocalypse to which Ameri- cans have apparently grown inured: more inequality, more punishment of the poor, more demoralization and pathology among them, the slow (or not-so slow) further breakdown of civic solidarities. A necessary if not sufficient condition for the reversal of these tendencies is the emergence of a vital Left, but this is precisely what is thwarted by the obsession with group difference. It is not that such a Left would automatically know what to do; rather, that taking seriously the need to compose a majority, it might at least begin to ask the right questions. Without the revitalization of the Left, however, the breakdown of the commons will most likely continue to be administered by "conservatives" who conserve nothing; who combine buccaneer laissez-faire with a mystique of unattainable "family values" to create a voting majority that federates much of the anxious middle class, mainly men, mainly whites, with the rich, all joined in the collective satisfaction of not being black or poor.

So the cultivation of separate identities is myopic for the Left above all. Instead of thinking deeply about how to produce majorities, leftists tend to list minorities as if they might simply gravitate to each other by magic. In truth, on the Left and among multiculturalists, majoritarian thinking is frowned on as a sign of accommodation.* Leftists have too long been comfortable as minorities, too quick to flatter themselves as "cultures of resistance." This is, in part, because university culture is hospitable to minoritarian recklessness and identity obsessions; in part because present economic conditions divide more than unite; in part because, like it or not, leftist professionals benefited disproportionately, if unwillingly, from Reagan's flush years. With tenure or its equivalent, with children in private schools, their worlds are decoupled from the worlds of their putative allies in the working classes.

But minoritarian thinking is also a generational heritage, an unwitting, authentically tragic extension of the born-to-lose protest spirit of the late 1960s. Then, a New Left that had begun as a movement with majority support, in civil rights, became—had to become—a minority pitted against the Vietnam War. To contribute even to a left-of-center Democratic majority at the moment of civil rights triumph, in the mid-1960s, would have amounted, in Staughton Lynd's words, to "coalition with the Marines." The separatisms that followed Black Power spawned a growing satisfaction with minority status. Charged with the spirit of blunt confrontation, these separatisms were ill-prepared for, and heedless of, inevitable backlash.

It was in the wake of a revolution of rising expectations that affirmative action, set-asides, token representation, race-based political districts,

---

* Or there are attempts to finesse the problem away. Feminists, for example, are prone to claim that they are already intrinsically majoritarian because women compose, after all, a majority—as if women thought or acted as a unified bloc. Then there are the leftists who brush away defeats by claiming to speak for the nonvoting majority—as if nonvoters retain moral title to the nation, as a sort of consolation prize.

and other racial preferences came to loom so large in the agenda of liberals and the Left. But these segments of the Johnson and Nixon domestic programs presupposed a certain abundance. Who got seated at the table and in what order mattered less if the table was piled high. As prosperity receded, however, so did the constituency for affirmative action. Such programs and the rhetoric that attended them became wedges into the already dwindling constituency of the Democratic Party. Polarization was foreordained. As Yale law professor Stephen L. Carter argued in a complex book, *Reflections of an Affirmative Action Baby,* whose most subtle and constructive contribution was missed by reviewers of every stripe, there remains a strong case for affirmative action in school admissions (though not university tenure) and hiring (but not the higher reaches). But the higher the position, the weaker the arguments, until by the time a president (George Bush) nominates to the Supreme Court a man of minimal achievements (Clarence Thomas) and calls him "the best man for the job," the arguments for racial preference break down altogether. Many forms of affirmative action can be defended on grounds of fairness, though some cannot, but even the best are most convincing when they do not invite the less comfortable to pay the steepest price. It is, again, a matter of proportion. The argument is overloaded on both sides. Many advocates of affirmative action and race-based districts exaggerate what they have accomplished for the worst-off blacks, while opponents inflate the damage done to *their* sides.

There are many reasons why the least comfortable white men in particular feel insecure, but one that swells up to huge symbolic proportions is the feeling of indignity provoked by the sense that there is, for them, no particular benefit in restraining their resentment—or voting Democratic. What is at stake, in practical political terms, is large and immediate. Out of the election wreckage of November 1994, one clump of statistics stuck out like an assault rifle. Fifty-four percent of males voted for House Republicans, as against 46 percent who voted for Democrats. Women voted in exactly the opposite proportions. "It was," wrote Richard Morin and Barbara Vobejda in the *Washington Post,* "the largest gap since gender differences were first reported on exit polls in 1982." The numbers were still more skewed for *white* males. Sixty-two percent voted Republican. Speaker Tom Foley lost his Washington district despite carrying a majority of women because he got only 45 percent of the male vote (almost all white). George W. Bush took two-thirds of the white male vote against Ann Richards in the race for governor of Texas and won. Despite exceptions, the overall pattern was clear. As white men went, so went the nation,* in no small part because the white men who came out to vote were disproportionately the most splenetic. These were the men who in a cynical, spiteful time had not given up on politics. They thought they could make the proverbial difference. And they did.

The Republican tilt of white men is the most potent form of identity politics in our time: a huddling of men who resent (and exaggerate) their relative decline not only in parts of the labor market but at home, in the bedroom and the kitchen, and in the culture. Their fear and loathing is, in part, a panic against the relative gains of women and minorities in an economy that people experience as a zero-sum game, in which the benefits accruing to one group seem to amount to subtractions from another. Talk about identity politics! These white men, claiming they deserve color-blind treatment, identify with their brethren more than their wives or sisters, or minorities. But economic jitters are only one force behind the conspicuous loathing of Bill Clinton and Democrats of all factions. Symbols are fuel. The rage of dispossession has been at work, seething, for example, in the savage assaults on Hillary Rodham Clinton and the frenzy directed against Clinton's partial acceptance of gays in the military.

Then, too, victories are won not by census figures and questionnaires but by turnout. It was the Clinton-haters who came out to vote, while an extraordinary number of Democrats voted their alienation and disgruntlement, and stayed home. The white men most fundamentalist in their Protestantism and most dedicated to the National Rifle Association came out to vote because their antagonism to illegal immigrants, welfare moth-

---

* Only once in thirty years has the white male presidential plurality failed to predict the winner. In 1976, Gerald Ford took only 51 percent of the white male vote against Jimmy Carter and lost—his white males weren't a big enough majority to compensate for Republican losses among blacks. In 1980, Ronald Reagan picked up 59 percent of white males, a majority that grew in 1984 to an astounding 67 percent. In 1988, George Bush picked up 63 percent, against Michael Dukakis, and in 1992, 41 percent against Bill Clinton's 37 percent, the remainder going to Ross Perot. Thanks to Perot, in other words, Bush was the first Republican candidate to lose the majority of white males since Barry Goldwater.

ers, and beneficiaries of affirmative action outweighed anything Democrats offered. In general, those who benefit most from government-sponsored privileges—the old, the cattle-grazers, and the house-rich—vote most, while the unemployed, the poor, the young, minorities, and industrial workers vote least. (The proportion of blue-collar workers who vote in presidential elections declined by one-third between 1960 and 1988.) Those who most resent taxes vote to punish those beneath them. Suburban homeowners refuse to pay taxes for the urban schools from which they have withdrawn their children. The groups who need government most have seceded from politics, feeling that politics has seceded from them.*

A Left that was serious about winning political power and reducing the inequality of wealth and income would stop lambasting all white men, and would take it as elementary to reduce frictions among white men, blacks, white women, and Hispanics. Could it be more obvious that the Left and the Democrats alike are helpless unless they offer all these constituencies something they benefit from in common? At the same time, a Left is not a Left unless it defends the scapegoated poor, tries to deliver them (along with the not-so-poor) training, decent jobs, and provision for children, acknowledging that the present welfare state is not kind to the poor. But multiculturalism by itself does not contribute to that political revival. The most insistent multiculturalists do not seem to recognize that there is no Left, there is only more panic, unless a plausible hope emerges for a greater equality of means. The right to a job, education, medical care, housing, retraining over the course of a lifetime—these are the bare elements of an economic citizenship that ought to be universal.

---

* Perhaps voter registration reforms will bring substantially more Democrats to the polls, perhaps not. But even if they eventually overcome active opposition from Republican politicians and foot-dragging on the part of local Democrats who were perfectly content with the status quo, there remains a self-defeating culture of disgust among traditional Democratic voters. Their reflex belongs to the secessionist mind-set. Why bother voting, secessionists feel, if politics is hopelessly disappointing? According to the census, whites voted at a rate of about 45 percent, blacks at about 35 percent, Hispanics at about 30 percent. Of those Americans earning $50,000 per annum or more, 61 percent voted (a slight increase from the 59.2 percent who voted in the previous off-year election in 1990), while of those earning between $5,000 and $10,000 per annum, only 23.3 percent voted (down from 30.9 percent in 1990). In California, Hispanics constitute about 27 percent of the population, but in the crucial 1994 vote, where Proposition 187 punished illegal immigrants and their children, they constituted only 14 percent of eligible voters and only 8 percent of the state vote.

Yet today, virtually unopposed, the market is trumpeted as the sole source of economic growth and the undisputed marker of social health. No one proclaims the virtues of the unbridled market more strenuously than those who benefit from tax breaks and acceptable subsidies. Utopian capitalists, the most potent purists left in the world, proclaim that the market delivers precisely the goods that need delivery and rewards the right winners; as for the rest—well, too bad for the losers. But the market is compatible with immense inequality and social chaos. Corporate secession across borders bleeds away the nation's capacity to bring its citizens together. An unbridled market generates mass panic and beckons gangsterism, theocracy, and authoritarian crackdowns. It fuels fantasies of a "moral community" surrounded by fortifications, of a smug "West" permanently embattled, closed, and unreconstructed.

Of popular movements that actually exist, the ecology movement alone on the Left has serious potential for crossing the identity trenches. Freedom needs a commons that remains green. Most Americans understand that the so-called conservatives have no interest in conserving the earth. But even here, commonality politics does not emerge automatically. Environmentalists who enjoy professional life cannot afford to forget that the dangers to public health from headlong industrial development fall disproportionately on the working classes, whose factories are frequently vile, whose neighborhoods are more likely to be the sites of toxic dumps and poisoned air than the neighborhoods of the better-off, and whose jobs may be at risk if logging is stopped or automakers are ever forced to shift from gasoline to energy sources that would not further heat up the atmosphere.

But let there be no illusions. All left-of-center forces in the world today are chastened if not demoralized, and for good reason. For a generation, throughout the industrial world, most socialist and social democratic parties, and the groupings of intellectuals around them, have lost ground. This is not only, perhaps not even mainly, because of the shadow of the Gulag and the sordid record of the former command economies of the East. It is largely because the various Lefts start with a built-in disadvantage. They operate on a national scale while corporations and capital flows are transnational. The Left wants to mobilize in behalf of democracy and equality, while capital, the least democratic institution of all, slips through the mesh. In power, social democracies end up presiding over mass unemployment.

It is this mobilization for equality and against arbitrary power that is the Left's main business—if there is to be a Left. Just how can a democratic society regulate the demons of technology and the strains of competition? How can multinational corporations be brought under democratic control without resorting to the heavy hand of the state? In the United States, though, the mind-set of identity politics—including the panic against political correctness—aborts the necessary discussion. Cultivating unity within minority groups, the obsession with difference stands in the way of asking the right questions.

To recognize diversity, more than diversity is needed. The commons is needed. To affirm the rights of minorities, majorities must be formed. Democracy is more than a license to celebrate (and exaggerate) differences. It cannot afford to live in the past—anyone's past. It is a political system of mutual reliance and common moral obligations. Mutuality needs tending. If multiculturalism is not tempered by a stake in the commons, then centrifugal energy overwhelms any commitment to a larger good. This is where multiculturalism as a faith has proved a trap even—or especially—for people in the name of whom the partisans of identity politics purport to speak. Affirming the virtues of the margins, identity politics has left the centers of power uncontested. No wonder the threatened partisans of "normality" have seized the offensive.

The dialogue today is inflamed and incoherent in part because the symbolic stakes are overloaded on every side. There is a lot of fantasy in circulation. The melting pot never melted as thoroughly as Henry Ford would have liked; the golden years were mighty white. And the monocultures of Afrocentrists and goddess-worshippers, however foolish, are far less prevalent than their advocates wish or their antagonists fear. But if the Right magnifies the multiculturalist menace, identity partisans inflate the claims they make for multiculturalism. All suffer from a severe lack of proportion. Most of all, while critics of identity politics are looting society, the politics of identity is silent on the deepest sources of social misery: the devastation of cities, the draining of resources away from the public and into the private hands of the few. It does not organize to reduce the sickening inequality between rich and poor. Instead, in effect,

what the left should be doing

it struggles to change the color of inequality. In this setting, the obsession with cultural identity at the expense of political citizenship distracts what must be the natural constituencies of a Left if there is to be one: the poor, those fearful of being poor, intellectuals with sympathies for the excluded.

Make no mistake—the path of commonality offers no utopian destination. It offers, in fact, difficulties galore. Majorities come and go; they are not easy to stitch together under the best of circumstances. A diversity of customs and rages is here to stay—and nowhere more than in amazingly profuse, polychrome, polyglot America. Plainly people are motivated by loyalties to clan, religion, race. Meanwhile, capital moves across frontiers at the speed of light as labor lumbers along at a human pace. Capital can always threaten to take off for lower-wage pastures and bring national reformers to their knees. At the same time, the nation-states that people expect to protect them against the flux may be obsolescent in an age of global markets, but they haven't gotten the news. They exist. They have weight. They wave flags; they recruit armies; they build monuments; people are willing to kill and die for their symbols. By contrast, commonality offers—what? The discredited red flag? The blue banner of UN bureaucracy? The green flag is fine, as far as it goes, and so is the flag of human rights, but neither stirs enough human hearts.

Still, we will not see what lies on the other side of the politics of identity unless, unflinchingly, without illusions, we look, look again, and are willing to go on looking. For too long, too many Americans have busied themselves digging trenches to fortify their cultural borders, lining their trenches with insulation. Enough bunkers! Enough of the perfection of differences! We ought to be building bridges.

Acknowledgments

I began this book on sabbatical leave from the department of sociology at the University of California, Berkeley. The French-American Foundation made it possible for me to finish in Paris, as the 1994–95 holder of the Chair in American Civilization at the École des Hautes Études en Sciences Sociales. There, under the aegis of the Centre d'Études Nord-Américaines, I benefited from the hospitality of Jean Heffer and François Weil, and from discussions with them and with Sophie Body-Gendrot, Marianne Debouzy, Nelcya Delanoë, Denis Lacorne, Dominique Schnapper, Alain Touraine, Sylvia Ullmo, and Michel Wieviorka.

I am grateful to many. For chapter 1, I had the benefit of interviews with David Anderson, Yasmin Anwar, Richard Arum, Carol Chinn, Harry Chotiner, Toni Cook, Fred Ellis, Kitty Epstein, Allen Graubard, Sheila Jordan, Jan Malvin, Gary Nash, Pedro Noguera, Meredith Story, Renee Swayne, Steven Weinberg, and Shelley Weintraub. Jan Malvin and Gary Nash gave me the use of many documents and tapes. For the fourth part of chapter 6, I thank Akira Iriye, Morton Keller, Albert Shanker, David Vigilante, and again Gary Nash for their letters.

Over many years of wrestling with the conundrums of culture and politics, I have benefited from conversations and correspondence with Marshall Berman, Kenneth Cmiel, Troy Duster, Richard Flacks, Maurice Isserman, Jeremy Larner, Robert Jay Lifton, Ruth Rosen, and Richard Zinman. Useful tips and facts came from Richard Alba, Frédérick Douzet, Steven Lukes, Michael Norman, Thomas Piazza, and Mary C. Waters. Eric Alterman rescued the book at one of many bad moments. Jon Kannegaard suggested I upgrade a subtitle into the title. I have stood on the shoulders of many writers, most acknowledged in notes, but in particular wish to single out two predecessors: Robert Hughes for *Culture of Complaint* and Russell Jacoby for *Dogmatic Wisdom.*

Earlier drafts or sections were read and criticized by David Biale, Norman Birnbaum, Shana Cohen, Barbara Epstein, Herbert J. Gans, Adam Hochschild, Arlie Hochschild, Jerome Karabel, Michael Kazin, Richard Rothstein, and John Torpey, all of whom helped and all of whom I cannot have satisfied, although not for lack of trying.

Earlier versions of parts of this book appeared in *Contention, Dissent, Harper's,* the *New York Observer,* and *World Policy Journal,* and in the books *Higher Education Under Fire,* ed. Michael Bérubé and Cary Nelson (London: Routledge, 1994) and *A New Moment in the Americas,* ed. Robert S. Leiken (New Brunswick, NJ: Transaction Publishers, 1994). I am grateful to the respective editors for permission to reprint.

Jennifer Fosket and especially Marco Calavita helped greatly with fact-checking, the latter thanks to the good offices of the Department of Culture and Communication of the School of Education at New York University.

Master editor Tom Engelhardt once again posed a few thousand imperative and difficult questions, of which I hope to have done justice to a few. Master editor Sara Bershtel then, with great finesse, pressed me to make more sense. Assistant editor Riva Hocherman helped. My agent, Ellen Levine, was grand.

Fletcher Haulley, Justin Haulley, and Shoshana Haulley, whether they knew it or not, provided distraction and forbearance.

Laurel Cook helped, and helped, and sublimely helped again.

Notes

Epigraphs

Page ix.

Frederick Douglass: *Life and Times of Frederick Douglass* (London: Collier Macmillan, 1892), p. 154.

Part I.

Plato: *Philebus*, Section 17A, in John Peters's free translation, in turn paraphrasing Paul Ricoeur.

Part II.

Henry James: *The American Scene*, edited and with an introduction by John F. Sears (New York: Penguin Books, 1994), p. 92.

Patrick Buchanan: Speech to the Republican National Convention, Houston, Texas, 1992.

Part III.

Ralph Waldo Emerson: Joel Porte, ed., *Emerson in His Journals* (Cambridge, Mass.: Harvard University Press, 1982), p. 305. The entry dates from April 17, 1843.

Part IV.

William Blake: *The Marriage of Heaven and Hell* (New York: Oxford University Press, 1975 [1790]), p. 7.

1. A Dubious Battle in Oakland

7 **Columbus Day of 1992:** Unless otherwise attributed, information in this chapter is drawn from my interviews with David Anderson (September 14, 1993), Yasmin Anwar (October 10, 1992), Richard Arum (December 18, 1992), Carol Chinn (November 5, 1992), Harry Chotiner (January 18, 1993), Toni Cook (December 16, 1992), Fred Ellis and Kitty Epstein (December 9, 1992), Allen Graubard (October 18, 1992), Sheila Jordan (January 23, 1993, and September 21, 1993), Jan Malvin (October 27, 1992), Gary Nash (February 4, 1993), Pedro Noguera (October 12, 1992), Meredith Story (May 22, 1993), Renee Swayne (February 1, 1993), Steven Weinberg (January 29, 1993), and Shelley Weintraub (October 24, 1992, August 22, 1994, and March 3, 1995).

8 **"Understanding Eurocentrism":** Gary B. Nash et al., *A More Perfect Union* (Boston: Houghton Mifflin, 1991), p. 28.
"could be very damaging": David L. Kirp, "The Battle of the Books," *San Francisco Examiner, Image* Magazine, February 24, 1991, pp. 17–19.

9 **eighty-five single-spaced pages:** The document is untitled. Berkeley, California: Communities United against Racism in Education, 1990, pp. 1, 47.
CURE pointed to . . . "people to fear": CURE document, pp. 9, 12, 13, 16, 24, 49, 2.

10 **CURE and other . . . "imagine being enslaved":** CURE document, pp. 2, 4, 7, 16, 26, 47, 8, 9, 14, 17, 81.
African-American woman: Kirp, "Battle of the Books," p. 19.

12 **the authors plausibly defended:** Gary B. Nash, "General Observations and Executive Summary of Issues Relevant to Multiculturalism in *Houghton Mifflin Social Studies,*" n. p., n. d. [1990]. Kindly made available to me by Gary Nash.
pictures of Mohammed: Robert Reinhold, "Class Struggle," *The New York Times Magazine,* September 29, 1991, p. 46.
As for the Jewish objections: "Modifications to the Text, *A Message of Ancient Days,* Which Were Requested by the Jewish Community But Not Made by the Publishers, Houghton Mifflin," bound with "Listing of Changes of Concern to Jewish Community Made by Houghton Mifflin in the Text, *A Message of Ancient Days,*" n. p., n. d. [1990]. Kindly made available to me by Jan Malvin.

13 **Between 1969 and 1994:** Peter Schrag, "California's Elected Anarchy," *Harper's,* November 1994, p. 56.
That framework: California State Department of Education, *History–Social Science Framework for California Public Schools* (Sacramento: California State Department of Education, 1988), p. 6.

14 which lacked a history series: Reinhold, "Class Struggle," p. 28.

15 Nash's books included: Gary B. Nash, *Red, White, and Black: The Peoples of Early America*, 2nd ed. (Englewood Cliffs, N.J.: Prentice-Hall, 1974), p. 2.

16 a student body: U.S. Bureau of the Census, San Francisco–Oakland, 1990. Data kindly furnished to me by Frédérick Douzet.

17 "sheer Eurocentric arrogance": Jacqueline Frost, "School Boards Told to Reject 'Racist' Books," *Oakland Tribune*, March 19, 1991, p. A12. **"a bone"** . . . **"dark-skinned":** Gary B. Nash et al., *A Message of Ancient Days* (Boston: Houghton Mifflin, 1991), pp. 97–98.

20 Frances FitzGerald: *America Revised: History Textbooks in the Twentieth Century* (Boston: Little, Brown, 1979), passim.
Houghton Mifflin's eighth-grade book: Gary B. Nash et al., *A More Perfect Union* (Boston: Houghton Mifflin, 1991), pp. 4, 10, 18, 26, 27.

26 At the sixth-grade level: Although the state had not approved the Scholastic book, the board was able to get a waiver to use it.

28 "positive materials": Dr. Mary Hoover and Dr. Kitty Kelly Epstein, "Should Bay Area Schools Adopt Social Studies Series Textbooks? NO: History of 90% of Oakland Students Is Distorted," *Oakland Tribune*, June 2, 1991.

29 in 1989 . . . **12 percent of whites:** Edward N. Wolff, *Top Heavy: A Study of the Increasing Inequality of Wealth in America* (New York: Twentieth Century Fund Press, 1995), pp. 7, 17.
46 percent of black children: U.S. Bureau of the Census, Housing and Household Economic Statistics Division, "Poverty and Wealth," 1994.
life expectancy gap: Alan L. Otten, "Life Expectancy Gap Widens Between Races," *Wall Street Journal*, August 12, 1994, p. B1.
males in Bangladesh: Colin McCord, M.D., and Harold P. Freeman, M.D., "Excess Mortality in Harlem," *New England Journal of Medicine*, Vol. 322, No. 3 (January 18, 1990), p. 174.

30 John U. Ogbu: "Understanding Cultural Diversity and Learning," *Educational Researcher*, Vol. 21, No. 8 (November 1992), pp. 6–7. See also John U. Ogbu, "Minority Status and Schooling in Plural Societies," *Comparative Education Review*, Vol. 27, No. 2 (June 1983), pp. 168–90; "Variability in Minority School Performance: A Problem in Search of an Explanation," *Anthropology and Education Quarterly*, Vol. 18, No. 4 (1987), pp. 312–34.
community college . . . **134 percent:** Marco Calavita, telephone interview with Joni Finney, Associate Director, California Higher Education Policy Center, San Jose, March 31, 1995.

32 Two years after: For a partial substitute, fourth-grade classes were using a sequence of three lesson plans, each good for six weeks, including one on the California Indians, put together by Shelley Weintraub and other teachers with the help of a group at the University of California, Berkeley. This was all the substitute curriculum they had time to produce under the waiver provision of the state law. Telephone interview, Shelley Weintraub, August 2, 1994. See also Dexter Waugh, "Oakland Teachers Make History," *San Francisco Examiner*, October 22, 1993.

33 who declined: U.S. Bureau of the Census, San Francisco–Oakland, 1990. Data kindly furnished to me by Frédérick Douzet.

34 Sean Wilentz: "Sense and Sensitivity," *The New Republic*, October 31, 1994, p. 46.

2. *"A Prodigious Amalgam"*

40 Allan Bloom: Quoted in William J. Bennett, "Why the West?" an address at Stanford University, April 18, 1988.
"victory culture": Tom Engelhardt, *The End of Victory Culture* (New York: Basic Books, 1995).

41 a school board in Florida: "School Board Will Recognize Other Cultures, but as Inferior," *New York Times*, May 13, 1994, p. A16.

42 "Who are we?": Subsequently, this sort of thing seems to have become a newsmagazine staple. For example, *Newsweek*'s feature story on July 10, 1995, pp. 18–23, was headlined, "What is an American?"
moderate Republicans: "America-First Policy Is Rejected," *New York Times*, October 7, 1994, p. A28.
can only be attained: Molefi Kete Asante at the University of Iowa, answer to audience question, March 29, 1994.

43 Tocqueville: Alexis de Tocqueville, *Democracy in America* (New York: Vintage, 1954), Vol. I, chapter 12.
"democracy of nationalities": The phrase is Horace M. Kallen's. Kallen added that these nationalities would "cooperat[e] voluntarily and autonomously through common institutions," and that "the common language of [America's] great tradition would be English." Horace M. Kallen, *Culture and Democracy in the United States* (New York: Boni and Liveright, 1924), pp. 123–24.

44 All these factors combined: Bernard Bailyn, *The Ideological Origins of the American Revolution* (Cambridge, Mass.: Harvard University Press, 1967), p. 51.
American nation is never: Benedict Anderson, *Imagined Communities: Reflections on the Origin and Spread of Nationalism* (London: Verso, 1983), p. 193.
"un-American": *Oxford English Dictionary* (1971), pp. 3467–68. The reference is to Morris Birkbeck, *Notes on a Journey in America* (New York:

A. M. Kelley, 1971 [1818]): "Ninety marble capitals have been imported at vast cost from Italy, . . . and shew how un-American is the whole plan" (p. 29).

Congress rejected a petition: Arthur Mann, *The One and the Many: Reflections on the American Identity* (Chicago: University of Chicago Press, 1979), p. 152, citing Marcus Hansen, *The Immigrant in American History* (1940), p. 132.

44 **Jonathan Boucher:** Quoted in Henry F. May, *The Enlightenment in America* (New York: Oxford University Press, 1976), p. 3. On Boucher's defense of inequality, see Bailyn, *Ideological Origins,* pp. 314–18.

Native American Party: "Declaration of Principles of the Native American Convention, Assembled at Philadelphia, July 4, 1845," in Stanley Feldstein and Lawrence Costello, eds., *The Ordeal of Assimilation: A Documentary History of the White Working Class* (New York: Anchor Books, 1974), pp. 147, 151, 152.

fear lest national integrity: Still the classic source is John Higham, *Strangers in the Land: Patterns of American Nativism, 1860–1925* (New York: Atheneum, 1963).

less than 2 percent: Mann, *The One and the Many,* p. 150.

45 **"composite nationality":** Frederick Jackson Turner, *The Frontier in American History* (New York: Holt, Rinehart & Winston, 1962 [1920]), p. 27.

"not a nation": Herman Melville, *Redburn: His First Voyage* (New York: 1849), p. 214, quoted in Mann, *The One and the Many,* p. 54.

46 **Marx's hypothetical revolutionaries:** Karl Marx, *The Eighteenth Brumaire of Louis Bonaparte* (New York: International Publishers, 1963 [1852]), p. 18.

John Quincy Adams: Quoted in Moses Rischin, ed., *Immigration and the American Tradition* (Indianapolis: Bobbs-Merrill, 1976), p. 4.

Emerson: *Emerson in His Journals,* sel. and ed. by Joel Porte (Cambridge, Mass.: Harvard University Press, 1982), p. 347.

Israel Zangwill: Quoted in Mann, *The One and the Many,* pp. 99, 100, 114. Herbert J. Gans points out that Zangwill was thinking of Americans of European origin alone, and that eventually he got his wish in the form of today's category of "European Americans." (Personal communication, September 26, 1994.)

Langston Hughes: "Let America Be Again," in Arnold Rampersad and David Roessel, eds., *The Collected Poems of Langston Hughes* (New York: Knopf, 1994), pp. 189–91.

Walter Lippmann: "National Purpose," in John K. Jessup et al., *The National Purpose* (New York: Holt, Rinehart & Winston, 1960), p. 125.

46 Ronald Reagan: I saw Ronald Reagan deliver this line on television but cannot locate the original.

Is there a Spanish: When I made this point in a lecture in Paris (November 3, 1994) by asking whether, in particular, there was a French dream, the sociologist Alain Touraine responded that there was indeed a French dream—the Cartesian model of universal reason. I take his point. But as I didn't have the wit to point out at the moment, this French dream does not announce itself by that name. To call it a "dream" would be to diminish it, to render it airy.

48 who disliked authority: Bailyn, *Ideological Origins,* chapter 3.

republican idea: Gordon S. Wood, *The Creation of the American Republic, 1776–1787* (New York: Norton, 1969).

49 cheap land: I am indebted to the historian Barbara Epstein for making this point. (Personal communication, September 18, 1994.)

fierce utopian streak: These figures were not marginal in their time. When the Scottish utopian Robert Owen visited the United States in 1825 to purchase land for an experiment in rational living (the result: New Harmony, Indiana), he gave a triumphal speech on February 25 to a throng in the House of Representatives that included the president of the United States, James Monroe, President-elect John Quincy Adams, House Speaker Henry Clay, numerous members of Congress, Supreme Court Justices, and Cabinet members. Owen addressed them thus: "If the leading men of these States, forgetting every little and unworthy party and sectarian distinction, will now cordially unite, they may, with ease, break asunder the bonds of ignorance, superstition, and prejudice, and by this acting they could not fail to dispel error, and to give and secure mental freedom and happiness to the world. To effect this change, the greater ever yet made in human affairs, no sacrifice on their parts will be necessary. If they possess, as I trust they do, sufficient moral courage to will this deed, and without delay to express that will openly and decisively to the world, then will mental slavery soon cease everywhere, and the victory over ignorance and poverty, and sin, and misery will be achieved." Quoted in Michael Harrington, *Socialism* (New York: Saturday Review Press, 1970), pp. 111–12.

Edward Everett Hale's: *The Man Without a Country,* 2nd ed. (New York: Ticknor & Fields, 1897), p. 7. In a foreword to the 1897 edition (p. iv), Hale writes of his patriotic intention to criticize anyone who would dare renounce his nationality. He adds: "The Civil War has taught its lesson so well that the average American of the year 1896 hardly understands that any such lesson was ever needed. The United States *is* a nation, now" (p. iii).

50 school textbooks: Ruth Miller Elson, *Guardians of Tradition: American*

Schoolbooks of the Nineteenth Century (Lincoln: University of Nebraska Press, 1964), chapters 4 and 5.

Alien Act . . . ideological grounds: William Preston, *Aliens and Dissenters: Federal Suppression of Radicals, 1903–1933* (Cambridge: Harvard University Press, 1963), pp. 22–30.

51 **after the Civil War:** Leah Greenfeld, *Nationalism: Five Roads to Modernity* (Cambridge: Harvard University Press, 1992), pp. 480–81. See, for example, Edward Everett Hale's assertion of 1897 in note above.

"Prior to 1917": Gary Gerstle, *Working-Class Americanism: The Politics of Labor in a Textile City, 1914–1960* (Cambridge, Eng.: Cambridge University Press, 1989), p. 1.

Immigrants clustered: John Bodnar, *The Transplanted: A History of Immigrants in Urban America* (Bloomington, Ind.: Indiana University Press, 1985), pp. 120–30, 175–89.

Cincinnati: Bodnar, *The Transplanted*, p. 119.

William Steinway: Bodnar, *The Transplanted*, p. 141.

52 **"Under the inroads":** John Higham, "Integrating America: The Problem of Assimilation in the Nineteenth Century," *Journal of American Ethnic History*, Vol. I, No. 1 (Fall 1981), pp. 19–20.

heightened attacks . . . purification crusades: Higham, *op. cit.* On alcohol, see Joseph Gusfield, *Symbolic Crusade: Status Politics and the American Temperance Movement*, 2nd ed. (Urbana: University of Illinois Press, 1986), and Michael Kazin, *The Populist Persuasion* (New York: Basic Books, 1995), chapter 4. On prostitution, see Ruth Rosen, *The Lost Sisterhood: Prostitution in America* (Baltimore: Johns Hopkins University Press, 1982).

New York City harbored: George Chauncey, *Gay New York: Gender, Urban Culture, and the Making of the Gay Male World, 1890–1940* (New York: Basic Books, 1994).

Benjamin Harrison: It was not, however, until 1898, one day after the United States declared war on Spain, that New York State decided that students must recite the pledge daily. Other states followed suit. David R. Manwaring, *Render Unto Caesar: The Flag-Salute Controversy* (Chicago: University of Chicago Press, 1962), pp. 2ff.

53 **Lincoln:** The Lincoln Memorial, dedicated in 1922, was yet another post–World War I monumentalization of national order, unity, and justice fused and frozen into the martyr figure of Lincoln.

Frederick Jackson Turner: Turner wrote these words in 1893. Quoted in Mann, *The One and the Many*, p. 118.

"Star-Spangled Banner": The anthem came to baseball during the 1918 World Series. It caught on, and was then played on the opening day of subsequent seasons. It was not, however, made an official national anthem until declared so by Herbert Hoover and Congress in 1931. Only after 1945 was it played before every game. See Benjamin G. Rader, *Baseball: A History of America's Game* (Urbana: University of Illinois Press, 1992), p. 156.

54 **In 1916, Wilson:** Higham, *Strangers in the Land,* p. 199.

Theodore Roosevelt: Mann, *The One and the Many,* pp. 112, 158, 118.

Randolph Bourne: "Trans-national America," in *History of a Literary Radical,* ed. Van Wyck Brooks (New York: B. W. Huebsch, 1920), pp. 266–99.

Free speech and antiwar advocates: Higham, *Strangers in the Land,* pp. 217–22; Preston, *Aliens and Dissenters,* pp. 88–151.

55 **Theodore Roosevelt:** Mann, *The One and the Many,* p. 100.

Henry Ford: Werner Sollors, *Beyond Ethnicity: Consent and Descent in American Culture* (New York: Oxford University Press, 1986), pp. 89–91. "Ask anyone of them what nationality he is," wrote a contributor to the company paper, *Ford Times,* in an article called "The Making of New Americans" in November 1916, "and the reply will come quickly, 'American!' 'Polish-American?' you might ask. 'No, American,' would be the answer. For they are taught in the Ford school that the hyphen is a minus sign."

universalist-feminist Jew: Mann, *The One and the Many,* pp. 102–16.

national origin principle: Mann, *The One and the Many,* pp. 132–34.

56 **John Dewey:** "Nationalizing Education," quoted in Sollors, *Beyond Ethnicity,* p. 88.

"House I Live In": Music by Earl Robinson, lyrics by "Lewis Allen," the pseudonym of Abel Meeropol, who later adopted the sons of Julius and Ethel Rosenberg. Sinatra's 1945 recording accompanied an Academy Award–winning short film of the same name, in which Sinatra breaks up a fight caused by ethnic scapegoating. (Information courtesy of Richard Flacks.)

Working Class melted: The apotheosis of the "common man" had roots in Gompers' American Federation of Labor as far back as the 1890s. See Michael Kazin, *Populist Persuasion,* p. 55.

"If you like America": *New Masses* back cover, XXIX (Sept. 27, 1938), as quoted in Paul Buhle, *Marxism in the USA* (London: Verso, 1987), p. 179.

57 **Leon Samson:** *Toward a United Front: A Philosophy for American Workers* (New York: Farrar & Rinehart, 1933), p. 16.

one of whose forebears: *Dictionary of American Biography,* Supplement 4, p. 2.

In his best-selling: James Truslow Adams, *The Epic of America* (Boston: Little, Brown, 1931), p. viii. Adams forswears formal authorship of the phrase, affirming that the dream is a "concept" that is "generally considered as being 'typically American'" (pp. vii–viii). In any event, only after the publication of Adams's book does the phrase begin to circulate in the speeches of politicians and the titles of plays and novels. I am grateful to Michael Norman for uncovering the source of this phrase and referring me to Anthony Brandt's summary "The American Dream," *American Heritage*, April–May 1981, pp. 24–25, and other references.

58 **"ugly scars":** Adams, *Epic*, pp. 404–5.

Adams concluded: Adams, pp. 416–17.

Mary Antin wrote: *They Who Knock at Our Gates: A Complete Gospel of Immigration* (Boston: Houghton Mifflin, 1914), pp. 138–39, quoted in Sollors, *Beyond Ethnicity*, p. 64.

59 **twoness:** W. E. B. Du Bois, *The Souls of Black Folk* (New York: Everyman's Library [Knopf], 1993), p. 9.

another American tradition: Werner Sollors *(Beyond Ethnicity*, p. 168) makes this point, citing James Weldon Johnson's novel, *Autobiography of an Ex-Colored Man* (1912), and Abraham Cahan's *The Rise of David Levinsky* (1917). The contemporary classic in this genre is Ralph Ellison's *Invisible Man*.

"DON'T SPEAK": This poster was on exhibit at the Italo-American Museum of San Francisco in 1994.

60 **multiethnic platoons:** Jeanine Basinger, *The World War II Combat Film: Anatomy of a Genre* (New York: Columbia University Press, 1986), pp. 51–53, 56, 61.

"We are a mongrel": Basinger, p. 51.

dark-skinned members: Basinger, pp. 57–58, 75. Basinger points out: "The minorities almost always die, and die most horribly" (p. 75).

Pima Indian Ira Hayes: Karal Ann Marling and John Wetenhall, *Iwo Jima: Monuments, Memories, and the American Hero* (Cambridge, Mass.: Harvard University Press, 1991), pp. 99, 101.

Restrictions on Chinese: John W. Dower, *War Without Mercy: Race and Power in the Pacific War* (New York: Pantheon, 1986).

the rare Italian: Evidence of the confinement and deportation of a few suspicious Italians was on display at the Italo-American Museum of San Francisco in 1994.

61 **middle-class individualists:** I borrow the term from Herbert J. Gans's underappreciated *Middle-Class Individualism* (New York: Free Press, 1988).

61 Nathan Glazer has written: *"Beyond the Melting Pot* Twenty Years After," *Journal of American Ethnic History,* Vol. I, No. 1 (Fall 1981), p. 47.

62 Servicemen's Readjustment Act: Kenneth T. Jackson, *Crabgrass Frontier: The Suburbanization of the United States* (New York: Oxford University Press, 1985), p. 233.

63 available only to the very rich: Jackson, p. 243.

Levittown's tract houses: Jackson, p. 235.

As early as the 1820s: Stuart M. Blumin, *The Emergence of the Middle Class: Social Experience in the American City, 1760–1900* (Cambridge: Cambridge University Press, 1989), p. 242.

Walt Whitman: Editorial in the *Brooklyn Daily News,* cited in Blumin, p. 1.

the term "middle-class": Blumin, pp. 275, 287, 291.

more Americans identified: Mary R. Jackman and Robert W. Jackman, *Class Awareness in the United States* (Berkeley: University of California Press, 1983), p. 18; James A. Davis and Tom W. Smith, *General Social Surveys, 1972–1986: Cumulative Codebook* (Storrs, Conn.: NORC-Roper Center, 1986), question 184, p. 218, cited in Gans, *Middle-Class Individualism,* p. 174, n. 13.

64 The small screen: These paragraphs on television draw on Todd Gitlin, "Looking Through the Screen," in Gitlin, ed., *Watching Television* (New York: Pantheon, 1987), p. 3, and "Flat and Happy," *Wilson Quarterly,* Autumn 1993, pp. 47–55.

66 David Sarnoff: "Turn the Cold War Tide in America's Favor," in John K. Jessup et al., *The National Purpose,* p. 51.

the editor of the report: John K. Jessup, "A Noble Framework for a Great Debate," in *The National Purpose,* p. 8.

69 America as a civilization: This was the title of a 1957 book by the liberal pundit Max Lerner.

Oglesby refused: "Trapped in a System," November 27, 1965, in Massimo Teodori, *The New Left: A Documentary History* (Indianapolis: Bobbs-Merrill, 1969), pp. 183–87.

Jerry Rubin: Todd Gitlin, *The Whole World Is Watching: Mass Media in the Making and Unmaking of the New Left* (Berkeley: University of California Press, 1980), p. 171.

"I don't like the sight": W. A. Swanberg, *Norman Thomas, The Last Idealist* (New York: Charles Scribner's Sons, 1976), p. 486.

70 By the fall of 1968: Gitlin, *Whole World,* p. 174.

As late as 1967: Tom Wells, *The War Within: America's Battle Over Vietnam* (Berkeley: University of California Press, 1994), pp. 135–37. Thomas was one of the few political elders who had welcomed the New Left at all. When, in 1962, the social-democratic parent organization of Students for a Democratic Society, the League for Industrial Democracy, had cracked down on SDS for ideological unreliability, Thomas had taken the side of SDS. That this self-same socialist dignitary could in 1965 be naive about where responsibility lay for the Vietnam War was the sort of revelation that fed the estrangement of young radicals. Some were shocked. Others, especially red diaper babies, had their dyed-in-the-wool suspicions confirmed—that the partisans of "even-numbered internationals," the social-democratic Second and Trotskyist Fourth, were only too willing to surrender to American foreign policy.

72 **the projects usually less:** On SDS community organizing projects, see Todd Gitlin and Nanci Hollander, *Uptown: Poor Whites in Chicago* (New York: Harper & Row, 1970); Kirkpatrick Sale, *SDS* (New York: Random House, 1973), pp. 95–115, 131–50; Sara Evans, *Personal Politics: The Roots of Women's Liberation in the Civil Rights Movement and the New Left* (New York: Knopf, 1979), pp. 126–55; James Miller, *"Democracy Is in the Streets"* (New York: Simon and Schuster, 1987), pp. 208–17. On attempts to organize working-class youth against the draft, see Michael Kazin, *The Populist Persuasion* (New York: Basic Books, 1995), p. 213. On New Left antiwar work in the military, and GI dissent generally, see David Cortright, *Soldiers in Revolt: The American Military Today* (Garden City, N. Y.: Anchor Press, 1975); Terry H. Anderson, "The GI Movement and the Response from the Brass," and David Cortright, "GI Resistance During the Vietnam War," in Melvin Small and William D. Hoover, eds., *Give Peace a Chance: Exploring the Vietnam Antiwar Movement* (Syracuse: Syracuse University Press, 1992), pp. 93–128; and Terry H. Anderson, *The Movement and the Sixties* (New York: Oxford University Press, 1995), pp. 166–67, 229–30, 319–22, 332, 376–77.

left to the imagination: This paragraph is influenced by Michael Kazin's argument in *The Populist Persuasion,* chapter 8.

73 **its first trade deficit:** John B. Judis, "Why Your Wages Keep Falling," *The New Republic,* February 14, 1994, p. 26.

insolent chariot: The phrase comes from John Keats, *The Insolent Chariots* (Philadelphia: Lippincott, 1958).

74 **Reagan denounced:** Lou Cannon, *Reagan* (New York: Perigee, 1984), pp. 212–15.

according to his own pollster (footnote): Cannon, *Reagan,* p. 272.

76 **"The time has come":** *A Time for Choosing: The Speeches of Ronald Reagan, 1961–1982* (Chicago: Regnery Gateway, 1983), pp. 184–85. The date of the speech was February 6, 1977.

Reagan brought together: On the making of Reagan's conservative infrastructure, see Sidney Blumenthal, *The Rise of the Counter-Establishment: From Conservative Ideology to Political Power* (New York: Times Books, 1986).

78 **"the kind of men and women":** *A Time for Choosing*, p. 232. This was a favorite citation of Reagan's. He repeated it in his celebrated 1983 "evil empire" speech to the National Association of Evangelicals (below, p. 79) —though not in his 1982 "crusade for freedom" Westminster speech, perhaps having been informed that Paine was, to Tory eyes, both a renegade and a revolutionary.

sprayed that famous Teflon: During his first month in office, for example, the total number of times Reagan was criticized by anyone, from any point of view, on the front page of the *New York Times* or the *Washington Post* was—two; and one of these came from his right, in the person of Jack Kemp complaining that Reagan wasn't planning to cut taxes on the rich.

the press that attributed to Reagan: Elliot King and Michael Schudson, "The Myth of the Great Communicator," *Columbia Journalism Review*, November–December 1987, pp. 37–39.

"probably one of the most important . . . imperfect world": Reagan, *A Time for Choosing*, pp. 107, 120, 119.

79 **"an evil empire":** Reagan, *A Time for Choosing*, pp. 179, 178.

two out of three white men: "Portrait of the Electorate," *New York Times*, November 5, 1992, p. B9.

81 **"There is no":** Irving Kristol, "My Cold War," *The National Interest*, Spring 1993, p. 144.

82 **As prosperity seeped away:** This paragraph parallels the argument of Thomas Byrne Edsall, with Mary D. Edsall, in *Chain Reaction: The Impact of Race, Rights, and Taxes on American Politics* (New York: Norton, 1991).

3. The Fragmentation of the Idea of the Left

84 **Joseph de Maistre:** *Considérations sur la France*, 2nd ed. (London; Bâle, 1797), p. 102, translated by K. Anthony Appiah, "Identity, Authenticity, Survival: Multicultural Societies and Social Reproduction," in Charles Taylor et al., *Multiculturalism: Examining the Politics of Recognition*, ed. Amy Gutmann, paper ed. (Princeton, NJ: Princeton University Press, 1994), p. 150.

85 **difference against a backdrop:** This distinction is one of shadings, not absolutes, for differences are always thought and felt against a background of what does not differ, and commonalities are always thought and felt in relation to differences. Still, the shadings matter. When people feel their differences more strongly than they feel their commonalities, it matters little whether philosophers think their commonalities should weigh more heavily.

exhaustion of that core belief: At this writing, Latin America may be the exceptional continent. The decline of military regimes and the recent experience of economic growth have given democratic ideas a boost. Latin American intellectuals from the moderate Right through the social-democratic Left share an enthusiasm for the future that their North American colleagues can only envy.

already clear in 1945: Ferenc Fehér, *The French Revolution and the Birth of Modernity* (Berkeley: University of California Press, 1990), p. 2.

87 **seating arrangements:** James H. Billington, *Fire in the Minds of Men: Origins of the Revolutionary Faith* (New York: Basic Books, 1980), p. 27.

88 **"politics of recognition":** Charles Taylor, *Multiculturalism and "The Politics of Recognition"* (Princeton, NJ: Princeton University Press, 1992). **Even Mazzini:** Quoted in Mitchell Cohen, "Rooted Cosmopolitanism," *Dissent,* Fall 1992, p. 480. Italics in the original.

89 **Marx dripped scorn:** For this point I am indebted to Marshall Berman.

90 **Germany's "True" Socialists:** Karl Marx and Friedrich Engels, "Communist Manifesto," in Robert C. Tucker, ed., *The Marx-Engels Reader* (New York: Norton, 1972), p. 356.
"species being": Marx, "Economic-Philosophical Manuscripts of 1844: Selections," in Tucker, ed., *Marx-Engels Reader,* pp. 52–103.
"entire sections . . . disappear[ed]": Marx and Engels, "Communist Manifesto," pp. 343–44.
"constantly revolutionizing . . . image": Marx and Engels, "Communist Manifesto," pp. 338–39.

91 **denationalized:** The term is James H. Billington's. *Fire,* p. 275.
"national differences . . . vanishing": Marx and Engels, "Communist Manifesto," p. 350.
"point out . . . nationality": Marx and Engels, "Communist Manifesto," p. 346.

92 **"radical chains":** Karl Marx, "Critique of Hegel's *Philosophy of Right:* Introduction," in Tucker, ed., *Marx-Engels Reader,* p. 22.

95 **"a cry of grief . . . malaise":** Émile Durkheim, *Socialism and Saint-Simon* (Yellow Springs, Ohio: Antioch Press, 1958), p. 7.
"The current Marxism": Michael Bérubé, "Pop Goes the Academy," *Village Voice Literary Supplement,* April 1992, p. 11. For a general critique of this tendency, see Todd Gitlin, "The Anti-Political Populism of Cultural Studies," in Marjorie Ferguson and Peter Golding, eds, *Beyond Cultural Studies* (Thousand Oaks, Calif.: Sage, forthcoming).

97 **principle was tailored:** Significantly, one of the first pamphlets defending

the radical potential of the student movement was Carl Davidson's "On Student Syndicalism" (Chicago: Students for a Democratic Society, 1966). The point about the student movement's relative independence of leaders was made by Irving Louis Horowitz and William Friedland in *The Knowledge Factory: Student Power and Academic Politics in America* (Chicago: Aldine, 1970), pp. 79–80.

98 **"Student as Nigger":** Originally published in the *Los Angeles Free Press*, 1967. Reprinted in Jerry Farber, *The Student as Nigger: Essays and Stories* (New York: Pocket Books, 1972).

99 **socialism would take:** I cannot find an exact source for this much-cited *bon mot* attributed to Wilde by Michael Walzer in *Obligations: Essays on Disobedience, War, and Citizenship* (Cambridge, Mass.: Harvard University Press, 1970), p. 230. Neither could Walzer, when I asked him. Such is a supreme reputation for wit that it does not suffer when mere documentation is wanting.

100 **structure of feeling:** This term is Raymond Williams's. See *Marxism and Literature* (New York: Oxford University Press, 1977), pp. 128–35.
Donald L. Horowitz: "Ethnic Identity," in Nathan Glazer and Daniel P. Moynihan, eds., *Ethnicity: Theory and Experience* (Cambridge, Mass.: Harvard University Press, 1975), p. 137.

4. The Coloring of America?

107 **non-Hispanic whites:** Mary C. Waters, "The Social Construction of Race and Ethnicity: Some Examples from Demography," unpublished paper presented at American Diversity: A Demographic Challenge for the Twenty-First Century, Center for Social and Demographic Analysis Conference, Albany, New York (April 1994), p. 22, citing U.S. Bureau of the Census, *Population Projections of the United States by Age, Sex, Race, and Hispanic Origin: 1992 to 2050*, Current Population Reports, P25–1092 (1992).
By the early years: Sam Roberts, *Who We Are* (New York: Times Books, 1993), p. 63. Roberts's figures are drawn from the 1990 census.
57 percent of American adult women: Roberts, p. 178.

108 **Between 1950 and 1970 . . . 3.0 percent:** 1970 figures from U.S. Bureau of the Census, "USA Statistics in Brief: 1988," n.p.; 1990 figures from Paul R. Campbell, *Population Projections for States, by Age, Race, and Sex: 1993 to 2020*, U.S. Bureau of the Census, Current Population Reports, P25–1111 (1994), Appendix A, Table A-1. Nineteen seventy was the first year the Census Bureau counted the category called "Hispanic."
In 1960 . . . women: U.S. Bureau of the Census, *School Enrollment— Social and Economic Characteristics of Students* (1993).

interracial couples: Waters, "Social Construction of Race and Ethnicity," p. 18.

Kwame Anthony Appiah (footnote): Kwame Anthony Appiah, *In My Father's House: Africa in the Philosophy of Culture* (New York: Oxford University Press, 1992), chapter 2, "Illusions of Race."

109 births of mixed-race babies: *USA Today*, December 11, 1992, cited in Waters, "Social Construction of Race and Ethnicity," p. 18.

"The number of children": Lawrence Wright, "One Drop of Blood," *New Yorker*, July 25, 1994, p. 49.

in 1986, outside the South . . . 4.2 percent: In 1986, among marriages by Southern black women, only 1.7 percent were to white men. Of course, a large number of blacks do not marry. Still, these figures, gathered by a Dutch demographer from marriage license data in 33 states, included about half of all marriages formed between 1968 and 1986 and defy the conventional wisdom to such a degree as to command attention. Matthijs Kalmijn, "Trends in Black/White Intermarriage," *Social Forces*, Vol. 72, No. 1 (September 1993), p. 124. Thanks to Richard Alba for calling this article to my attention.

of "mixed blood" to start with: The U.S. Census asks people to categorize themselves by both race and ethnicity. In 1980, nearly 7.4 million Americans gave either their race or their ethnicity as "American Indian." Of them, 84 percent mentioned Indian ancestry, or "ethnicity," but recorded their "race" as something other than Indian. Keep in mind, too, that many of the 16 percent, or roughly 1.2 million, who recorded themselves as "Indian" in race, cannot presume that their ancestors in perpetuity were "pure bloods." Purity of blood is a racist fantasy, not a human fact. Terry P. Wilson, "Blood Quantum: Native American Mixed Bloods," in Maria P. P. Root, ed., *Racially Mixed People in America* (Newbury Park, Calif.: Sage Publications, 1992), p. 124, citing research by C. M. Snipp, "Who Are American Indians? Some Observations about the Perils and Pitfalls of Data for Race and Ethnicity," *Population Research and Policy Review* 5 (1986), p. 249.

Some of these statistics: *Time*, Fall 1993, "The New Face of America," pp. 2, 64–65. Despite *Time*'s well-intentioned cover prose, a headline writer slipped from interethnic grace by writing, on an interior page, this subhead: "For all the talk of cultural separatism, the races that make up the U.S. are now *crossbreeding* at unprecedented rates." Italics mine.

By the year 2000: This is the Census Bureau's middle-range projection. U.S. Bureau of the Census, *Population Projections of the U.S. by Age, Sex, Race and Hispanic Origin, 1993–2050* (1993). The Census Bureau projections cited in this chapter presuppose the annual number (not percentage) of immigrants is fixed at the 1990 level.

According to the Census Bureau . . . 67 percent: Campbell, *Population Projections,* Table 3, Table A-1, p. 23. Note that "Hispanic" is not a racial category. Not all Hispanics are white. This is why the percentages add up to more than 100 percent. For simplicity's sake, I have omitted the small numbers (about 1,500,000 in 1990, less than 1 percent of the population) of those classifying themselves Native Americans, a category that includes American Indians, Inuits (Eskimo), and Aleutian Islanders.

110 **Hispanic population should surpass:** Robert Pear, "New Look at the U.S. in 2050: Bigger, Older and Less White," *New York Times,* national edition, December 4, 1992, pp. A1, A10.

non-Hispanic white population: Ibid.

According to census . . . the year 2029: Campbell, *Population Projections,* Table 3, Series A.

decline, by 2050: Waters, "Social Construction of Race and Ethnicity," p. 22, citing U.S. Bureau of the Census, *Population Projections of the United States by Age, Sex, Race, and Hispanic Origins: 1992 to 2050,* Current Population Reports, P25–1092 (1992).

Contrary to popular mystique: Campbell, *Population Projections,* Table 2, Series A, pp. 5–7.

descendants of new immigrants: Pear, *op. cit.*

Whites are already a minority: Roberts, *Who We Are,* p. 100.

111 **less than 1 percent:** Roberts, *Who We Are,* p. 101.

California and Texas: Roberts, *Who We Are,* p. 80.

only 57.2 percent: U.S. Bureau of the Census, *1990 Census of the Population: General Population Characteristics: California* (1992). Somewhat less heterogeneous are the three next largest states: Texas, New York, and Florida. Still, California, Texas, New York, and Florida, the four most populous states, together account for 31 percent of the U.S. population, 27 percent of the electoral college, and 28 percent of the vote—although nonwhites are famously underrepresented on the registration rolls and in the voting booths. (U.S. Bureau of the Census, *Statistical Abstract of the United States: 1994.)*

"one drop of blood": Paul R. Spickard, "The Illogic of American Racial Categories," in Root, ed., *Racially Mixed People in America,* p. 15. Spickard points out that even here, the black ancestor could not be defined biologically, but only socially—it was a question of how he or she was regarded.

112 **Alonso and Waters performed:** William Alonso and Mary C. Waters, "The Future Composition of the American Population: An Illustrative Projection," paper presented at the 1993 winter meetings of the American Statistical Association, Fort Lauderdale, Florida, p. 15.

claimed Irish origin: Michael Hout and Joshua Goldstein, "How 4.5 Million Irish Immigrants Became 50 Million Irish-Americans: Demographic and Subjective Aspects of the Ethnic Composition of White Americans," *American Sociological Review,* Vol. 59 (February 1994), pp. 64–82.

113 **"Almost no White American extended family":** Paul R. Spickard, "Pacific Islander Americans and Multiethnicity: A Vision of America's Future," paper presented at the Social Science History Association Annual Meeting, Baltimore, Maryland, 1993, quoted in Waters, "Social Construction of Race and Ethnicity," p. 25.

1990 student meeting: Paul Rogat Loeb, *Generation at the Crossroads: Apathy and Action on the American Campus* (New Brunswick, N.J.: Rutgers University Press, 1994), chapter 15, p. 199.

Henry Louis Gates, Jr.: *Loose Canons: Notes on the Culture Wars* (New York: Oxford University Press, 1992), p. 122.

racial makeup of New York City: Telephone interview, Deborah Meier, July 17, 1994.

The actual figures: U.S. Bureau of the Census, *1990 Census of the Population: General Population Characteristics: New York* (1992).

114 **Roy Wilkins:** Wilkins went on, writing about Stokely Carmichael: "You can face a lion one way when you have real artillery, but if you have a powder puff, you have to handle yourself differently—if you want to keep your people alive. For all Stokely's reckless talk of guns and power back then, I still don't think he could tell the difference between a pistol and a powder puff." Roy Wilkins, with Tom Mathews, *Standing Fast: The Autobiography of Roy Wilkins* (New York: Da Capo, 1994 [1982]), p. 317.

what automatically follows: The same point can be made about "Asian Americans," a category that ropes together, in Cynthia L. Nakashima's words, "middle-class third- and fourth-generation Japanese Americans, wealthy immigrants from Taiwan, and welfare-dependent Southeast Asian refugees." ("An Invisible Monster: The Creation and Denial of Mixed-Race People in America," in Root, ed., *Racially Mixed People in America,* p. 175.)

origin was given as Hispanic: Roberts, *Who We Are,* p. 80.

115 **radicals who claim:** Professor Carlos Muñoz, Jr., of the Chicano Studies Department at the University of California, Berkeley, at a Stanford University conference around 1990. Muñoz proposed "Latino" as a label of choice, though of course "Latino" sustains the European reference of "Hispanic." There are no semantic solutions to the conundrums of complex identity.

Mexican-American assistant principal: Personal communication, Richard Rothstein, September 27, 1994.

Chicanos criticized: Harold Meyerson, "Fractured City," *The New Republic*, May 25, 1992, p. 24.

1994 midterm election: "Times Poll: A Look at the Electorate," *Los Angeles Times*, November 11, 1994, p. A5. The pro-187 figures for other populations were whites, 63 percent; blacks, 47 percent; Asians, 47 percent.

Their ethnicity is . . . an "option": Mary C. Waters, *Ethnic Options: Choosing Identities in America* (Berkeley: University of California Press, 1990).

116 **Korean-American shopkeeper:** The jury rejected the prosecutors' charge of second-degree murder as well as a lesser charge of involuntary manslaughter. The verdict in this case was delivered the same day as high-visibility testimony in the Clarence Thomas–Anita Hill hearings, which may partly explain its relatively limited publicity. The verdict ended up on the front page of the *Los Angeles Times*, but less conspicuously than the Thomas–Hill story. Andrea Ford and Tracy Wilkinson, "Grocer Is Convicted in Teen Killing," *Los Angeles Times*, October 12, 1991, p. A1.

In the wake: Joel Kotkin and David Friedman, *The Los Angeles Riots: Causes, Myths and Solutions* (Washington, D.C.: Progressive Policy Institute, 1993); Mario-Rosario Jackson et al., "An Analysis of Selected Responses to the Los Angeles Civil Unrest of 1992," *Contention*, Vol. 3, No. 3 (1994), pp. 3–21.

In San Francisco: Michael Harris and William Cooney, "S.F. and NAACP Settle Suit," *San Francisco Chronicle*, December 31, 1982, p. A1; Nanette Asimov, "Lowell High Fails Desegregation Test," *San Francisco Chronicle*, September 9, 1993, p. A15; "Clone Lowell High, Education Panel Says," *San Francisco Chronicle*, December 22, 1993; Debra J. Saunders, "Clipping Children's Wings," *San Francisco Chronicle*, July 18, 1994, p. A19.

117 **Compton:** The population was 51 percent Latino, but there were no Latinos on the city council, and while 78 percent of city employees were black, only 11 percent were Latino. Patrick J. McDonnell, "As Change Overtakes Compton, So Do Tensions," *Los Angeles Times*, August 21, 1994, p. A1, and Emily Adams, "Compton Mayor Offers Plans to Ease Tensions," *Los Angeles Times*, September 8, 1994, p. B3.

Theodore Roosevelt: Cited in Alonso and Waters, p. 15.

Tom Buchanan: F. Scott Fitzgerald, *The Great Gatsby* (New York: Scribner's, 1925), p. 13. Expressing some combination of sympathy and annoyance, or perhaps simply changing the subject, the tennis star Jordan Baker chimes in: "You ought to live in California"—in 1925, California is synonymous with a white bastion!

whites are less than half as likely: Catherine Whitaker, *Black Victims* (Bureau of Justice Statistics, 1990), cited in Andrew Hacker, *Two Nations* (New York: Scribner's, 1992), p. 47.

On television news: Robert M. Entman, "African Americans According to TV News," *Media Studies Journal,* Summer 1994, pp. 31–32.

118 **Black and Hispanic enrollments:** Ruth Sidel, *Battling Bias: The Struggle for Identity and Community on College Campuses* (New York: Viking, 1994), pp. 37–38.

blacks whose unemployment rates: Hacker, *Two Nations,* p. 103.

In 1990, 12.1 percent: *Money Income of Households, Families, and Persons in the United States,* Series P-60, No. 174 (Bureau of the Census, 1991), cited in Hacker, *Two Nations,* p. 98.

blacks are 0.1 percent: "The Corporate Elite," *Business Week* (November 25, 1991), cited in Hacker, *Two Nations,* p. 108.

4.5 percent of college teachers . . . 3.6 percent of engineers: Hacker, *Two Nations,* pp. 111, 113, citing census figures.

in 1983 . . . twenty to one: Edward N. Wolff, *Top Heavy: A Study of the Increasing Inequality of Wealth in America* (New York: Twentieth Century Fund, 1995), p. 2.

120 *Newsweek***'s March 29, 1993:** The following is adapted from Todd Gitlin, "Commentary," *New York Observer,* April 12, 1993, p. 4.

121 *Business Week:* "White, Male, and Worried," *Business Week,* January 31, 1994.

122 **a high school in Anaheim:** Louis Freedberg, "School Club for the New Outsiders," *San Francisco Chronicle,* January 15, 1992, p. A1.

whites were 42 percent: Office of Student Research, University of California, Berkeley, in Troy Duster et al., *The Diversity Project: Final Report* (Berkeley: Institute for the Study of Social Change, 1991), p. 2.

123 **29 percent of a national sample:** Joe R. Feagin and Hernán Vera, *White Racism: The Basics* (New York: Routledge, 1995), p. 137, citing the National Opinion Research Center's 1990 General Social Survey.

Whites who said they supported antidiscrimination laws: Feagin and Vera, *White Racism,* citing Howard Schuman, Charlotte Steeh, and Lawrence Bobo, *Racial Attitudes in America* (Cambridge, Mass.: Harvard University Press, 1985), pp. 86–125.

In 1989: Paul M. Sniderman and Thomas Piazza, *The Scar of Race* (Cambridge, Mass.: Harvard University Press, 1993), pp. 102–104. According to Piazza (personal communication, December 23, 1994), there was no significant difference between men and women.

when Sniderman: Sniderman and Piazza, *The Scar of Race,* chapter 6.

124 **the bloc accountable:** Todd Gitlin, "Republicans Told White Guys: You

Can Get It Up Again," *New York Observer,* November 28, 1994, p. 4. See chapter 8.

a victim like the victims: See Feagin and Vera, *White Racism,* p. 146.

"potential rapist": Daphne Patai and Noretta Koertge, *Professing Feminism* (New York: New Republic/Basic Books, 1994), pp. 130–31.

sometimes exaggerated: For an example of a most-likely fabricated story of racist abuse that inflamed opinion on one campus, see Loeb, *Generation at the Crossroads,* pp. 179–85, 204–6.

verbal viciousness and violence: Feagin and Vera, *White Racism,* pp. 34–43; Ruth Sidel, *Battling Bias,* pp. 5–7, 57–60, 82–87. Statistics on these matters are difficult to evaluate. Sidel, like others, cites reports by the National Institute Against Prejudice and Violence (pp. 7–8) maintaining that some 800,000 to one million college students, not all of them members of racial minorities, have suffered "ethnoviolence," or racist abuse, usually verbal, at least once. In *Dictatorship of Virtue: Multiculturalism and the Battle for America's Future* (New York: Knopf, 1994, pp. 203–10), Richard Bernstein argues that such incidents, while "certainly unfortunate, . . . [do] not at all prove that ethnoviolence is dramatically on the rise" (p. 205). Fair enough. There are indeed cases in which public argument against affirmative action is wrongly taken as prima facie evidence of "racism"—a view especially hard to sustain when large numbers of black Americans are themselves opposed to affirmative action. The serious problem not to be talked away consists of outspokenly racist attacks, which may or may not be on the rise, but in any event should not have to turn to lynching before being taken seriously. "Scattered incidents" and "sporadic" violence (pp. 204, 205) are easier to dismiss by those who are not tagged members of the target group.

"If you want to go": Troy Duster et al., *The Diversity Project: Final Report* (Berkeley: Institute for the Study of Social Change, 1991), p. 37.

125 **"Being white":** *Diversity Project,* p. 53.

5. Marching on the English Department While the Right Took the White House

127 **Erik H. Erikson:** Erik H. Erikson, *Identity, Youth and Crisis* (New York: Norton, 1968), p. 224.

As Erikson wrote: Erikson, *Identity, Youth and Crisis,* p. 42.

Erikson warned: Erikson, *Identity, Youth and Crisis,* p. 24.

128 **"Ethnicity" was crystallized:** Herbert J. Gans, "Symbolic Ethnicity: The Future of Ethnic Groups and Cultures in America," *Ethnic and Racial Studies,* Vol. 2, No. 1 (January 1979), p. 8.

129 Oakland Youth Council: Nat Hentoff, *The New Equality* (New York: Viking, 1965), p. 49.

"I'm from America": *Malcolm X Talks to Young People: Speeches in the U.S., Britain, and Africa* (New York: Pathfinder, 1993), p. 11.

"We need allies": Malcolm X, in George Breitman, ed., *The Last Year of Malcolm X: The Evolution of a Revolutionary* (New York: Merit Publishers, 1967), p. 43.

130 To call yourself "Afro-American": Basic Unity Program, Organization of Afro-American Unity, in Breitman, *The Last Year of Malcolm X*, p. 121.

Mississippi Freedom Democratic Party: Anne Romaine, " 'We Come from a Distance' (The story of the Mississippi Freedom Democratic Party Through the Convention of 1965), An Oral History," Charlottesville, Virginia, privately printed, 1969; Todd Gitlin, *The Sixties: Years of Hope, Days of Rage* (New York: Bantam, 1987), pp. 151–62.

131 cultural and political pluralism: The pluralist meaning was the one articulated in Stokely Carmichael and Charles V. Hamilton, *Black Power: The Politics of Liberation in America* (New York: Random House, 1967).

Those who advocate: Julius Lester, *Look Out, Whitey! Black Power's Gon' Get Your Mama!* (New York: Grove, 1969 [1968]), p. x.

"another language": Lester, p. 91.

it was pointless: Lester, p. 91.

"It is clear": Lester, p. 137.

Stokely Carmichael: Quoted in Lester, pp. 132–33.

132 "The struggle of blacks": Lester, p. 139.

openly armed Black Panther Party: Soon, Lester himself was writing perceptively and courageously that the Panthers were orchestrators of media events and not the deeply based organizers they purported to be. SNCC and the Panthers were briefly joined, then divorced when the Panthers resorted to gunplay. See Clayborne Carson, *In Struggle: SNCC and the Black Awakening of the 1960s* (Cambridge, Mass.: Harvard University Press, 1981), pp. 278–96, and Hugh Pearson, *The Shadow of the Panther* (Reading, Mass.: Addison-Wesley, 1994), pp. 159–63.

Inspired . . . kinky "Afros": Maxine Leeds, " 'Black Is Beautiful': Personal Transformation and Political Change," Ph.D. dissertation, Department of Sociology, University of California, Berkeley, 1995, chapter 4.

133 Maulana Ron Karenga: Personal communication, Maxine Leeds, May 20, 1995, citing research by Waldo Martin; William L. Van Deburg, *New Day in Babylon: The Black Power Movement and American Culture, 1965–1975* (Chicago: University of Chicago Press, 1993), p. 172.

134 James Baldwin: *The Fire Next Time* (New York: Vintage, 1993 [1963]), p. 94. Italics in original.

135 Nathan Glazer: "The Peoples of America," in *Ethnic Dilemmas, 1964–1983* (Cambridge, Mass.: Harvard University Press, 1983), p. 20. (Originally published in *The Nation,* September 20, 1965.)
"practically no survey": Andrew Greeley, "The Rediscovery of Ethnicity," *Antioch Review,* Vol. 31, No. 3 (Fall 1971), p. 351.

136 Gunnar Myrdal's impression: "The Case against Romantic Ethnicity," *Center Magazine 7* (July–August 1974), p. 28; cited in Arthur Mann, *The One and the Many: Reflections on the American Identity* (Chicago: University of Chicago Press, 1979), p. 38.
survey evidence: David Colburn and George E. Pozzetta, "Race, Ethnicity, and the Evolution of Political Legitimacy," in David Farber, ed., *The Sixties, From Memory to History* (Chapel Hill, N.C.: University of North Carolina Press, 1994), p. 131.
white ethnic groups: Rudolph J. Vecoli, "The Coming of Age of the Italian Americans," *Ethnicity* 5 (1978), pp. 137–38; John F. Stack, "Ethnicity, Racism, and Busing in Boston: The Boston Irish and School Desegregation," *Ethnicity* 6 (1979), pp. 21–28; Colburn and Pozzetta, "Race, Ethnicity, and the Evolution of Political Legitimacy," pp. 131–37.
Herbert J. Gans: "Symbolic Ethnicity."

137 sided with the Palestinians: Jonathan Kaplan, *Broken Alliance: The Turbulent Times between Blacks and Jews in America* (New York: New American Library, 1989), pp. 76 ff., 198 ff.

138 Radical Jewish Unions: Interview, David Biale, August 23, 1994, and David Biale, quoted in Sara Bershtel and Allen Graubard, *Saving Remnants: Feeling Jewish in America* (New York: Free Press, 1992), pp. 245–46.
radical activist Arthur Waskow: *Jewish Bulletin,* March 25, 1994, p. 33.
"those of us in the ethnic bag": Baroni, "I'm a Pig Too," *Washingtonian Magazine,* July 1970, quoted in Mann, *The One and the Many,* p. 34.

139 The new ethnicity was articulated: Gans, "Symbolic Ethnicity," pp. 5 ff.
"I want to have": Michael Novak, *The Rise of the Unmeltable Ethnics: Politics and Culture in the Seventies* (New York: Macmillan, 1972), p. 71.
"I am born of PIGS": Novak, p. 53.
"In recent months": Novak, p. 53. Around 1975, a high school classmate of mine who had become a sociologist spoke to me of similar anger: *his* grandfather, his *Sicilian* grandfather, had spent time in prison for no crime at all, had been poor all his life, but there was no legitimate sanction to be Sicilian, let alone to demand reparations for America's bad treatment. When we knew each other in high school, in the late 1950s, it had never occurred to me that he had an "ethnicity" at all.

"Where in America": Novak, p. 53.

"The recent increase": Novak, pp. 7–8.

Their **ancestors were not slaveowners**: Novak, p. 60.

140 **the Left was making a mistake**: Novak, p. 14.

"we are, in a word": Novak, p. xvi.

"Why do the educated classes": Novak, p. 58.

"To ethnics, America is almost": Novak, p. 65.

Novak overlooked evidence: Howard Schuman, "Two Sources of Anti-war Sentiment in America," *American Journal of Sociology,* Vol. 78, No. 3 (November 1972), p. 517.

142 **many men dismissed**: *New Left Notes,* July 10, 1967; Kirkpatrick Sale, *SDS* (New York: Random House, 1973), pp. 362–63n.; Sara Evans, *Personal Politics* (New York: Vintage, 1980), pp. 190–92.

generational animus: I owe this point to an unpublished manuscript by Ruth Rosen.

gay liberation welled up: See, among other works, Martin Duberman, *Stonewall* (New York: Dutton, 1993).

144 **unprecedented triumphs**: There is a tremendous literature on the consequences of the women's and gay movements, but see in particular Flora Davis, *Moving the Mountain: The Women's Movement in America Since 1960* (New York: Touchstone/Simon and Schuster, 1992); Eric Marcus, *Making History: The Struggle for Gay and Lesbian Equal Rights, 1945–1990* (New York: HarperCollins, 1992); and Paul Berman, "Democracy and Homosexuality," *The New Republic,* December 20, 1993, pp. 17–35.

145 **racial caste system**: For example, the historian Peter H. Wood observed that of 407 articles published in the prestigious *William and Mary Quarterly* between 1960 and 1976, a mere 26, or 6.4 percent, directly concerned blacks, racism, or slavery. More articles discussed slavery in Massachusetts than in Virginia. Peter H. Wood, " 'I Did the Best I Could for My Day': The Study of Early Black History during the Second Reconstruction, 1960–1976," *William and Mary Quarterly,* 3rd Series, XXXV (April 1978), pp. 185–225. See also the discussion in Nathan Irvin Huggins, "The Deforming Mirror of Truth," introduction to the revised edition, *Black Odyssey* (New York: Pantheon, 1990), pp. xxxiii–xxxiv.

Clark Kerr: Clark Kerr, *The Uses of the University* (Cambridge, Mass.: Harvard University Press, 1963).

146 **Roger Kimball and Richard Bernstein**: Roger Kimball, *Tenured Radicals: How Politics Has Corrupted Our Higher Education* (New York: HarperCollins, 1991), pp. xv, 166–67; Richard Bernstein, *Dictatorship of Virtue: Multiculturalism and the Battle for America's Future* (New York: Knopf, 1994), p. 6.

148 separatist rancor: A compelling treatment of women's studies programs is Daphne Patai and Noretta Koertge, *Professing Feminism* (New York: New Republic/Basic Books, 1994). Patai and Koertge have had the courage to put on paper what many other feminists have been saying *sotto voce* about women's studies for years.

149 University of Michigan: Andrea Press, personal communication, December 1991.

Native American graduate student: Ruth Rosen, personal communication, April 1992.

150 gay English professor: Reported on the Canadian Broadcasting Corporation, January 1994.

a Berkeley activist: Sumi Cho, panel discussion, American Civil Liberties Union of Northern California, July 1991.

153 "best blacks": Stephen L. Carter, *Reflections of an Affirmative Action Baby* (New York: Basic Books, 1991), pp. 47–69.

taxi drivers: Ellis Cose, *The Rage of a Privileged Class* (New York: Harper Perennial, 1995), p. 55.

storekeepers to open their doors: It has been widely reported that jewelers refuse to buzz in young black men. In *The Alchemy of Race and Rights* (Cambridge, Mass.: Harvard University Press, 1991), law professor Patricia J. Williams recounts having seen a sweater she liked in a Soho store window on a Saturday afternoon, only to be refused admittance by the white store clerk, who claimed the store was closed, although several white shoppers were going about their shopping (pp. 44–45).

startled and hostile: Brent Staples, *Parallel Time: Growing Up in Black and White* (New York: Pantheon, 1994), pp. 202–3.

ran out of elevators: Henry Louis Gates, Jr., *Loose Canons: Notes on the Culture Wars* (New York: Oxford University Press, 1992), p. 135.

went out of their way: Sometimes inferiority claims were based on test scores, as in the case of the Georgetown University law student who rifled admissions files to show that black law school admittees had lower grades and test scores than whites. ("Georgetown Reprimands Author of Article," *New York Times*, May 21, 1991, p. A14.) In 1994, pseudoscientific genetic claims were back in fashion, with Charles Murray and Richard J. Herrnstein's atrociously argued and roundly refuted *The Bell Curve* (New York: Free Press) on the best-seller list.

earn less than whites: Black men earned 72 percent as much as white men in 1989. For women, the ratio was 92 percent. But the improvement slackened after the 1960s. For men, the ratio rose by only 3.6 percent between 1969 and 1989 (the period when affirmative action was said to have done them so much good), while for women, it rose 12.2 percent. In

1989, black college graduates were 2.24 times as likely to be unemployed as white college graduates. Andrew Hacker, *Two Nations* (New York: Scribner's, 1992), pp. 101, 104, citing census reports.

154 peer pressure: White, black, Latino, and Asian students report these pressures in Troy Duster et al., *The Diversity Project: Final Report* (Berkeley: Institute for the Study of Social Change, 1991).

Regarded with suspicion: See also Terry Wilson, "Blood Quantum: Native American Mixed Bloods," in Maria P. P. Root, ed., *Racially Mixed People in America* (Newbury Park, Calif.: Sage Publications, 1992), p. 114. This suspicion runs rife through the racially obsessive history of the United States, marked not only by state laws against miscegenation, designed to fortify and preserve "white purity," but by comparable barriers erected by racial and ethnic minorities, including Japanese Americans, Jews, and others. See Paul R. Spickard, "The Illogic of American Racial Categories," in Root, ed., *Racially Mixed People,* pp. 15–16, 20–21.

Orrin Hatch (footnote): Quoted in Kathleen Quinn, "Author of Her Own Defeat: Lani's Lesson for Academia," *Lingua Franca,* September/October 1993, p. 58.

155 black poor are left desperate: In *The Truly Disadvantaged: The Inner City, the Underclass and Public Policy* (Chicago: University of Chicago Press, 1987), William Julius Wilson has argued, controversially, that the upward mobility of the black middle classes had the unintended consequence of abandoning the black ghettos to social disintegration. (See especially pp. 55–57, 109–15, and 143–44.) For criticisms, see reviews by Adolph Reed, Jr., in *The Nation,* February 6, 1988, pp. 167–71, and Christopher Jencks in *The New Republic,* June 13, 1988, pp. 23–32.

157 one egregious 1993 case (footnote): I interviewed the parents of one of these students, Richard Wolff and Harriet Fraad-Wolff, on January 18, 1994. See also Richard Pérez-Peña, "Private Colleges Are Criticized for Their Brand of Justice," *New York Times,* June 1, 1994, p. B22, and Sarah Kerr, "Droit de Vassar," *Lingua Franca,* Vol. 4, No. 5 (July-August 1994), pp. 32–39.

158 these administrators (footnote): See Alan Wolfe, "The New Class Comes Home," *Partisan Review,* Fall 1993, pp. 729–37.)

more than doubling: See figures cited in chapter 1, page 30.

160 sociology played a part: Dennis H. Wrong, "The Influence of Sociological Ideas on American Culture," in Herbert J. Gans, ed., *Sociology in America* (Newbury Park, Calif.: Sage Publications, 1990), pp. 19–30.

Robert Jay Lifton: *The Protean Self: Human Resilience in an Age of Fragmentation* (New York: Basic Books, 1993). Even the ethnic identities affirmed with such sureness by college students shift, melt, and reform as one ages. Clarence Thomas is far from the only conservative middle-aged African American who went through a collegiate phase in which he admired Malcolm X.

161 David Riesman: *The Lonely Crowd* (New Haven: Yale University Press, 1950).

revision is routine: Orrin E. Klapp, *Collective Search for Identity* (New York: Holt, Rinehart & Winston, 1969), pp. 15–19, 74.

Half of the Fortune: *Time,* "New Face of America," Fall 1993, "It's a Mass Market No More," pp. 80–81.

162 "American Indian" . . . 10 million: Karl Eschbach, "Changing Identification among American Indians and Alaska Natives," *Demography,* Vol. 30, No. 4 (November 1993); Nampeo R. McKenney and Arthur R. Crewce, "Measurement of Ethnicity in the United States: Experiences of the U.S. Census Bureau," paper presented at the Joint Canada–United States Conference on the Measurement of Ethnicity, April 1–3, 1992, Ottawa, Canada, p. 189. Both are cited in Mary C. Waters, "The Social Construction of Race and Ethnicity: Some Examples from Demography," unpublished paper presented at American Diversity: A Demographic Challenge for the Twenty-First Century, Center for Social and Demographic Analysis Conference, Albany, New York (April 1994), pp. 7–8.

capitalizing Deaf: Andrew Solomon, "Defiantly Deaf," *New York Times Magazine,* August 28, 1994, pp. 38–45, 62, 65–68.

163 the yawning gulf: Herbert J. Gans, "Second Generation Decline: Scenarios for the Economic and Ethnic Futures of the Post-1965 American Immigrants," *Ethnic and Racial Studies,* Vol. 15, No. 2 (April 1990), pp. 173–92.

164 naturally cooperative: See Patai and Koertge, *Professing Feminism,* chapter 7.

Africans naturally inventive: Professor Molefi Kete Asante of Temple University, a leading "Afrocentrist" and editor of the *Journal of Black Studies,* writes that he wishes to "present the African as subject rather than object" ("Multiculturalism: An Exchange," *The American Scholar,* Spring 1991, p. 270). But he also believes that the Arabs who invaded northern Africa more than a millennium ago are not "real" Africans (lecture, University of Iowa, March 29, 1994). That is, only blacks of "Negroid" features qualify as the founders of geometry, philosophy, and so on. If the Greeks produced anything of value, it is because they were "really" Africans. This poses for Dr. Asante a problem he does not seem to have faced: If Plato *was* black, why not read him? But what is most astounding about Asante's jerry-built cosmology and race-based idea of "knowledge" is that serious university professors fear to ask embarrassing questions of him. The fear of being considered "racist" cows them.

165 Sister Souljah: Quoted in Gregory Stephens, "Sister Souljah and the issue of black racism," *In These Times,* August 5–August 18, 1992, p. 18.

6. The Recoil

166 "Western liberal values" . . . **"culture":** Roger Kimball, *Tenured Radicals,* paperback ed. (New York: HarperCollins 1991), pp. 192, 206.
"reason": John Searle, presentation to National Association of Scholars, San Francisco, May 1993.

167 "thought police . . . watch what you say": *Newsweek,* December 24, 1990, cover.

168 "Tenured radicals": George Will, "Curdled Politics on Campus," *Newsweek,* May 6, 1991. The pull-quote is only slightly compressed from Will's own words.
NEXIS database: *Democratic Culture,* Vol. 3, No. 1 (Spring 1994), p. 2. In his critical review of Richard Bernstein's *Dictatorship of Virtue* in the *New York Times* (October 28, 1994, p. C27), Nicholas Lemann gives different figures for "politically correct" and "political correctness": seven appearances in 1981, 5,007 in 1992. (Actually, Lemann gives seven for *1991,* but this is almost certainly a typographical error, since Lemann means to counterpose these figures to Bernstein's own figures on the boom in references to "multiculturalism" between *1981* and 1992.)
Jackie Mason: Comedy Central proceeded to file suit against Mason, charging: "People could get confused. It tends to dilute the rights to the name that we've built up and spent a lot of money on." "Newsclips," *Democratic Culture,* Vol. 3, No. 1 (Spring 1994), p. 14.

169 Richard Bernstein: "The Rising Hegemony of the Politically Correct," *New York Times,* News of the Week in Review, October 28, 1990.

170 rarely punitive: The gravest case of the punishment of a faculty member, the two-year suspension without pay of tenured University of New Hampshire professor J. Donald Silva because of charges that he had leveled sexual innuendoes, ended with his reinstatement by a federal judge and a settlement in which the university agreed to pay damages, back salary, and legal fees. See Richard Bernstein, *Dictatorship of Virtue,* pp. 98–106, and "University to Reinstate a Professor," *New York Times,* December 4, 1994, p. 35. The most serious case I know of a "politically correct" witch hunt against students concerns two Vassar students unjustly punished by a malign combination of student finger-pointing and an inquisitorial administration. (See above, p. 157–58, footnote.)

171 freedom against slavery: Brent Staples wrote in an editorial note in the

New York Times ("Politically Correct: False Slogan," April 17, 1991) that the slogan "seeks to reduce all differences of opinion to a single one: the difference between liberals and conservatives."

172 **Hilton Kramer:** "Confronting the Monolith," *Partisan Review,* Vol. LX, No. 4 (1993), pp. 569–71.

Roger Kimball: "From Farce to Tragedy," *Partisan Review,* Vol. LX, No. 4 (1993), p. 568. Kimball's was one of the more hysterical contributions to *Partisan's* by no means unanimous issue, "The Politics of Political Correctness."

"over the last couple of years": Kimball, p. 565.

173 **citing Churchill's statement:** Kimball, p. 569.

D'Souza's flying tour: Dinesh D'Souza, *Illiberal Education: The Politics of Race and Sex on Campus* (New York: Free Press, 1991).

Stanford University's: The best reportorial critique is Fran Smith, "The Big PC Monster on Campus," *West* Magazine (of the *San José Mercury News*), October 17, 1993, pp. 20–24.

"perhaps the text which best": D'Souza, pp. 71–73.

all eight courses assigned: The complete list of assigned authors for the 1988–89 school year is reproduced as an appendix to Denis Lacorne, "Des Coups de Canon dans le Vide? La 'Civilisation Occidentale' dans les Universités Américaines," *Vingtième Siècle* (Paris), No. 43 (July–September 1994), pp. 16–17.

174 **One might also argue:** See Todd Gitlin, "The Anti-Political Populism of Cultural Studies" among other contributions to Marjorie Ferguson and Peter Golding, eds., *Beyond Cultural Studies* (Thousand Oaks, Calif.: Sage Publications, forthcoming).

D'Souza, to bolster: D'Souza, pp. 20, 68. The quote, from Christopher Clausen, originally appeared in Clausen's "It Is Not Elitist to Place Major Literature at the Center of the English Curriculum" *(Chronicle of Higher Education,* January 13, 1988, p. A52). D'Souza plucked it from a widely cited *Wall Street Journal* article (by David Brooks, February 2, 1988) deliciously, if predictably, entitled "From Western Lit to Westerns as Lit."

Gerald Graff: *Beyond the Culture Wars: How Teaching the Conflicts Can Revitalize American Education* (New York: Norton, 1992), p. 21.

national surveys: Graff, pp. 23–24.

175 **bitter struggle:** Graff, p. 24.

Walt Whitman: Leo Marx, address to the convention of the American Studies Association, New Orleans, November 1, 1990.

excesses of the anti-PC: For general critiques of D'Souza, see Todd Gitlin, "An Intolerance of the New Intolerance," *Los Angeles Times Book Review,* April 14, 1991, pp. 2, 19, from which I have borrowed some phrases; Louis Menand, "Illiberalisms," *New Yorker,* May 20, 1991, pp. 101–107; Russell Jacoby, *Dogmatic Wisdom: How the Culture Wars Divert Education and Distract America* (New York: Doubleday, 1994), pp. 8, 9, 11, 21–22, 25, 33, 36, 42, 47, 104. On Harvard University in particular, see Jonathan Wiener, "What Happened at Harvard," *The Nation,* September 30, 1991, pp. 384–88. On the University of Michigan, see a leaflet distributed at an Ann Arbor conference unfortunately called "The PC Frame-Up," November 1991.

Leonard Jeffries: Arthur Schlesinger, Jr., *The Disuniting of America* (Knoxville, Tenn.: Whittle, 1991), pp. 33–34, 63; James Traub, *City on a Hill: Testing the American Dream at City College* (Reading, Mass.: Addison-Wesley, 1994), pp. 232–71.

176 **"about half a dozen":** Jonathan Wiener, "School Daze," *The Nation,* November 7, 1994, p. 526.

Richard Bernstein: *Dictatorship of Virtue,* pp. 83–85.

Robert Alter: "The Persistence of Reading," *Partisan Review,* Vol. 60, No. 4 (1993), p. 512.

Morris Dickstein: "Correcting PC," *Partisan Review,* Vol. 60, No. 4 (1993), p. 547.

177 **Paul Berman:** *Debating P.C.* (New York: Dell, 1992).

Patricia Aufderheide: *Beyond PC: Toward a Politics of Understanding* (St. Paul, Minn.: Graywolf Press, 1992).

Michael Bérubé and Cary Nelson: *Higher Education Under Fire* (New York: Routledge, 1995).

Barbara Epstein: "Political Correctness and Collective Powerlessness," *Socialist Review,* Vol. 21, No. 3–4 (July–December 1991), pp. 13–35.

Henry Louis Gates, Jr.: "Multiculturalism and Its Discontents," *Contention,* Vol. 2, No. 1 (Fall 1992), pp. 69–77.

David A. Hollinger: "Postethnic America," *Contention,* Vol. 2, No. 1 (Fall 1992), pp. 80–96, subsequently reworked and expanded into a book of the same name, published by Basic Books in 1995.

178 **"missing children":** Nina Eliasoph, "Drive-In Morality, Child Abuse, and the Media," *Socialist Review,* Vol. 16, No. 6 (November–December 1986), pp. 7–8, citing the *Denver Post* of May 15, 1985.

179 **Dinesh D'Souza's:** *Illiberal Education,* chapter 2.

so many California high school: Troy Duster et al., *The Diversity Project: Final Report* (Berkeley: Institute for the Study of Social Change, 1991), p. 3.

bonus grade-point credit: Jerome Karabel, personal communication, August 20, 1994.

24 percent of *white* students: Duster et al., *Diversity Project,* p. 4.

Harvard: Jerome Karabel and David Karen, "Go to Harvard, Give Your Kid a Break," *New York Times*, op-ed page, December 8, 1990.

180 **news net:** The term is used by Gaye Tuchman, *Making News: A Study in the Construction of Reality* (New York: Free Press, 1978), pp. 21–25.

181 **Maynard Parker:** Interview, Jerry Adler, November 9, 1992.

Other top *Newsweek* editors: Interview, Jerry Adler, November 9, 1992.

183 **protracted crusade:** The canonical study is still Richard Hofstadter's *Anti-Intellectualism in American Life* (New York: Knopf, 1963).

"Destructive" . . . **1974–75:** Leonard Silk and David Vogel, *Ethics and Profits* (New York: Simon and Schuster, 1976), chapter 4. The quotations are from pp. 109, 111, 112, 118.

Neoconservatives: Peter Steinfels, *The Neoconservatives: The Men Who Are Changing America's Politics* (New York: Simon and Schuster, 1979); B. Bruce-Briggs, ed., *The New Class?* (New Brunswick, N.J.: Transaction Books, 1979).

"What is happening": William E. Simon, *A Time for Truth* (New York: Reader's Digest Press, 1978), p. 44.

"nothing less . . . mankind' ": Simon, pp. 229–30.

184 **"Funds generated . . . arguments":** Simon, pp. 230, 231, 232.

"the only thing . . . counterintelligentsia": Simon, p. 238.

right-wing publicists: Sidney Blumenthal, *The Rise of the Counter-Establishment: From Conservative Ideology to Political Power* (New York: Times Books, 1986).

In 1978, Simon and Kristol: Sara Diamond, "The Funding of the NAS," in Patricia Aufderheide, ed., *Beyond PC*, p. 89.

185 **"for a moment . . . intimidation":** Quoted in Fran Smith, *West*, October 17, 1993.

186 **George Will:** "In this low-visibility, high-intensity war, Lynne Cheney is secretary of domestic defense. The foreign adversaries her husband, Dick, must keep at bay are less dangerous, in the long run, than the domestic forces with which she must deal. Those forces are fighting against the conservation of the common culture that is the nation's social cement." "Literary Politics," *Newsweek*, April 22, 1991, p. 72. In 1992, the *Chronicle of Higher Education* reported in considerable detail that Lynne Cheney had "politicized the agency's grant system" by systematically heeding conservative objections to research grant proposals that they considered *outré*, even when peer reviews were strongly supportive. (Stephen Burd, "Chairman of Humanities Fund Has Politicized Grants Process, Critics Charge," *Chronicle of Higher Education*, April 22, 1992, pp. A1, A32–A33.) No prominent national coverage resulted.

187 **Between 1981 and 1986:** Ernest Benjamin, "A Faculty Response to

the Fiscal Crisis: From Defense to Offense," in Michael Bérubé and Cary Nelson, eds., *Higher Education Under Fire*, p. 54.

during the Reagan and Bush years: Paul Lauter, " 'Political Correctness' and the Attack on American Colleges," in Bérubé and Nelson, eds., *Higher Education Under Fire*, p. 84.

In Illinois . . . in 1992: Lauter, " 'Political Correctness,' " pp. 75–76.

188 **About half:** Benjamin, "Faculty Response," p. 59.

spoke Italian: This example, Casa Italiano, exists at Berkeley.

If he came from: Ruth Sidel, *Battling Bias: The Struggle for Identity and Community on College Campuses* (New York: Viking, 1994), pp. 124–29.

If he had friends: This could be true for women, too, of course. The editor of the conservative *Berkeley Review* said publicly that it was such an experience that had turned her against affirmative action.

189 **"make it sound":** Lynne V. Cheney quoted by Associated Press, "Plan to Teach U.S. History Is Said to Slight White Males," *New York Times*, October 26, 1994, p. B12.

"politically correct": Cheney on the *MacNeil/Lehrer NewsHour*, quoted in "A Blueprint of History for American Students," editorial, *San Francisco Chronicle*, October 29, 1994.

"really out of balance": Cheney quoted by Guy Gugliotta, "Up in Arms About the 'American Experience,' " *Washington Post*, October 28, 1994, p. A4.

"politicized" products: Lynne V. Cheney, "The End of History," *Wall Street Journal*, October 20, 1994.

"flimflammed": Cheney quoted in Gugliotta, "Up in Arms."

190 **She had been impressed . . . "human sacrifice":** Cheney, "End of History."

191 **"They would sacrifice":** Cheney quoted in Gugliotta, "Up in Arms."

Cheney quoted . . . "any emphasis": Cheney, "End of History."

"consensus": Except where otherwise noted, all quotations from Nash in the following discussion are from my telephone interview, November 13, 1994.

"The process was as reasonable": Morton Keller, personal communication, December 12, 1994.

"I was deeply impressed": Akira Iriye, personal communication, January 3, 1995.

192 **"A classic":** Charles Krauthammer, "History Hijacked," *Washington Post*, November 4, 1994, p. 25.

"Where is Plymouth Rock . . . ?": LynNell Hancock with Nina Archer Biddle, "Red, White—and Blue," *Newsweek*, November 7, 1994, p. 54. In fact, the Pilgrims arrived at Plymouth on page 58. Perhaps Hancock was upset about the absence of the rock proper. Daunting, that rock, its actual dimensions never mentioned in the tales of the landing. Anyone reared on the old unreconstructed textbooks, impressed by the saga of the landing, courts disappointment on beholding the actual modest stone officially marked off Plymouth beach.

Rush Limbaugh: Quoted in Gugliotta, "Up in Arms."

John Leo . . . "colonial officials": "The Hijacking of American History," *U.S. News and World Report,* November 14, 1994. See Leo's *Two Steps Ahead of the Thought Police* (New York: Simon & Schuster, 1994).

In the *Wall Street Journal:* Shanker quoted in Gary Putka, "Historians Propose Curriculum Tilted Away from West," *Wall Street Journal,* November 11, 1994. At the time he made this comment, Shanker had seen only the penultimate version of the World History Standards—because, he says (personal communication, May 4, 1995), the UCLA group's "strategy was to freeze out people who disagreed with them," and hence they did not send an advance copy of the final document to the president of the American Federation of Teachers. Shanker's comments on the U.S. standards in his weekly Sunday *New York Times* column (November 6, 1994) were more measured than his early newspaper quotes. The standards, he wrote here, were "substantive and demanding," included "more social history" in "an attempt to correct previous distortions," namely the dominance of political history in earlier textbooks, and the "invisibility" of groups "that did not play major roles in politics." "A good first draft of an extremely difficult assignment," Shanker concluded here, calling for "knowledgeable historians to critique and rework the standards to provide the balance that is lacking."

the book asked students: National Center for History in the Schools, *National Standards for World History: Exploring Paths to the Present, Grades 5–12, Expanded Edition* (Los Angeles: National Center for History in the Schools, 1994), pp. 146–47. Italics in the original.

193 Washington was mentioned: National Center for History in the Schools, *National Standards for United States History: Exploring the American Experience Grades 5–12, Expanded Edition* (Los Angeles: National Center for History in the Schools, 1994), pp. 76, 79, 85, 88.

Robert Fulton . . . Cyrus McCormick: National Center for History in the Schools, *National Standards for United States History,* p. 101.

Bell . . . Salk: National Center for History in the Schools, *National Standards for World History,* p. 262 (Einstein, Edison); National Center for History in the Schools, *National Standards for History for Grades K–4: Expanding Children's World in Time and Space* (Los Angeles: National Center for History in the Schools, 1994), pp. 51 (Salk), 64 (Bell).

"it's absurd to say": Gary B. Nash, personal communication, December 28, 1994.

194 Project codirector . . . "citizenship": National Center for History in the Schools, "Fact Sheet," November 1, 1994, p. 2. According to Nash (personal communication, December 28, 1994), Crabtree wrote this statement and he edited it.

thirteen of the references: National Center for History in the Schools, *National Standards for United States History*, pp. 178–79.

all nineteen references: National Center for History in the Schools, *National Standards for United States History*, pp. 214–15.

make the cases . . . Alamo: National Center for History in the Schools, *National Standards for United States History*, pp. 100, 115.

Leo was right: "Hijacking."

Andrew Carnegie's *Wealth*: National Center for History in the Schools, *National Standards for United States History*, p. 136.

195 conduct a mock trial: National Center for History in the Schools, *National Standards for United States History*, p. 44.

"the Horatio Alger model": National Center for History in the Schools, *National Standards for United States History*, pp. 139, 143.

not a catechism: At least one supporter of the standards, however, seemed more extravagant than Cheney. Mabel Lake Murray, a member of the National Alliance of Black School Educators who served on one of the consulting panels, was quoted in *Newsweek:* "Black children have been brainwashed since they started school in America to celebrate white heroes, concepts and values. What needs to happen now is a reverse brainwashing." LynNell Hancock, "Red, White—And Blue," p. 57.

"While the standards do reflect": Morton Keller, personal communication, December 12, 1994.

"a new American revolution": UCLA News press release, "National Standards for United States History, Produced by UCLA Center, to Bring 'Revolution to History Education,' " October 26, 1994, p. 1. The quote turned up in the October 27 *Los Angeles Times* editorial, "Now a History for the Rest of Us," in Guy Gugliotta, "Up in Arms," *Washington Post*, October 28, 1994, p. A4, and in Hugh Dellios, "Battle over History May Itself Prove Historic," *Chicago Tribune*, October 30, 1994, p. 1.

"the sad and the bad": Cheney quoted in Hancock, "Red, White—And Blue," p. 57.

"The study of history": National Center for History in the Schools, *National Standards for United States History*, p. 7.

196 "to consider multiple perspectives": The only pundit to strike a glancing blow at this aspect of the standards was Charles Krauthammer, but he did it ham-handedly. Krauthammer wrote in his syndicated column that the question was not just what but how to teach. Deeper than "ideological slant" was that "the larger project of the new history is to collapse the distinction between fact and opinion. . . . In the new history, there are no facts independent of ideology and power, no history that is not political. . . . Its purpose is to empower students against . . . elites by teaching them their own counter-narrative, heavy on McCarthy, light on Edison." Krauthammer was tendentious in claiming that Nash proposed to substitute mock trials and debates for the teaching of facts, or that he worshipped opinion. Krauthammer, in short, had his facts wrong. But he did approximate a fact: Nash did not propose to teach facts in the old-fashioned way.

The Causes of the American Revolution: National Center for History in the Schools, *National Standards for United States History:* p. 9.

not just conservatives: See, for example, John Patrick Diggins's critique of the new standards, arguing that "the study of history cannot be separated from the study of outstanding leaders" and that the great Westerners should be studied because they are precisely the embodiments of the virtues of free inquiry. ("Historical Blindness," *New York Times,* November 19, 1994), p. 23.

197 Morton Keller: Personal communication, December 12, 1994.

198 Theodore K. Rabb: Rabb added that another newspaper had rejected his article "because it did not have enough 'red meat' and refused to make a partisan case." "Whose History? Where Critics of the New Standards Flunk Out," *Washington Post,* Outlook Section, December 11, 1994, p. C5.

Akira Iriye: Personal communication, January 3, 1995.

7. Where We're Coming From

200 To paraphrase Marx: "Men make their own history, but they do not make it just as they please; they do not make it under circumstances chosen by themselves, but under circumstances directly encountered, given, and transmitted from the past." Karl Marx, "The Eighteenth Brumaire of Louis Bonaparte," in Lewis Feuer, ed., *Basic Writings on Politics and Philosophy: Karl Marx and Friedrich Engels* (Garden City, N.Y.: Anchor Books, 1959), p. 320.

To paraphrase Marshall Berman: *The Politics of Authenticity: Radical Individualism and the Emergence of Modern Society* (New York: Atheneum, 1970), p. 325: "You may not be interested in politics, but politics is interested in you." Trotsky: "You may not be interested in the dialectic, but the dialectic is interested in you."

201 "interpretive community: Stanley Fish, *Is There a Text in This Class? The Authority of Interpretive Communities* (Cambridge, Mass.: Harvard University Press, 1980), pp. 13–14. See also his *There's No Such Thing as Free Speech, and It's a Good Thing, Too* (New York: Oxford University Press, 1994).

There are only stories: For example: "[S]ocial science is not very different from interpretation. It is basically the telling of stories." Michael J. Piore, *Beyond Individualism* (Cambridge, Mass.: Harvard University Press, 1995), p. 175, citing John S. Nelson, Allen Megill, and Donald N. McCloskey, eds., *The Rhetoric of the Human Sciences: Language and Argument in Scholarship and Public Affairs* (Madison: University of Wisconsin Press, 1987).

202 Iroquois Confederation: The strong form of the evidence, sometimes exaggerated, is presented in Donald Grinde Jr., "Iroquois Political Theory and the Roots of American Democracy," pp. 227–80 of Oren Lyons et al., *Exiled in the Land of the Free: Democracy, Indian Nations, and the U.S. Constitution* (Santa Fe: Clear Light Publishers, 1992). See also the review by Rodney A. Smolla, "Last in War, Peace and the Supreme Court," *New York Times Book Review,* April 11, 1993, p. 22.

caricature of evidence: In the current climate, it is apparently necessary to add that the claim is laughable. An excellent refutation is David Brion Davis, "The Slave Trade and the Jews," *New York Review of Books,* December 22, 1994, pp. 14–16.

Those who deplore false universals: The artful Richard Rorty is the best-known philosopher to espouse this point of view. See the brilliant critique of his approach by Norman Geras, "Language, Truth, and Justice," *New Left Review,* No. 209 (January/February 1995), pp. 110–35. A widely cited feminist compendium of this epistemology is Elizabeth Kamarck Minnich, *Transforming Knowledge* (Philadelphia: Temple University Press, 1990).

204 Historians: See Peter Novick's study, *That Noble Dream: The "Objectivity Question" and the American Historical Profession* (Cambridge, Eng.: Cambridge University Press, 1988).

biographers: See Janet Malcolm, *The Silent Woman: Sylvia Plath and Ted Hughes* (New York: Knopf, 1994). Malcolm's fine judgment on the blindnesses of the biographers of Sylvia Plath is unfortunately not matched in her more notorious likening of journalists to criminals in *The Journalist and the Murderer* (New York: Knopf, 1990).

curdled into cliché (footnote): Open a collection of leading feminist criticism, like *Conflicts in Feminism,* edited by Marianne Hirsch and Evelyn Fox Keller, (New York: Routledge, 1990), for example, and you see these terms everywhere. Here, a prominent feminist literary theorist, Elizabeth Abel, refers to "the roles of race and class in a diversified construction of subjectivity." There, the influential feminist film theorist Teresa de Lauretis writes: "Most feminists . . . agree that women are made, not born, that gender is not an innate feature (as sex may be) but a sociocultural construction. . . ." (Teresa de Lauretis, "Upping the Anti *[sic]* in Feminist Theory," pp. 256–57.)

Joan W. Scott (footnote): "Multiculturalism and the Politics of Identity," in Micheline R. Malson, Jean F. O'Barr, Sara Westphal-Uhl, and Mary Wyer, eds., *Feminist Theory in Practice and Process* (Chicago: University of Chicago Press, 1989), p. 7.

"[D]ifferences are created" (footnote): Joan W. Scott, in Michael Bérubé and Cary Nelson, eds., *Higher Education Under Fire: Politics, Economics, and the Crisis of the Humanities* (New York: Routledge, 1995), p. 321.

Dennis Wrong (footnote): "The Influence of Sociological Ideas on American Culture," in Herbert J. Gans, ed., *Sociology in America* (Newbury Park, Calif.: Sage Publications, 1990), pp. 19–30.

205 **hard science:** Which is not to say that hard science has been immune to perspectivist attacks. Far from it. The anti-objectivist spirit has been riding high since the publication of Thomas Kuhn's *The Structure of Scientific Revolutions*. For defenses of scientific methods against recent radical—including feminist—attacks, see Susan Haack, "Knowledge and Propaganda: Reflections of an Old Feminist," in *Partisan Review*, Fall 1993, pp. 556–64; Paul R. Gross and Norman Levitt, *Higher Superstition: The Academic Left and Its Quarrels with Science* (Baltimore: Johns Hopkins University Press, 1994), valuable despite its exaggerations; and Daphne Patai and Noretta Koertge, *Professing Feminism* (New York: Basic Books, 1994), chapter 6.

207 **populated by more than:** I am staying out of the argument as to whether this compound self is modern or postmodern. Postmodernists argue that, amid the flux and surfeit of selves, there is no fixed central self—that the self is inhabited, "saturated," by a whole population of "ghost" selves arising from the multiple roles we play, the multiple images that envelop us, and so forth. (Kenneth Gergen, *The Saturated Self.*) Modernists think that there is a central self—a sun, as it were, around which the planetary subidentities revolve (Anthony Giddens, *Modernity and Self-Identity*). I am inclined toward the modernists, but for purposes of my argument, it doesn't matter.

Leon Wieseltier: "Against Identity," *The New Republic*, November 28, 1994, p. 30.

"determined" in the sense: This reading of "determination" is borrowed from Raymond Williams, *Marxism and Literature* (New York: Oxford University Press, 1977), pp. 83–89.

208 absurd at best: An example of the latter. In 1989, a measure was proposed at the University of California, Santa Cruz, requiring that any faculty member dating a student notify the head of the department and take him- or herself off any committee holding any power over the student. A female professor objected to the sweeping nature of the policy and proposed, instead, that the relationship only be reported when the professor held that power over the student before the dating began. Said another female professor to her: "You're a white male!" The unintended comedy bespeaks the dead-end logic of "essentialism."

209 Whatever relativists may say: This point is well put in Dan Sperber, "Apparently Irrational Beliefs," in Martin Hollis and Steven Lukes, eds., *Rationality and Relativism* (Cambridge, Mass.: MIT Press, 1982), p. 161.

it ill behooves him: Not so fast: the Nietzschean mood, at least in graduate schools of English, is such that the renowned antifoundationalist English Professor Stanley Fish *is* eager to say so. Which raises the question, Why go to the trouble? If might suffices to make right, why go to the trouble of trying to persuade? The cynical answer is that the academy is a place where victories are won not by mobilizing tanks but by mobilizing arguments; when in the academy, fake it the way other academics do.

211 "We never . . . further questions": *Wittgenstein's Lectures: Cambridge, 1930–1932*, ed. Desmond Lee (London: Blackwell, 1980), quoted in Ray Monk, *Ludwig Wittgenstein: The Duty of Genius* (New York: Free Press, 1990), p. 301.

Max Horkheimer and T. W. Adorno: *Dialectic of Enlightenment*, translated by John Cumming (New York: Seabury, 1972 [1944]), pp. xiii, 24, 4, 13, 21.

212 Thomas Kuhn's: *The Structure of Scientific Revolutions* (Chicago: University of Chicago Press, 1962).

213 Kuhn's protestations: Kuhn, "Afterword," in Paul Horwich, ed., *World Changes: Thomas Kuhn and the Nature of Science* (Cambridge, Mass.: MIT Press, 1993), pp. 311–41.

Zygmunt Bauman: *Modernity and the Holocaust* (Ithaca, NY: Cornell University Press, 1989).

measure the rain forest: Horkheimer and Adorno, *Dialectic of Enlightenment*, p. xiv.

214 unfolding of one of the Enlightenment's: The political theorist Sheldon Wolin has pointed out that the critics identify the Enlightenment with its German wing, which was weak, to put it mildly, on liberal politics and democratic potential, and strong on the totalist potential of Reason. The

American Enlightenment, by contrast, drew heavily from the Scottish Enlightenment and was strong on individual rights. Wolin, "Democracy in the Discourse of Postmodernism," *Social Research*, Vol. 57, No. 1 (Spring 1990), p. 13. See also Jürgen Habermas, *The Philosophical Discourse of Modernity*, translated by Frederick Lawrence (Cambridge, Mass.: MIT Press, 1987).

Charles Taylor (footnote): *Multiculturalism and "The Politics of Recognition"* (Princeton, N.J.: Princeton University Press, 1992), pp. 30, 38–39.

215 **basis for common human rights:** The founding father of perspectivism, Michel de Montaigne, made this point in the sixteenth century in the course of respecting the "difference" of cannibals. "We call contrary to nature what happens contrary to custom; nothing is anything but according to nature, whatever it may be. Let *this universal and natural reason* drive out of us the error and astonishment that novelty brings us." "Of a Monstrous Child," from *The Complete Essays of Michel de Montaigne*, translated by Donald Frame (Stanford: Stanford University Press, 1958), p. 539 (my emphasis). In his interesting book, *Cosmopolis* (Berkeley: University of California Press, 1990), Stephen Toulmin invites attention to the tradition of Montaigne as an alternative to the tradition of Descartes, which, in abstracting the mind from the body, clamps a single standard for truth over the wild multiplicity of the world.

Voltaire was anti-Semitic: See, for example, Peter Gay, *The Enlightenment: An Interpretation: The Science of Freedom* (New York: Norton, 1969), p. 391.

Hume, Kant, Hegel, and Jefferson: Henry Louis Gates, Jr., *Loose Canons: Notes on the Culture Wars* (New York: Oxford University Press, 1992), pp. 60–61.

Jefferson in particular: In Paris, noting the Declaration of the Rights of Man and Citizen, Jefferson urged Madison to propose a Bill of Rights to the American Constitution—in order that the United States preserve its reputation as the avant-garde of liberty. See Gordon S. Wood, "The Origins of the American Bill of Rights," *The Tocqueville Review*, Vol. XIV, No. 1 (1993), pp. 41–42.

Richard Rorty's words: *Objectivity, Relativism, and Truth* (Cambridge, Mass: Cambridge University Press, 1991), p. 207.

Horkheimer and Adorno: *Dialectic of Enlightenment*, p. xiii.

216 **Lata Mani:** "Multiple Mediations: Feminist Scholarship in the Age of Multinational Reception," *Feminist Review*, 35 (Summer 1990), p. 26. Mani also writes: "Claims to universality and objectivity have been shown to be the alibis of a largely masculinist, heterosexist, and white Western

subject" (p. 25). Hundreds of other examples from recent briefs for idei.
politics could be offered.

as Richard Rorty writes: *Contingency, Irony, and Solidarity* (New York: Cambridge University Press, 1989), p. 44.

Norman Geras: "Richard Rorty and the Righteous among the Nations," *Socialist Register 1994* (London: Merlin Press, 1994), pp. 32–59. The quotation from Rorty's essay "Solidarity" appears on p. 33.

217 Michael Walzer: *What It Means to Be an American* (New York: Marsilio, 1992), pp. 7–8.

Walzer maintains: "Multiculturalism and Individualism," *Dissent*, Spring 1994, pp. 185, 190–91.

218 "connoisseurs of diversity": Rorty, *Objectivity, Relativism, and Truth*, p. 207.

8. The Fate of the Commons

225 Average real wages: U.S. Department of Labor, Bureau of Labor Statistics, Current Employment Statistics Survey, 1995.

percentage of *full-time* workers: U.S. Bureau of the Census, *The Earnings Ladder* (revised), June 1994.

Since 1973: Richard J. Barnet, "Lords of the Global Economy," *The Nation*, December 19, 1994, p. 754.

In 1979 . . . *nineteen* times: *New York Times*, National Edition, May 4, 1994, p. A15, citing Thomas G. Mortenson, a higher education policy analyst.

This is class division: For further examples of the widening class breach in higher education, see Russell Jacoby, *Dogmatic Wisdom* (New York: Doubleday, 1994).

226 average chief executive officer: Barnet, "Lords of the Global Economy," p. 754.

almost one in four: The precise figure in 1955 was 24.7 percent. U.S. Department of Labor, Bureau of Labor Statistics, Directory of National Unions and Employees Associations, 1979 (September 1980).

fewer than one in six: The precise figure in 1994 was 15.5 percent. U.S. Department of Labor, Bureau of Labor Statistics, Employment and Earnings, January 1995.

Even many workers: But note, too, that many others who would join unions if permitted are defeated, or at least discouraged, by unfavorable government policies—rules kept unfavorable, for the most part, because of the dwindling political power of unions. Commission on the Future of Labor–Management Relations, *Fact Finding Report* (Washington, D.C.: U.S. Department of Labor and U.S. Department of Commerce, 1994), p. 77,

one source alluded to by Richard Rothstein in his *L. A. Weekly* column for September 2–8, 1994. I am grateful to Richard Rothstein for the reference.
"Strong organizations" . . . **Gay Rights parade:** Michael J. Piore, *Beyond Individualism* (Cambridge, Mass.: Harvard University Press, 1995), pp. 19–20. Piore cites a historical precedent (p. 146): "In mass production industries, the racial and ethnic distribution of jobs and organization of tasks was used as a deliberate managerial tactic to divide the labor force and forestall class identification and union organization." See also L. A. Kauffman, "The Diversity Game: Corporate America Toys with Identity Politics," *Village Voice,* August 31, 1993, pp. 29–33.

228 none of the consequences: Americans whose origins lie in Mexico—or Vietnam or Korea—stir up panic and paranoia in considerable part because their appearance is superimposed on the old white purism.

229 Orlando Patterson: *Slavery and Social Death: A Comparative Study* (Cambridge, Mass.: Harvard University Press, 1982).
slavery is central: Two recent compilations from within an enormous literature are Barbara L. Solow and Stanley L. Engerman, eds., *British Capitalism and Caribbean Slavery: The Legacy of Eric Williams* (Cambridge, Eng.: Cambridge University Press, 1987), and Barbara L. Solow, ed., *Slavery and the Rise of the Atlantic System* (Cambridge, Eng.: W. E. B. Du Bois Institute for Afro-American Research/Cambridge University Press, 1991). In the latter, Franklin Knight writes: "Without African slaves and the transatlantic slave trade, the potential economic value of the Americas could never have been realized, since neither Portugal nor Spain had the reserves of labor necessary to develop their new possessions" (p. 72).

230 cosmopolitan credo: A fine evocation of cosmopolitanism appears in Michel Feher's "The Schisms of '67: On Certain Restructurings of the American Left, from the Civil Rights Movement to the Multiculturalist Constellation," in Paul Berman, ed., *Blacks and Jews* (New York: Delacorte Press, 1994), pp. 275ff.

231 Staughton Lynd's words: "Coalition Politics or Nonviolent Revolution?" *Liberation,* June/July 1965, p. 19.

232 wedges into the already dwindling: Thomas Byrne Edsall, with Mary D. Edsall, *Chain Reaction: The Impact of Race, Rights, and Taxes on American Politics* (New York: Norton, 1991). See also William Julius Wilson's convincing defense of "race-neutral" programs: "Race-Neutral Programs and the Democratic Coalition," *The American Prospect,* Spring 1990, and a good sampling of other relevant arguments in Nicolaus Mills, ed., *Debating Affirmative Action* (New York: Delta, 1994).

Stephen L. Carter: *Reflections of an Affirmative Action Baby* (New York: Basic Books, 1991), pp. 88–90.

Out of the election wreckage: The following paragraphs draw on my column, "Republicans Told White Guys: You *Can* Get It Up Again," *New York Observer*, November 28, 1994, p. 4.

Richard Morin and Barbara Vobejda: " '94 May Be the Year of The Man," *Washington Post*, November 10, 1994, pp. A27, A33.

Sixty-two percent: Richard L. Berke, "Defections Among Men to G.O.P. Helped Insure Rout of Democrats," *New York Times*, November 11, 1994, p. A1.

233 **Despite exceptions:** In the California Senate race, Michael Huffington took 59 percent of white male votes but still lost narrowly to Democrat Dianne Feinstein. In Maryland, Republican Ellen Sauerbrey took 63 percent of white males and still lost narrowly to Democrat Parris Glendening. **In 1976 . . . Perot** (footnote): "Portrait of the Electorate," *New York Times*, November 5, 1992, p. B9.

234 **proportion of blue-collar workers:** J. E. Leighley and J. Naylor, "Socioeconomic Class Bias in Turnout 1964–1988: The Voters Remain the Same," *American Political Science Review*, Vol. 86, No. 3 (September 1992), pp. 725–36, cited in Eric Hobsbawm, *Age of Extremes: The Short Twentieth Century, 1914–1991* (London: Michael Joseph, 1994), p. 581.

According to the census (footnote): U.S. Bureau of the Census, *Voting and Registration in the Election of 1994* (June 1995). The actual figures reported by the census, based on a survey of 60,000 households, were, respectively, 50.1 percent, 38.9 percent, and 34.0 percent. But these are *claims* to have voted, and they are inflated. If the total population had voted in these percentages, the total turnout would have been somewhat more than 10 percent higher than in fact it was. I have therefore reduced the reported numbers by 10 percent.

Of those Americans earning $50,000 (footnote): Associated Press, "Low-Income Voters' Turnout Fell in 1994, Census Reports," *New York Times*, June 11, 1995.

Hispanics constitute (footnote): Efrain Hernandez and Richard Simon, "Despite Gains, Latino Voters Still Lack Clout," *Los Angeles Times*, December 4, 1994, pp. A1, A39–40.

235 **Corporate secession:** See David A. Hollinger, *Postethnic America* (New York: Basic Books, 1995), p. 149.

Index